Ambition, Rank, and Poetry
in 1590s England

Ambition, Rank, and Poetry
in 1590s England

John Huntington

UNIVERSITY OF ILLINOIS PRESS
URBANA AND CHICAGO

♾ This book is printed on acid-free paper.

Library of Congress Cataloging-in-Publication Data
Huntington, John, 1940–
Ambition, rank, and poetry in 1590s England /
John Huntington.
      p.   cm.
Includes bibliographical references (p.) and index.
ISBN 0-252-02628-4 (alk. paper)
1. English poetry—Early modern, 1500–1700—
History and criticism. 2. Literature and society—
England—History—16th century. 3. Chapman,
George, 1559?–1634—Political and social views.
4. Poetry—Authorship—Social aspects. 5. Social
classes in literature. 6. Ambition in literature.
I. Title.
            PR535.S6H86   2001
        821'.309355—dc21   00-010160

        C 5 4 3 2 1

Contents

Preface

This book aspires to the simple goal of making us conscious of how awareness of social rank and its economic and political consequences, its privileges and handicaps, motivates nonaristocratic poets in the 1590s and thereby conditions the meanings of their poems. The project itself is not simple. It entails highlighting motifs in the poetry that for various reasons scholarly criticism has ignored or repressed, and it means justifying such an emphasis. The different angle of interpretive vision brings out meanings and sharp distinctions that have been overlooked, illuminates the way a variety of poets, a number of whom have received very little attention in this era of canon-busting, are working with subtlety and passion to establish their places in the literary-social space, and gives us a glimmer of how their sensitivity to their own social position begins to generate distinctions that will later evolve into the taste culture which we now inhabit. At the center of my attention is the early work of George Chapman, a poet nowadays less honored than he was a generation or two ago, whose reputation has suffered from his being misread as a pedantic and ascetic moralist. Chapman makes explicit an agenda for increasing the value of poetry as cultural capital in a world in which epideictic compliment, aristocratic self-display, and moral education have been seen as the justifications for literature. He shares this agenda with a range of poets, from such canonic authors as Christopher Marlowe, Ben Jonson, and Edmund Spenser to such writers as the now-forgotten Matthew Roydon and the recently rediscovered Aemilia Lanyer. Chapman also, by his oblique criticisms of works by such varied writers as Philip Sidney, Barnabe Barnes, and even William Shakespeare, draws our attention to the social implications even of works of the conventional mainstream. This book is, finally, a sketch articulating how an understanding of the social meaning of the poetry affects our sense of literary history.

Over the last two decades the interpretation of literature has undergone profound changes, and any critic, even one who in some way is challenging the received methods and evaluations, is deeply in debt to the way the field has been altered. While I have tried to acknowledge my specific obligations in the notes, there are a few critics whose work has conditioned my thought in ways that are too large to do justice to by such individual notation. Recent students of the style and rhetoric of the Elizabethan court such as Daniel Javitch and Frank Whigham, from very different perspectives, have stressed the hegemonic coherence of the ideology of social rank and how it shapes the courtiers' own behaviors and maintains privileges.[1] From a different critical perspective, Richard Helgerson describes a poetic strategy and a social function that generally collaborate with the courtly ideology.[2] Louis Montrose's studies of the relation of poetic conventions to the realities of Renaissance economic life also see the poetry as in the service of the hegemonic structure.[3] If I pose an alternative to Stephen Greenblatt's ideas of the way subversion operates, it is not without a deep appreciation of how his work has freed us to think about Renaissance culture in complex critical ways.[4] Finally, Annabel Patterson's *Censorship and Interpretation* helped me get beyond simple models of social repression and see the writer in negotiation with the censor.[5] Also crucial for my understanding has been my reading of Pierre Bourdieu over the last fifteen years.[6] It was Bourdieu who led me to ask myself the simple question, why would a man of Chapman's social background, chronically in debt, choose to be a poet whom no one seems able to read? Everything else follows from that question.

Anyone working in this area owes a special debt to the small number of previous explorers who have worked heroically to make sense of Chapman's difficult verse. Millar MacLure and Raymond Waddington in their different ways tried to account for Chapman by invoking the traditions of the learned mysteries, and if I have disagreed with them, I have also learned from them. Richard Ide's comparison of Chapman and Shakespeare helped me understand the meaning and importance of *virtue* for Chapman. At a crucial moment early in my thinking about the book I found encouragement and liberation in Gerald Snare's *The Mystification of George Chapman,* which more than any other single work tries to get at Chapman as an artist in the modern sense.[7] I also want to use the occasion of the preface to acknowledge Vincent W. Beach Jr.'s useful annotated bibliography of Chapman criticism, a work which finds no occasion to appear in the notes.[8]

I wish to thank the following journals: *English Literary Renaissance* for permission to reprint portions of "'This Ticklish Title': Chapman, *Nennio,* and the

Critique of Nobility" (26 [1996]: 291–312); *Criticism* for portions of "Virtues Obscured: George Chapman's Social Strategy" (39 [1997]: 161–84); and *Modern Philology* for portions of "Furious Insolence: The Social Meaning of Poetic Inspiration in the 1590s" (94 [1997]: 305–26 [© 1997 by The University of Chicago]). The book, however, is much more than the sum of these three articles. Only when the individual points about nobility, obscurity, and furor have been established independently can the really important social argument be made: that the poets I am looking at are engaged in a social struggle that even if it comes to naught in the short run will change the ideals of English poetry.

I wish to thank the Institute for the Humanities at the University of Illinois at Chicago for a yearlong fellowship in 1995–96 during which the basic draft of the book was written. I also thank the College of Liberal Arts and Sciences for a one-semester sabbatical leave in spring of 1997. Colleagues in Chicago and elsewhere, especially David Bevington, Norman Boyer, Alan Hager, Michael Lieb, Peter Lindenbaum, Ned Lukacher, Bridget Gellert Lyons, Mary Beth Rose, and Richard Strier, have been a steady source of encouragement and discussion. Clark Hulse read portions of the work, and at important moments made delicate suggestions that have made all the difference. Judy Gardiner has served as a regular sounding board for the ideas of the book as they were developing, and her reading of the whole manuscript has saved me from many of the excesses to which such a work is prone. Working with Cathy Daly on her dissertation on Spenser and Ireland helped me to think about that poet's status and ambitions. Pat Hollahan of the University of Illinois Press has been the ideal copyeditor. And finally, Virginia Wright Wexman, as always, has urged me on, read anything, anytime, anywhere, and then patiently advised me whenever I got stuck.

Ambition, Rank, and Poetry
in 1590s England

Introduction

The simple axiom that culture is a site of social struggle conceals an extraordinary circularity: "Culture," says Bourdieu, "is a stake which, like all social stakes, simultaneously presupposes and demands that one take part in the game and be taken in by it; and interest in culture, without which there is no race, no competition, is produced by the very race and competition which it produces."[1] To be "taken in" by the game one must have already invested in it. Such initial commitment is inspired by a conviction that this is a race worth entering. Success will, it is imagined, lead to recognition, authority, and, important for poets coming from an impoverished background, economic reward. Those for whom such recognition and reward are not forthcoming can abandon the race, or they can try to change its terms, to criticize and revise them so that at least in some ways they can claim victory. The history of art in modern times is one of a constant process of such revision. In the early modern period, as poets from poor and unimpressive social positions compete with each other and with privileged poets, this dimension of the cultural competition increasingly entails a revision of the social purposes of culture. The competition becomes an attempt to impose a redefinition of art itself.

Renaissance scholars have long rejected summaries of a simple world picture, but that still has not prevented them from frequently generalizing about uniform social, religious, and intellectual meanings, from the interpretations of iconography or "Renaissance conventions" to statements about what is socially permitted. Bourdieu's sociology directs us not to such summary but to an awareness of the *differences* between the understandings possible at any one time from the various positions in social space. Without appealing to the freedom and individuality so often claimed for art and genius, we can nevertheless stress the local social motives and tactics that shape the rhetoric of each individual production and try to understand these productions in struggle against and alliance with other contemporary productions. The "practice" of art, to invoke another Bourdelian theme, takes place as tactical play within hegemonic rules.

Wealthy and titled poets, endowed with leisure, can indulge in art and easily appeal to standing traditions of courtiership and grace to justify their avocations. The dynamic of the social hierarchy grants them an inherent importance, so that even mediocre verse gets attention. Poor poets have a more difficult project. They lack the distance from necessity that would permit them to "waste" time. Having no other source of social recognition, for them poetry is their whole definition, their mode of self-assertion. Usually their livelihood is at least indirectly dependent on their poetry. The implications of this social dimension of the poetry, both for the poets themselves and for our understanding of what their poems are *doing,* have not been much observed by modern critics.[2] Yet the struggle as it was pursued in Elizabeth's last years reshaped the cultural landscape and is central to our modern ideas of why art is important.

To begin with a simple problem: Why at this time, before the development of the modern taste culture which has ways of converting cultural capital into economic wealth, should a poor man want to be a poet?[3] Economically, it is a mystery why in a society in which the highest arts are devoted to the praise and entertainment of aristocrats and the queen and in which the most fashionable forms, such as the sonnet, seem designed to allow a courtier to display his gracefulness, ambitious men, and at least one woman, of no social distinction and no fortune should undertake careers as poets.[4] We are familiar with a number of strategies by which a poor man could succeed in this difficult economy. Some, such as Robert Greene and Christopher Marlowe, sought commercial success, whether by voluminous publication of popular fiction, or by energetic production for the popular theater, or in the case of Thomas Nash by creating a reputation as a lively and disputatious personality. By all accounts, however, this was a very hard way to make a living. Others such as John Lyly succeeded economically by playing to the court, though this too was not an insured livelihood, as his difficulties in the 1590s prove.[5] Samuel Daniel and, later, Ben Jonson followed a more traditional route and found sufficient patronage early in their careers to bolster more commercial risks. Edmund Spenser supported a serious commitment to poetry by employment as a secretary, just as did John Donne, at least in the later 1590s. Shakespeare worked many fronts, dedicating poems to an aristocratic patron, writing plays for the commercial theater, and working as an actor and shareholder in a theater company. These men may not have been particularly happy with their places, but still the picture they give of poets scrambling by various, often multiple, enterprises to find a way to practice their craft makes some economic sense, and as long as we do not probe the economics too deeply, it is easy for us to treat them as engaged in a common pursuit with more privileged poets and sharing with them a common poetic purpose.

There was one important poet, however, whose strategy makes no sense in this picture. Economically George Chapman belongs with these poets, but he stands strikingly apart. In his early work Chapman frequently complains about his poverty and the unappreciative audience, but he at the same time takes considerable pride in writing a poetry which he insists most readers will not understand. His earliest poems address not a potential economic patron but a fellow poet, Matthew Roydon, known to have had his own financial troubles. Though Chapman clearly understands how one succeeds in a patronage system and though he participates actively in the commercial theater, he begins his career as a poet belligerently advocating and practicing an obscurity that, given his social ambitions, seems self-defeating and illogical.

Chapman seems to have attended both universities, and in his early title pages at least he titled himself "Gent." He was not, therefore, without some social capital from the start. Yet, poverty plagued Chapman all his life, from almost a decade before he began publishing until late in his career when he was a recognized poet and playwright. Thanks to the researches of Mark Eccles, we know the story of how in 1585 Chapman was approached in a friendly fashion by a man named John Wolfall, who offered to supply a bond of surety for a loan to furnish Chapman money "for his proper use in Attendance upon the then Right Honorable Sir Rafe Sadler Knight." Chapman's courtly ambitions led him into a trap. He apparently never received any money, but he would be plagued for many years by the papers he had signed. Wolfall had the poet arrested for debt in 1600, and when in 1608 Wolfall's son, having inherited his father's papers, sued again, Chapman's only resort—this, let us remember, is late in a career that began long after the original scam—was to petition the Court of Chancery for equity. The younger Wolfall complains on his side that Chapman "whoe att the first being a man of verry good parts and expectacion, hath sethence [presumably since 1585] very unadvisedly spent the most part of his tyme and his estate in ffruitless and vayne Poetry."[6] We cannot expect to know Chapman's personal motives for entering the literary arena, but with Wolfall junior we can appreciate the reasons militating against such a career. And, though Wolfall does not bring up the matter, we can ask why a poet in such recurring financial difficulty should write a poetry that takes considerable pride in being unpopular.

The anomaly of Chapman is the key to a pervasive consciousness which will require us to reconfigure the whole picture. In Chapman's practice we see what is elsewhere hidden, evidence of an intense but muted social struggle wherein the value of cultural capital is being renegotiated. Different social needs produce different ideals of poetry. By questioning the nature and purposes of poetry, Chapman and a group of poor fellow poets initiate a line of inquiry that leads finally to a criticism of the established social hierarchy, its values and its basis. They are energetically attempting to create a "serious" poetry that will be neither the sign of what they see as the trivial wit and grace that the court promotes nor the tools of moral pedagogy that the moral and religious poets (and the enemies of poetry) demand.[7] Bourdieu would describe them as attempting to improve the exchange-rate of their cultural capital. They invoke a variety of classical and continental models for their enterprise, so it is deceptively easy to read them as simply involved in a grand, unified poetic tradition, but because of their lowly social position the tradition always means something different for them than it does for aristocrats or for moral educators. It is their idea of the high social value of poetry itself, not just a device for some other end—pleasing a patron, wooing a woman, displaying one's skill, teaching morality to schoolboys—that links Chapman with Marlowe, Spenser (in some of his guises), Jonson, and more minor poets such as Thomas Watson, Thomas Lodge, Aemilia Lanyer, and Matthew Roydon.

These poets are sometimes confused with earnest moralists such as Stephen Gosson, Gabriel Harvey, Barnabe Barnes, and the mysterious Henry Willobie, who, while they have in some senses poetic ambitions, finally commit themselves to a moral crusade that distrusts poetry and drama altogether. Some members of this group come from an educated, middle-class background and turn to a moral didacticism only after first attempting a conventional literary career, writing plays in the case of Gosson or scandalous amorous lyrics in that of Barnes.[8] Since the moralists often share with the poets we are interested in a sense of outrage at the values and behavior of the aristocracy, their moral agenda confuses the reading of the larger field; their utilitarian and ethical idea of poetry has often been mistaken by modern critics, who have generally failed to distinguish the social discourses involved, as identical to the moral position of the other social factions. In their mature stance, however, they are hostile to poetry as anything other than moral and religious instruction, and the work they produce has not attracted the attention of later ages as literature.

Against these enemies of poetry appears the extraordinary image of Sir Philip Sidney. At his death in 1586, when all his work was still available only in manuscript, Sidney was honored publicly as a soldier and courtier more than as a literary figure. But in the 1590s, with the publication of the *Apology for Poetry, Astrophel and Stella,* and the various versions of *Arcadia,* he comes to be treated as a literary model. The tradition that might be said to culminate in Yeats's "In Memory of Major Robert Gregory" is set in motion in the 1590s by the image of the accomplished, amorous courtier who dashes off masterpieces in a variety of genres while serving his country and his religion. This has seemed an attractive vision in recent years, and in the absence of a critical text to compete with the *Apology* it has become common to treat Sidney as the spokesman for all English Renaissance poets.[9]

As we shall see, on a number of occasions Chapman pointedly opposes Sidney's ideas of poetry. For Chapman, Christopher Marlowe, scandalous for what Meres calls his "Epicurisme and Atheisme,"[10] murdered unheroically in a tavern in 1593, represents a much more attractive intellectual position. Marlowe, the scholarship boy from Canterbury who makes his literary place not by virtue of his social position but by audacious and shocking learning, is a model for a kind of wild, popular genius. The public stage that so outraged the enemies of poetry, a form Sidney never worked in, is a major source of Marlowe's reputation at his death, but he is also well known by the end of the decade as the poet who wrote *Hero and Leander* and "Come Live With Me and Be My Love." If Sidney for obvious reasons is not concerned with how a poor poet makes a living or about such a poet's social status, for equally obvious reasons Marlowe finds the economic plight of impoverished talent an inescapable concern. It is one of the aims of this book to bring out Marlowe's social perspective and its special sense of the sociocultural significance of poetry itself.

Though criticism has sought to understand Marlowe's relation to such canonic figures as Shakespeare and Spenser, Chapman is the figure who most emphatically represents this tradition after Marlowe's death. Chapman's completion of Marlowe's *Hero and Leander* in 1598 is but the most obvious sign of a sympathy that binds the two poets. The link, however, is not so much personal as a shared sense of resentment. In his early poetry Chapman, in ways that have been almost entirely overlooked by modern scholars and critics, attacks the courtly tradition of literature in the name of a high art, what he calls the "absolute poem," that speaks to a cultural elite. Chapman, more than any other poet of the period after Marlowe, articulates the defining edge of this emerging formation.

These three groups—the moralists, the aristocrats, and the poor poets—render well-marked positions in the poetic field at the end of the century, but they do not by any means account for every poet. Donne, for instance, while he too is acquainted with poverty, loves learning, and admires Ovid, attempts a career trajectory rather different from that of any of the poets we have mentioned. Poetry is never more than an avocation with him, and while he cannot share Sidney's aristocratic tastes, his ambitions prevent him from the kind of complaint about the established social possibilities we will find in Marlowe and Chapman. However, Donne's anomalous position should make us aware of the inadequacy of the categories themselves as defining a "literary system." It is a principle of the "field" as Bourdieu understands it that it be a space in which we articulate positions by remarking differences on a number of axes. Thus, though two poets might share an economic origin, on other axes, such as religion or profession, they may well diverge. Helgerson's categories of Professional, Prodigal, and Laureate, suggestive as they are, insofar as they define absolute categories rather than points related in a field, oversimplify the situation.

My aim is to understand distinctions and linkages that would have been strongly felt in the period but have become obscure to later students. As a rule, literary historians have preferred the implausible drama of personalities when the significant disagreements and claims to association in the period were generated by more intrinsic social situations. The Nash-Harvey controversy in particular has presented literary history with a misleading model for the way the literary rivalries that matter were enacted in the period. Nash and Greene were quite extraordinarily theatrical men, and they seem to have delighted in taking issue with Richard Harvey's clumsy and very oblique attack on them for their vigor in pursuing the Martin Marprelate controversy. Theories about "the rival poet" or "the School of Night" get much of their inspiration from the Nash-Harvey model. The alliances between poets as evidenced by public claims of friendship and affection are also often wrongly treated as genuinely personal. I would agree with S. K. Heninger that differences of rank make it unlikely that Spenser had anything like a "friendship" with Sidney.[11] Chapman may drop the names of the earls of Derby and Northumberland in his first letter to Matthew Roydon, but these are strategic claims of association, hardly signs that he knew these powerful men.[12] It would be naive of us to be deaf to the social strategy of claims of friendship with nobility such as we find in the verse letters and dedications of Donne, Jonson, and Lanyer, even if the acquaintance has a basis in fact.

By the same token, we should not be naive about the motives for disagreement. We need to remember that the harshest intellectual controversies are often not between adversaries of distinct persuasion—all conversation has generally ceased in such cases—but between thinkers who if viewed from any distance look identical. At the psychological level Freud calls this "the narcissism of minor differences," and it is a pattern that recurs at the political and sociological levels.[13] To the established middle class Marx and Bakunin seem colleagues and anarchy a synonym for communism. But for Marx the errors of Bakunin are more dangerous than those of Adam Smith. As Bourdieu puts it, "Social identity lies in difference, and difference is asserted against what is closest, which represents the greatest threat" (*Distinction,* 479). Just so, from our historical distance, the angry defenses of poetry by poets of the English Renaissance may look like a unified attack mounted by the artists against the philistines who disregard poetry, but a closer analysis will show that the anger is not against the enemies of poetry but against fellow poets who in a different social space use poetry for different purposes. The people Chapman attacks by calling them "ignorants"[14] are not the illiterate or even the practical Burleighs but those poetasters who make a claim to art and learning and in so doing distort and debase them. Chapman's anger is directed against courtly *sprezzatura* itself which, by making poetry an illusion of graceful improvisation, would diminish its high and mysterious purpose which, so the socially struggling poets Chapman represents would want to claim, merits recognition and valuation above the false dignities of rank and fortune. In other words, *sprezzatura* is a demonstration of social privilege.

The social formation the Marlowian group of writers represents has been difficult to perceive in part because, alert to the dangers of complaining about the injustices of a system that privileges inherited power and to the benefits of the association with the wealthy, they tend to conceal their critique and to promote the illusion that they somehow share social space with their social superiors. Aspiring poets, whatever their dark, private feelings about the social situation, often strive to appear in contexts that associate them with aristocratic and courtly poets. Matthew Roydon's elegy for Sidney, which I will argue advocates a poetic ideal that is contrary to the one Sidney himself stood for, hides its oppositional stance by appearing with the countess of Pembroke's own elegy for her brother in *The Phoenix Nest* and in the volume of Spenser's poems that contained *Colin Clouts Come Home Again*.[15] Thomas Lodge, for all his claims in "To Rowland" to write obscure hymns, is best known as a writer of popular prose romances. Chapman is particularly hard to separate from the crowd clustering around the court. By the late 1590s he is mentioned as an important poet and playwright by such dutiful recorders of fashion as Meres and Harvey. He wrote popular comedies in the late 1590s and later under James wrote a court masque and a notorious epithalamium for a notorious aristocratic union. Despite their anger at the economic plight of poor poets and at the state of culture, these poets are not above realizing success when they can. Though it is relatively marginal, the group is not, in Raymond Williams's terms, "oppositional."[16] Its members are careful to speak their complaints about society's false honors and the neglect of merit in an ambiguous language so as not to offend powerful groups, whether economic patrons or official censors. As J. W. Saunders long ago observed, all nonreligious authors try to "give the impression that their literature was written by gentry, for gentry, and about gentry."[17] Even for writers who could use the title "Gent," such an impression has its element of gamble, and the illusion of happy participation in an aristocratic exchange does not exclude feelings of envy.

Twentieth-century readers may unintentionally collaborate in concealing the social perspective; the themes of need and resentment that identify the group seem a little embarrassing, perhaps unpoetic, and we show our own breeding and cultural nobility by looking beyond the economic complaints and by overlooking the vulgar signs of resentment. Louis Martz's uneasiness with Marlowe's digression in the middle of *Hero and Leander* on the economic plight of scholar-poets is a surprisingly forthright expression of a pervasive sensitivity.[18] It has seemed an act of perverse ingenuity to dwell on the occasional moments of clear, abrasive social anger when so much of the work can be read as conventional. Thus, between the ambiguity of the poets' criticisms and the discreet decorum of the scholars it has been almost too easy to be unaware of the group's separateness. Yet at a deep level *need* itself is a theme and a structuring principle for the poetry of these men struggling to make a living. Lodge complains that need "tyrannises" and generates "dull conceits" and thereby makes exceptional poets appear conventional. Unless we recognize this elementary social issue—which once acknowledged shows up everywhere—we will misunderstand what motivates these poets, misunderstand the poetry, and fail to recognize what makes them important in their own time. We will therefore misread the history of literature.

The real stakes in the game of culture are always out of sight; that is what it means to play the game. The texts do not simply "say" what they say; they are tactical moves in a social struggle. They must be interpreted, and to this end we must work to discover the social motives behind arguments that have commonly been misconstrued as general "Renaissance" ideas. The hermeneutic closedness and adequacy of the moral reading of poets of the period that critics in the 1590s and in the 1950s worked hard to make seem so obvious as to be undoubtable, remain obstacles to reinterpretation. One project in what follows is to identify the disguised but explicit evidence of resentment and critique in the published texts. That is not a simple task.

Over the last fifty years we have come to a profound appreciation of the economic changes that were transforming English society in the late sixteenth century.[19] For aristocrats, both poets and the patrons of poets, a period of economic transition is a time to insist on the stable moral and political traditions of poetry: Horace's *dulce et utile*.[20] For commoners, on the contrary, here is an opportunity to realign the system of cultural power, to propose that artistry, wit, and learning are important qualities in themselves, apart from the rank of the person displaying them. By so doing, they can create what Bourdieu calls a "nobility of culture" to rival the nobilities of blood, power, and money. The project entails many facets: criticizing old traditions, finding revisionary models, and forming an alliance with a readership which will appreciate and support a new idea of poetry. Print and the stage are essential technologies for this project because they can generate an economics of culture not entirely dependent on patronage, though they are not in themselves liberating, for they can just as easily be used by forces of the traditional hegemony.[21] Also important as a way of creating the new social space is the practice of a poetry that will not advocate aristocratic manners and grace but will speak to the importance of poetry itself in the new economic situation and of poets, whatever their rank.

The critique implicit in the stance of these poets must be distinguished from the systematic process that Stephen Greenblatt describes by which "power" expresses "subversion" in order to contain it.[22] Greenblatt's idea of subversion reads ideological contradictions that accompany the process of enlightenment as potential negations of enlightenment. Thus Thomas Harriot's skeptical insight into the uses of religion to awe the superstitious, whether native Americans or faithful English, becomes in Greenblatt's reading a piece of a larger puzzle in which imperialist domination is rationalized (*Shakespearean Negotiations,* 39). Harriot's intellectual move is entirely co-opted by the larger mechanisms of "power." In the present inquiry I am interested in a different dynamic of social activity, one which works to construct a social place where none existed before, one anchored in the middle-class dilemma of how to make a living. Ambition leads poor poets to be cautiously critical of a social system that disregards merit and to resist the recontainment that characterizes the subversions Greenblatt examines.

If Greenblatt's pessimism tends to reduce subjectivity to an illusion in the larger system of power, another line of recent criticism tends to find "resistance" in nonhegemonic gestures and to find premonitions of a more modern, revolutionary consciousness in past figures.[23] The situation I am examining is more tangled than such a reading of resistance acknowledges; if these poets are not contained by power, they are nevertheless to some extent complicit with it. They are poets, after all, constructing their careers, and they have no intention of becoming religious martyrs or political agitators. They are less interested in changing society than in establishing the worth of their own accomplishments and thereby accumulating cultural capital. But, though the struggle is in terms of the definition of cultural value, it is still inescapably political in that it must, at some point, fault the dominant faction's values, and it will put forth its own virtues as a challenge to the hereditary basis of the aristocratic hegemony. This last strategy entails developing a critique of the social system as a way of revising the market for cultural capital in relation to the more material forms of capital.

Pierre Bourdieu's reading of modern taste culture is useful because it accounts for both the opportunities offered by the cultural field and the profound conservatism it also enforces. Bourdieu envisions a culture in which, again and again at every layer in thousands of infinitesimal judgments and validations, the already legitimate is relegitimized, nobility sanctified, and the miracle of social coherence takes place, a culture in which people acting by their own choice find their predetermined places in the reciprocating system wherein the chosen accept their election and the excluded know better than to try to break in. Though from a broad sociological perspective the system seems hopelessly deterministic, nevertheless at the local, individual level agency operates, and it is the "practice" of individuals that makes the system function. Agents are always negotiating for social benefits. Bourdieu's early work, as represented by *Outline of a Theory of Practice,* argues that it is at this level, when agents *choose* how to reciprocate—how rich a gift to give, how quickly to respond—that the anthropologist sees the actual workings of the system that the traditional structural codifications miss entirely.[24] An understanding of the meaning of such individual tactics is important if we are to grasp what is actually happening, why people act the way they do.

Such tactics operate at the very heart of the social system, but they are neither simple nor easily understood. The redundant complexity and subtlety of the hegemonic reproductive structure entails an equally subtle repertory of moves on the part of those who wish to play on the system. Within any field, agents compete for position and benefits, but always with a sense of what is possible that is itself shaped by the dynamics and history of the field. The system at any moment offers any individual a set of social possibilities and options, though they are never as free as they may appear to someone insensitive to the system's constraints and dangers. Therefore, as Bourdieu repeatedly insists, a reading that is not aware of how the producer's social position shapes his or her work will inevitably miss a central issue of any artistic production: "By ignoring the systems of social relations within which symbolic systems are produced and utilized, the strictly internal interpretation most frequently condemns itself to the gratuitousness of an arbitrary formalism. . . . The semiologist, who claims to reveal the structure of a literary or artistic work through so-called strictly internal analysis exposes himself to a theoretical error by disregarding the social conditions underlying the production of the work and those determining its functioning."[25] The problem is, as Bourdieu warns, one cannot show what an author is doing by simply "reading." Thus, "Circumspect and repeated re-readings" of Chapman without a sense of his social needs will demonstrate only how thoroughly he has rendered his meaning ambiguous.

We need to articulate Chapman's social attitudes within the larger field of poetic discourse at the time to understand both what his meaning is and why he should obscure it. The historical reconstruction of the field will need to begin with analysis of moments of specific difference by which poets distinguish themselves from others. We will identify four such points: the expression of resentment, the idea of true nobility, the championing of obscurity, and the invocation of poetic furor. As these specific points of difference become clearer we can use them to describe a field in which we can situate Chapman and his fellow poor poets. As we shall see, Chapman is, in a way that has not been previously understood, a poet with a political message.

I sketch this problematic to give depth to an issue inherent in Richard Helgerson's version of "the literary system." In laying out the expectations of the system that places Spenser, Jonson, and Milton, Helgerson reifies certain values in the game of culture. It is to a large extent the historic canonization of these three poets that creates by a back formation the illusion of "system" in the Renaissance. To be sure, Renaissance theorists themselves often worked hard to establish an authoritative system, but as Bourdieu would insist, their theories too are moves in the game, and the success of particular Renaissance theories is an instance of hegemony in action. If centuries later we have lost the ability to hear the alternative voices, that is testimony to the dominant class's success in shaping the canon that is passed on and, more subtly, the methods of interpreting that canon. The system appears to be securely in place because, given the more or less exclusive access to interpretive authority of a certain small group of people, mostly men, even those resentful poor poets who might imagine their interests best served by some alternative will appear to have adapted to the system. Outright rebels will have been destroyed, and the more subtle artists, who have tried to turn the system to their own advantage, will have been reread as part of the system that has always existed, either as Shelley-like idealists (Marlowe) or as boring pedants (Chapman). In these chapters we shall have occasion to reread a series of works from quite different sectors of the cultural field—works by Sidney, Spenser, Roydon, Barnes, Willobie, Shakespeare, Stubbes, and Lanyer, as well as Chapman—as social actions, often addressed to each other. My hope is by this concentrated reading to identify the themes and the social concerns that motivate one portion of the field.

If Bourdieu can teach us the redundant and unrecognized ways the social structure reproduces its hierarchies, nevertheless he analyses a society that is economically different from the late feudal–early modern culture of the Elizabethan period.[26] Before the modern system is in place (Bourdieu locates its establishment in France in the seventeenth century, but it is not fully operational until the nineteenth century), it cannot ever achieve the elaborated totality that Bourdieu explores because it cannot escape the domination of the powerful economic and ideological structures of inherited nobility. Taste culture cannot function as such until artists and intellectuals are "in a position to liberate their products from all social servitude, whether the moral censure and aesthetic programmes of a proselytizing church, or the academic controls and directives of political power, inclined to regard art as an instrument of propaganda."[27] In this earlier period, as Russell Fraser argues, the circle of privilege precedes and dominates culture;[28] the boorish lord is independent of taste, and those nobles who pay attention to the developing cultural economy adapt it to their own hegemonic purposes, thus anchoring the system in the undeniable and seemingly unchallengeable material reality of the fixed system of social rank. The privileged aristocracy of birth, supported by sumptuary laws, extremely limited access to education, and the violent and arbitrary power of authority, hardly seems to need "taste" to maintain the status quo. Given the blatant enforcement of established privilege by law, force, and tradition, in the early modern period, taste serves simply as another confirmation—perhaps there can never be too many such confirmations—of the supposed justice of the present order.

Yet one should not, as it were, idealize the purity of the rule of privilege. Though feudal conceptions of rank appear to offer a simple field for analysis, the system is never as systematic as it claims. Nobles may invoke ancient lineage, but in many cases the distinguished family owes its position to a social bounder only a few generations back. As we will see when we turn to *Nennio,* this is not an intellectual mystery even in the sixteenth century, but the system is so powerful that it can easily override occasional critiques. And it protects itself. Social reproduction is always complex and always requires an elaborate supporting system.[29] By the same token, the ambiguous possibilities of alternative social standings implicit in almost any dramatic situation in the Elizabethan period will in all likelihood receive a clear and to our ears perhaps biased reading by virtue of the field as it exists historically.

Rude mechanicals and princes display the rightness of their social placing in their every gesture. Part of the comedy of Bottom as viewed from a position sympathetic with the aristocracy is his audacious assumption that, just as he can play all the roles, he can be Titania's consort. To aristocrats, his very deafness to his violations of decorum signals his social inferiority, and the aristocratic members of the wedding party are, even in their general laughter at his improprieties, clear about the disruption he represents. It can be tolerated in this situation as comedy befitting a moment of revelry. There is never any sense that Bottom's taste culture is anything but inferior—that is, its comedy is available only to the aristocrats—and there is no possibility of exchange of cultural capital with the royal party. If implicit in Bottom's ambitions is a utopian possibility, an element of

Bakhtinian dialogism, it is uncovered only in the space of modern class tolerance. The fields of power and rank as they exist in the 1590s, rigorously restricted and controlled by the circle of privileged inheritance, will in turn limit the possibilities of meaning for poetry and drama.

Just as the historical field of social possibilities restricts the possible meanings of Bottom's ambitions, it limits the kinds of freedom a poet could claim or imagine. The Renaissance poet, especially a poor poet, cannot escape the exigencies of the social reality by an appeal to a transcendent aesthetic and all the distinctions associated with isolation and dedication that accrue to the modern artist. Therefore, one cannot simply read a poet of 1600 as a proto-modern, though that is what T. S. Eliot and Margaret Bottrall seemed to want to do with Chapman.[30] Chapman is responding to social needs different from those that drive modern culture, and the apparent modernity in his defense of obscurity is in fact an illusion. The tactics of the game we can learn from Bourdieu, but the actual economy is somewhat different. In general, the distinctions Bourdieu analyzes discriminate between the privileged and the newly wealthy who would aspire to cultured status without the long training (disguised as innate taste) that the position requires. Taste distinctions tend to reinforce the status quo. To be sure, the dominated fraction of the dominant class, because of the analogy between its position and that of the lower classes, often sympathizes with the dominated, but nevertheless its final allegiance is with the dominant and it tends to perpetuate the ruling culture's obfuscation of social reality. In the period we are concerned with, the situation is different because culture, insofar as it matters at all, tends to be thought synonymous with birth. Even if the rigidities of the social hierarchy are beginning to loosen thanks to economic changes, the ideology of birth is dominant and largely unquestioned. In this situation the distinctions of taste (or as they would be termed at this time, the "virtues of the mind") serve not to reinforce the status quo (though they still, of course, exclude the vulgar) but to put in play elements of a critique of the ideology of birth that is only just beginning to find expression. If by the later eighteenth century, as John Guillory argues, new, vernacular definitions of literacy may grant some status to the bourgeoisie while continuing to enforce the basic social structure,[31] in the early modern situation of the late Elizabethan period, certain disadvantaged men are just discovering how by asserting a higher standard of literacy they can challenge courtly privileges and the styles that signify them.

The necessarily oblique nature of social criticism under a patronage system accounts for the difficulty critics have had understanding the exact meanings of Chapman's social assertions.[32] Even though patrons might claim to support enlightened thought, they cannot, without undermining their own status and privilege, allow the class of patrons to be criticized, and so long as the dominant group is free from analysis, social thought is doomed to the repetition of aristocratic prejudices. The point is not to suggest that once patronage gives way to more market-driven forces then hegemonic prejudices will disappear; only that the censorship of this issue under patronage is intrinsic to the system. Provocative criticism of the system of rank and privilege as such will come mainly from religious activists like Phillip Stubbes or true blue Protestant poets like Henry Willobie who do not seek patrons. Anyone aspiring to a literary *career* as that is understood at the time must take considerable pains not to offend the class of patrons.[33] There are, to be sure, complaints about aristocrats in the literature of the period, but the people who make them generally do not attack the class itself but lament in carefully restricted language particular offenses and individuals. The best testament to the power of patronage to restrict discussion is the absence of any clear contemporary analysis of the Elizabethan social system. Insofar as a general analysis might raise questions about the supposedly inherent privileges of patrons, the analyst risks being silenced for speaking.

Quite apart from the specific problem of offending the patron by a criticism of patronage, thinking and speaking clearly about matters of social rank is always compromised by a deep, often unconscious, self-interest. The socially ambitious poet in particular will be working from a bias. As Bourdieu's axiom with which we began asserts, the race is a trap; the *habitus* that shapes each member of the social system, even one angry with it, invests the resentful poet with an undoubted appreciation of the profits of that system.[34] In the Renaissance this collaboration is particularly insidious, for many members of the fit audience the learned poet addresses will come from the very aristocratic class that might be criticized. By challenging the entitlements of superior ranks, the thankless poet denigrates the people of discrimination, those "nobles" who from the beginning, by educating and supporting poor men and rewarding intellectual accomplishment, have enabled the analysis. The very term "nobility" becomes ambiguous, identifying the public structure of rank by birth but also asserting the existence of a merit that has nothing to do with the artificial and fortunate accidents of genealogy.

Chapman and in less obvious ways Marlowe and Spenser speak in a way that those who share their sense of rank, aspiration, and resentment will appreciate, but that others, especially those wealthy and privileged people who see no need for such attitudes, will find opaque and trivial. The poor poet's very mode of speaking becomes expressive. Four centuries later in a very different cultural economy we have difficulty grasping what exactly that style expresses. Like the fluid negotiation with the censors that Anabell Patterson describes, this discourse becomes meaningful insofar as it risks exposure, and without a sense of that risk and the anger that justifies it we, like the censors, will find it entirely obscure. It both speaks "truth" that the powerful will not enjoy and by its risk articulates the line, the frontier, along which it hopes change will occur.

Once we grasp the social purpose of such a style we can rethink Chapman's poetic project. Modern criticism has treated Chapman as a moralist and a supporter of the aristocratic status quo. Gary Waller in his *English Poetry of the Sixteenth Century,* to take just one example, mentions Chapman only once, as a writer of "moralistic" poetry.[35] Jonathan Goldberg in his book on James I performs a brief analysis of *Bussy D'Ambois* in which he argues that Chapman is a spokesperson for the Jacobean idea of absolutist monarchy.[36] Given the traditions of modern Chapman criticism with its narrow interest in abstruse iconography, these are entirely understandable positions to take, but they are misconstructions of what Chapman is doing. The Chapman whom we discover when we tease out the social agenda is strikingly different from the stolid moralist of common criticism. He is witty, angry, and ingenious, and he takes pleasure in speaking in an entirely ambiguous way that requires us to use both what he calls our "light-bearing intellect"[37] and our sympathy with his social situation to find his meaning.

In one of his early comedies, *The Gentleman Usher,* Chapman has given us instructions how to read a message whose intention is to fool authorities but which must also be public. The lesson Chapman teaches us is important, because it opens up the period's sense of the suggestiveness of all discourse. It shows language as a medium by which messages can be sent through the censors themselves, while the censors, whether the governmental patriarchy, or earnest religious pedants, or in this case a foolish steward, can never be sure what is being said. And it shows that we need to attend to the strange suggestions of impossible social ideas we hear in fragments in a text. The discourse of thwarted lovers studied in this scene is analogous to that of the oppressed, of prisoners, and of poor poets.

At the middle of the play Margaret manipulates the foolish Bassiolo, the gentleman usher of the play's title, to carry a letter to her lover, Vincentio, which both says and unsays its message in such a way that Bassiolo, though he has studied its words, does not know what its message is. Margaret expects Vincentio, however, to hear the message clearly. As Margaret writes the letter we are instructed in a way of reading a hidden message:

Mar.   How spell you *foolish*?
Bas.   *F-oo-l-i-s-h.* [Aside] She will presume t'indite that cannot spell.
Mar.   How spell you *usher*?

Bas. 'Sblood, you put not in those words together, do you?

Mar. No, not together.

Bas. What is betwixt, I pray?

Mar. *As the.*

Bas. *Ass the?* Betwixt *foolish* and *usher?* Gods my life, *foolish ass the usher?*

Mar. Nay then, you are so jealous of your wit! Now read all I have written, I pray.

Bas. [*reads*] "*I am not so foolish as the usher would make me.*" O, so foolish as the usher would make me? Wherein would I make you foolish?

Mar. Why, sir, in willing me to believe he loved me so well, being so mere a stranger.[38]

I include the last turn to render the complexity of this interpretive moment, since the whole discussion is framed by Bassiolo's ignorance that Margaret and Vincentio are lovers using him as a go-between. To anyone in on the plot—as is the audience—the line "I am not so foolish as the usher would make me" is, as the evolution of the line reveals, a slighting of Bassiolo at many levels. But it remains harmless to the ignorant reader, and Bassiolo even takes some pride in what he reads as a revelation of Margaret's illiteracy and his superior knowledge.

The letter that is finally produced is entirely ambiguous, even nonsensical: "I am not so foolish to think you love me, being so mere a stranger. And yet I know love works strangely and therefore take heed by whom you speak for love, for he may speak for himself, not that I desire it, but if he do, you may speed, I confess. But let that pass. I do not love to discourage anybody. Do you, or he, pick out what you can. And so, farewell." In the play the audience hears the letter dictated but never read straight, and there is a suggestivity to the fragments in isolation that my rendering dampens, but my point is not how does the audience or Bassiolo read it, but how would Vincentio?[39] This is a text that allows anyone ("you, or he") to "pick out what you can," and each of these readers will most likely come up with a different interpretation. But of course the ambiguity is a trap for one reader and a game for the other. It is a model for how the play itself is to be read: the victim of criticism is to read it as flattery. The letter in its awkwardness allows for a "picked out" reading without ever sacrificing deniability. That the censors themselves read this way is neatly shown in the bureaucratic communication surrounding Hayward's *Henry IV* in 1599. Cyndia Susan Clegg quotes John Chamberlain's correspondence in which he cheerfully urges a friend to see if he can find a basis for censorship in the "toye": "I have got you a transcript of yt that you may *picke out the offence yf you can;* for my part i can find no such buggeswordes, but that every thinge is as yt is taken."[40]

The art of "picking out" meaning requires a reader patient with enigma and committed to the labor of understanding. Like the recipient of Margaret's letter, such a reader must through sympathy (i.e., it takes a lover to understand this strange love letter) find an important message in a text that an unsympathetic reader will find confused and trivial. We should recall Chapman's arch use of the word "trifle" to describe his serious work in his dedication of *Hero and Leander* to Lady Walsingham. The game of meaning he plays, with all its provocative evasiveness, is here explicitly set forth:

> I present your Ladiship with the last affections of the first two Lovers that ever *Muse* shrinde in the Temple of *Memorie;* being drawne by strange instigation to employ some of my serious time in so trifeling a subject, which yet made the first Author, divine *Musaeus,* eternall. And were it not that wee must subject our accounts of these common received conceits to servile custome; it goes much against my hand to signe that for a trifling subject, on which more worthines of soule hath been shewed, and weight of divine wit, than can vouchsafe residence in the leaden gravitie of any *Mony-Monger;* in whose profession all serious subjects are concluded. But he that shuns trifles must shun the world. (*Poems,* 132)

On the one hand the poet concedes that the poem is a trifle, but at the same time he asserts that such a trifle, inspired by "strange instigation," composed in "serious time," and revealing "worthines of soule" and "weight of divine wit," surpasses anything that might be constructed out of the "leaden gravitie of any *Mony-Monger.*" Just as eternal and divine wisdom can reside in a "trifle," so "brainles and passionate fooleries" may be found in the "reverend heapes of substance and austeritie" that belong to the "world." Yet, though the clean distinction between "trifles" and "reverend heapes" certainly attracts the poet, he rejects it as he makes it. "He that shuns trifles must shun the world": the aphorism might just as well tell us to engage the world as to shun it. It is in such almost uninterpretable enigmas that we find the heart of Chapman's style, which is in its most simple renderings profoundly puzzling, but not without serious meaning.

I

Morality, Rank, and the Cultural Field

In this initial chapter I want to understand how the privilege of rank touches the field of culture as it exists at the end of the sixteenth century in England, and to do this I will examine three texts which posed some difficulties for the dominant orders at the time but which may seem to us innocuous and unproblematic. The first text, Phillip Stubbes's *Anatomy of Abuses* (1583), has some notoriety as an early attack on the theater. The text has attracted attention recently mainly for its defense of traditional gender roles and behavior, but for us it will demonstrate the contortions a fervid moralist must perform if he is to speak openly. The second, *Willobie, His Avisa* (1594), is a lengthy set of poems admiring an innkeeper's virtuous wife, Avisa, who resists the importunities of five suitors. This text aroused vigorous hostility, both from poets and from the bishops, who had it called in and burnt in 1599, but to our eyes it is a pedantic and simple praise of a woman who repeatedly resists being seduced. Its controversial nature has puzzled twentieth-century scholars who have sought to uncover obscure and personal allegories. *Avisa* explicitly sets itself in competition with Shakespeare's *The Rape of Lucrece,* and it is this still unexplained connection that brings this otherwise apparently innocuous poem to modern attention. These two poems, controversial in their own time, I am using to explain how a social consciousness can express itself in this period when religion might be debated but rank was strictly protected. Behind the moral position of these texts lies a strong and angry consciousness of social rank, the privileges and presumptions of the nobility. It is the danger of such expression which accounts for the styles of these two texts and the strong reactions they provoked.

In the final section of this chapter we engage a third mysterious poem, Barnabe Barnes's *Parthenophil and Parthenophe* (1593), a poem now known, if it is known at all, for its lasciviousness, though the reaction of other poets and writers again seems out of proportion to the poem's affront to decorum. Unlike Stubbes and "Willobie," Barnes attempts to co-opt the exclusionary power of the dominant culture by outdoing it. He succeeded insofar as he became notorious. Hostility between social ranks accounts for the styles of these texts and the strong reactions they provoked, and an examination of them helps us understand the different strategies available to writers who felt excluded by or critical of the system. The difficulties these three texts pose will enable us to understand how limited are the possibilities of expression of social criticism in the then developing cultural field. It is with such minor texts in the background—the first two resistant to the dominant aristocratic culture, the last attempting to enter that culture—that we can then turn to Marlowe, Chapman, and other ambitious but poor poets and appreciate the task they face and inadequacy of the models they have for how to succeed.

In the eloquent and vigorous final chapters of *The War against Poetry*, Russell Fraser makes the case for understanding the Elizabethan attack on poetry not as simply a moral position but as an attempt to disrupt the "vicious circle" of privilege, which by a web of assumptions backed by powerful economic prerogatives "proves" that "Only the man of inherited means is the good man."[1] Fraser weaves the vicious circle of privilege by juxtaposing the arrogant and presumptuous statements of contemporary defenders of nobility with the facts of noble privilege as set forth by modern economic and cultural historians. A set of traditional ideological axioms sustains this vicious circle: the value and dignity of "blood," the contemptibility of "mechanical arts" and "trade," and the association of learning and the "Artes liberall" with leisure (pointedly distinguished from idleness), which tends to express itself in the ability to squander wealth. A cluster of moral and aesthetic misrecognitions in the service of economic power functions as a redundantly supported system that, while vulnerable at any number of specific points, nevertheless remains secure overall. The writers whom Fraser examines see poetry as an important ornament of privilege and therefore as the symbol against which they direct their broad class hostility. The "new man" (who has many faces: Puritan, Anglican, Catholic, businessman, scientist) "is bidding for a more substantial place. The aristocrat comes between him and the achieving of this place. But he does not attack the aristocrat directly: that is not thinkable in the sixteenth and early seventeenth centuries. . . . The tokens or accoutrements of privilege are called into question. This is, on one side, the genesis of the war against poetry. Its entail is aesthetic and vastly political. The closing of the theatres [in 1642] is coincident with, or rather it betokens a major shift in the understanding and evaluation of poetry. It betokens also the dispossessing of the privileged man" (*War against Poetry*, 142).

Since ultimately it is the monarch who may be threatened by the logic behind this attack, no one in the sixteenth or early seventeenth century is foolish enough to make that logic explicit. Therefore, while we find evidence of repression throughout the period, almost invariably we find that the texts being controlled are to our eyes innocuous or at worst entirely ambiguous. It may be, as Stephen Greenblatt argues, that authority has constructed subversion as a way of justifying and maintaining its own power and controlling the possibilities of dissent, in which case there are no truly subversive texts except those power projects. However, unless we are to believe that the whole citizenry agrees with or resignedly submits to power, dissatisfaction must be given some kind of voice. Fraser's accomplishment is to bring out the element of progressive social critique in what will probably seem to most modern critics to be reactionary and in the strict sense unpolitical texts.[2] Those who are protecting power may immediately recognize offense in such voices and texts, but we, living under a very different social dynamic, will need to learn to hear and understand the dissonance whose presence is signaled to us only by the authorities' disapproval.

It is this difficult and strictly regulated situation that accounts for the rambling and confused prose of Phillip Stubbes's *Anatomy of Abuses*.[3] Stubbes faces a delicate rhetorical situation: he must make a moral point without appearing to draw the political conclusions that follow. His simple argument is that the most dangerous sin is pride—most emphatically the pride exhibited in elegant apparel, in titles, and finally in idle pursuits, such as dancing and playgoing—because it distracts from the proper devotion to God. The logic of this equation would seem to lead inevitably to an apparent criticism of the court and the nobility. They, after all, most conspicuously take pride in titles and most ostentatiously display fine dress. Yet Stubbes also explicitly denies this conclusion. He repeatedly insists that his aim is not to fault the wealthy or the noble; he grants the social purpose of dignified costume for magistrates; he defends the sumptuary laws. Nevertheless, the strain on the argument is apparent. Much as he hates the pretensions of the cottager's overdressed daughter, his main hostility is directed against the wealthy and privileged. One cannot avoid the suspicion that his book is popular—and Stubbes is dangerous—because he expresses social antagonisms.

Whenever the issue of the privileges of the nobility arises, Stubbes is careful at some point to seem to blunt any critical intent, either by countering with a defense of the nobility, or by blurring the argument's focus. The logic at such moments never quite makes sense, however, and there are statements, usually immediately disavowed, which if isolated must be read as attacks on the nobility.

In a late passage that exemplifies this style of arguing at different levels and always maintaining deniability, Stubbes denounces titles. The passage artfully avoids offense to powerful people with titles by seeming to attack the ambitious pretensions of the newly rich and to defend the sumptuary laws: Philopono, Stubbes's spokesman in the dialogue, argues that men "affect money,"

> to be advanced and promoted to high dignities & honors upon earth. And they see, ye world is such that he who hath moni enough shalbe *rabbied* & maistered at every word, and withal saluted with the vaine title of worshipfull, and right worshipfull, though notwithstanding he be a dunghill Gentleman, or a Gentleman of the first head, as they use to terme them. And to such outrage is it growne that now adayes every Butcher, Shooemaker, Tailer, Cobler, Husband-man, and other, yea every Tinker, peddler and swinherd, every Artificer and other, *gregarii ordinis,* of the vilest sorte of Men that be, must be called by ye vaine name of Maisters at every word. But it is certain, that no wyse man, will intitle them, with any of these names, worshipfull and maister (for they are names and titles of dignitie, proper to ye Godly wyse, for some speciall vertue inherent, either els in respect of their birth, or calling due unto them,) but such Titivillers, flattering Parasits, and glosing *Gnatoes,* as flatter them, expecting some pleasure or benefit at their hands, which thing if they were not blowen up with the bellowes of pride, and puffed up with the wind of vainglori they might easily perceive. For certen it is, they do but mock and flatter them with these titles, knowing that they deserve nothing lesse. Wherfore, like good Recusants of that thing which is evill, they should refuse those vainglorious Names, remembring the words of our savior Christ, saying: be not called Maister, in token there is but one onely true Maister and Lord in Heaven. (K4–K4v)

It is the slipperiness of this that I want to emphasize. The passage begins with contempt for the pride evidenced in "high dignities & honors upon earth," but it quickly slides away from a criticism of all titles, first to the charge that it is money that determines title and then to indignant outrage at the pretensions of *gregarii ordinis* in laying claim to title. At this point Philopono is careful to insert a parenthesis explicitly sanctioning "names and titles of dignitie." Yet, the warning against the flattery of title might accuse all titles of "vainglori," and the conclusion that there is only one "Maister," God, were it not that the nobility has been explicitly exempted from the moral rules, would seem to be a clear criticism of all titles. The final turn could be read as asking the nobility to deny their titles, just as good recusants will abjure the pope.

The incoherent argument that what is damnable pride in the *gregarii ordinis* is somehow "proper" to others who "in respect of their birth, or calling due unto them" warrant titles may pass without remark because it seems to support social orthodoxy. It is moments like this that have led some recent scholars to read

Stubbes as a "conservative" supporter of the status quo.[4] But that is to mistake the disguise for the point, the gestures of obedient humility for love. For the hardworking lower orders it is the pride of the aristocracy that is most offensive. The parenthesis which excepts the nobility from the vanity of title has already itself been contradicted much earlier in the treatise in an equally evasive passage:

> Pride of the mouth, or of wordes, is, when we boast, bragge or glorie, either of our selves, our kinred, consanguinitie, byrth, parentage, and suche like: or when we extol our selves for any vertue, sanctimonie of lyfe, sincerytie of Godlynes, which eyther is in us, or which we pretend to be in us. In this kinde of Pride (as in the other) almost every one offendeth: for shal you not have all (in a maner) boast & vaunt themselves of their Ancestors, and progenitors? saying & crying with open mouth: I am a Gentleman, I am worshipful, I am Honourable, I am Noble, and I can not tell what: my father was this, my father was that: I am come of this house, and I am come of that: Whereas, Dame *Nature,* bryngeth us all into the worlde, after one sorte, and receiveth all againe, into the wombe of our mother, I meane, the bowelles of the earth, al in one and the same order and manner, without any difference or diversitie at all. (B6v)

This diatribe, while it attacks all claims of blood, poses as an innocent argument against boasting and bragging, that is, as a text on decorum rather than on the values of descent. Anyone sensitive to privilege, however, will hear its critique of the natural basis of privilege reverberating later in the argument against pride of title, even though—and this is a crucial issue—it is impossible to prove any treasonous challenge to the system of privilege.

The Anatomy of Abuses is littered with gestures at which the wealthy and noble might take momentary offense, while the worst that can be conclusively proven against Stubbes is that he holds them up to the Christian moral standard. "Do they think that it is lawfull for them to have millions of sundry sorts of apparell lying rotting by them, when as the poore members of Jesus Christ die at their doores for wante of clothing?" (E5). Stubbes translates "bursa avari, os est diaboli" as "The powch of a rich covetous Man, is the mouth of the devill, which is ever open to receive but always shut to give" (J7v). The Latin mentions greed, but "rich" is Stubbes's interpolation. When Spudeus, the other speaker in the dialogue, opines that "dainty fare & good cheer had both noorished ye body perfectly, and also prolonged life," Philopono responds as clearly as he ever does that the style of the wealthy is an abomination, but to themselves most of all:

> Experience, as my former intimations you may gather, teacheth clean contrary: for who is sicklier then they, that fare deliciously every day? who is corrupter? who belcheth more, who looketh wursse, who is weaker, and feebler then they? who hath

more filthie colour, flegme and putrifaction (repleat with grosse humors) then they? and to be briefe who dyeth sooner then they? Do wee not see the poor man that eateth brown bread wherof some is made of Rye, barlie, peason, beans oates and such other grose graines) [*sic*] & drinketh small drink, yea sometimes water, feedth upon milk, butter and cheese, (I say) doo wee not see such a one, helthfuller, stronger and longer living then the other, that fare daintily every day? (J2v–J3)

This is a beautiful example of what Bourdieu calls the "choice of the necessary," whereby that which one consumes for lack of choice is presented as a good in itself, as something one would choose even if one had other options.[5] And conversely, the dainties, which the poor cannot choose, are seen as deleterious, something one would reject anyway. By this sour grapes argument the dominated rationalize their situation, but we should be aware that in the act of rejecting that which they cannot have they also criticize it. The energy of the passage's beginning is motivated by social resentment, not by logic.

To undo the circle of rationalization of privilege, whose terrifying logic finally depends not on reason but power, one cannot speak openly, but one must nevertheless criticize. Stubbes seems to dance close to the edge at times, and it is the gratuitous moments of offense that cue us to watch for something more than what the contorted line of argument seems to conclude. Yet Stubbes is never a disloyal subject. If there are statements that verge on treason, there are also explicit defenses of nobility and the queen. Like his cousin a decade earlier, who, after the executioner has cut off his right hand for daring to advise the queen in print, holds up his bleeding stump and cries "God save the Queen," Stubbes writes a gesture that the authorities cannot discipline without seeming to punish obedience. And yet, one imagines, the authorities sense what is going on, and they will wait and watch for further offense. In the apparent illogic and self-contradiction of Stubbes's prose we see an instance of what Annabel Patterson calls the "hermeneutic of censorship." To read such prose we need to be aware of the powerful motive of social resentment which, if it may not be the whole motive, is never entirely separate from the moral and religious argument.

One of the more puzzling instances of disciplinary regulation is the bishop's ban of 1 June 1599, which ordered the burning of books by Hall, Marston, Guilpin, Davies, Marlowe, Nash, Harvey, and others.[6] Four days later two of these books, Hall's satires and Cutwode's *Caltha Poetarum*, were "staid," that is, they were not burnt, and "Willobies *Aviso*," not mentioned in the first list, was "to be Called in" (*Stationers' Register*, iii, 678). The list of books banned, like something out of Borges or Calvino, puzzles the thought and forces the question of exactly what in this cluster the bishops found offensive? Marlowe's translation of Ovid's elegies and Davies' epigrams were bound together, so it may have been impossible to ban one without the other, but the fact that they appeared as a unit may, conversely, point to their common purpose and audience. The sexual orientation of some of these works led scholars in the first part of this century to think that the ban was an attempt to enforce sexual morality. But the satires of Marston, Hall, and Guilpin, though of course they are not without some bawdy, are, all in all, less shocking for their sexuality than for their social anger. More recent scholarship has tended to see the ban as an attempt to quiet a trend toward satire, of which the erotic poems are a subcategory.[7] But that generic target still does not account for all the works of the list. After all, Hall's satires were quickly exempted. Both sides of the Harvey-Nash exchange seem to have angered authority.

Most mysterious of all is the inclusion in the second round of *Willobie, His Avisa,* which appeared in 1594 and was popular enough in some circles to justify a publisher's reprinting it six times in the next four decades. This long poem, in seventy-four cantos ranging in length from one to occasionally a dozen or even more six-line stanzas, has little that attracts the attention of the modern reader. Willobie, an apparently fictitious author, tells of the virtue of Avisa, an innkeeper's wife, who resists a series of five seducers.[8] Being neither lascivious nor obviously satiric, this celebration of virtue triumphant hardly seems to warrant censorship, and modern critics have therefore suspected a personal reference of some kind. G. B. Harrison read it as an attack, written by Matthew Roydon and sponsored by Ralegh, on the Essex-Southampton group. More recently B. N. de Luna has read the poem as an allegory of Queen Elizabeth's various refusals of marriage, identifying each of Avisa's suitors with one of the queen's. Remembering how offended the queen was when John Stubbes had the temerity to voice an opinion on the Alençon affair, the argument goes, the bishops thought fit to remove this audacious allegory, even though in de Luna's reading it is entirely approving of the queen. Yet *Willobie, His Avisa* was first published in 1594 and if personal libel or violation of royal prerogative were what made the poem offensive, one would hardly expect the authorities to wait until 1599 to discipline it.

I would suggest that the poem, and for that matter all the other poems included with it in the ban, are found offensive less because of their specific, individual arguments than because they represent a somewhat random sampling of a growing propensity to speak impertinently of aristocratic privileges and the social order that upholds them.[9] The bishops' problem is that even though disaffection is rife, few texts are sufficiently offensive in themselves to warrant selective prosecution. By burning a group of texts that in their eyes are disrespectful of authority and privilege the bishops hope to check what they see as a dangerous trend. This is their way of trying to discipline the strategy of promoting insolence under the guise of moral teaching or classical translation or imitation. *Willobie, His Avisa* is hardly a subversive poem in any strict sense. But the bishops may have suspected—and suspected rightly—that the poem's author may well have hoped that by celebrating a middle-class, married Englishwoman's virtue the text would be seen as irreproachable by the authorities even if it pointedly describes aristocrats behaving badly.

The argument that class offense was at the center of the bishops' concern in 1599 is made plausible by the appearance three years earlier of *Penelope's Complaint* by Peter Colse. In its introductory matter, this work makes explicit, angry reference to *Avisa,* and it is Penelope's high birth that Colse invokes in order to condemn the *Avisa* project. In his dedication to Lady Horsey, Colse claims that he is inspired to publish his poem by consideration of "the shipwracke that noble vertue chastitie is subject to" and that *Avisa* "(over-slipping so many praiseworthy matrons) hath registred the meanest." An author identified only as S.D., in a Latin poem addressed to Colse in the introductory material of *Penelope's Complaint,* is very angry that Avisa, an obscure woman from an obscure place, wife of an innkeeper and daughter of a peddler, should be made equal to Penelope, a famous woman and wife to an illustrious man.[10] In his own letter to the reader, Colse, after some haughty words about "desiring rather to teach the simple their uniforme cinque pace" than courtiers "their lofty galliards," denounces "vaineglorious *Avisa*" who seeks "by slaunder of her superiors, to eternize her folly." The aristocratic prejudice is so blatant that a modern reader might be tempted to wonder if Colse's production might not itself be a parody, but since it did not attract the bishops' attention, it seems more plausible to read it as simply a particularly unguarded statement of the expectations and privileges of rank of a sort not uncommon in this age.[11]

The promoters of *Avisa* must have been surprised and perhaps worried by the anger in defense of nobility their poem aroused. Sometime after Colse's *Penelope* a second edition of Avisa appeared with new introductory material: a defense of *Avisa* by "Hadrian Dorrell" and the new poem, "The Victorie of English Chastitie, under the fained name of Avisa," which tries to deflect the discussion to issues of national pride.[12] Dorrell insists that Avisa is fictional, and he, somewhat willfully, misinterprets Colse's phrase, "registered the meanest," ignoring Colse's obvious snobbery and defending *Avisa* on the grounds that "Chastitie had not beene the meanest, but rather one of the greatest gifts, that God giveth to men or women" (239). Without ever acknowledging a bias in the poem against the nobility and gentry, he insists that the lechers come from "all estates and degrees, and all Countries and Common-wealthes" (241). The new material makes much

of the universality of chastity and pretends that in putting Avisa ahead of Pene-
lope the offense was as much against Greece as against nobility.

At this level *Avisa* seems to generate attention and rebuke because it poses a
middle-class woman as a valid subject for poetry and therefore may imply that
such a figure is the social equal of legendary aristocratic women. It is an early
gesture of what John Guillory calls "imaginary politics," whereby social and eco-
nomic issues are addressed by demanding that the traditional canonic represen-
tations be changed.[13] We may share Guillory's skepticism about the effectiveness
of imaginary politics (it resembles the classic idealist fallacy of hoping to change
the base by reforming the superstructure), but at the same time we must recog-
nize the social struggle the cultural assault represents.

It is not simply Avisa's class that distinguishes Willobie's poem. Just as Fraser
argues that a social and political issue is being broached by the attack on poetry,
I want to argue that in *Avisa* we see evidence that the same party that has de-
nounced poetry, that is, the Protestant middle class, changing its strategy some-
what, here challenges the aristocratic uses of poetry by posing an alternative poetic.
At this point it is appropriate to draw attention to another dimension of *Willo-
bie, His Avisa:* more than the poem's late addition to the list of the bishops' ban,
what has drawn modern scholarly attention to it is the pointed reference to Shake-
speare in an introductory poem in which Avisa is put forward as a better model
of virtue than such famous classical women as Penelope and Lucrece.

> *In Lavine Land though Livie bost,*
> There hath beene seene a *Constant* dame:
> Though *Rome* lament that she have lost
> The *Gareland* of her rarest fame,
>> Yet now we see, that here is found,
>> As great a *Faith* in *English* ground.
>
> Though *Collatine* have deerely bought,
> To high renowne, a lasting life,
> And found, that most in vaine have sought,
> To have a *Faire* and *Constant* wife,
>> Yet *Tarquyne* pluckt his glistering grape,
>> And *Shake-speare,* paints poore *Lucrece* rape. (128)

Like other aspects of this mysterious poem, the tone here is ambiguous: the end
of this passage could be read as praise of Shakespeare.[14] But a more likely read-
ing would see Shakespeare as the poet of a false ideal of virtue. This author finds
Lucrece has "lost / the Gareland of her rarest fame," implying that whatever other
fame she may attain, the rape has robbed her of her virtue (constancy and chas-

tity).[15] The mention of Shakespeare at this point, however, is not necessary either to identify Lucrece, who is a famous example of virtue, nor to explain why Willobie would see her rape as having compromised her. In its oblique way the introductory poem is setting up a rivalry not just between Avisa and Lucrece but between this poem and Shakespeare's. If Peter Colse and the bishops find *Avisa* offensive, then in the competition here being adumbrated Shakespeare becomes a champion of a posture that bishops and aristocrats can praise. Female chastity might seem an unambiguous virtue, but as a closer inspection will show it has significant social nuances.

Shakespeare immensely complicates Lucrece as the embodiment of "virtue," both by exploring her inner sense of pollution and by linking her virtue to the theme of male rivalry and the founding of the Roman republic.[16] These complications rest on a set of unemphasized but unmistakable aristocratic presumptions.[17] To deliver her note to Collatine Lucrece calls a "sour-fac'd groom," and the narrative dwells on the confusion his lower-class humility and her aristocratic sense of pollution and guilt create:

> The homely villain cur'sies to her low,
> And blushing on her with a steadfast eye,
> Receives the scroll without or yea or no,
> And forth with bashful innocence doth hie;
> But they whose guilt within their bosoms lie,
>   Imagine every eye beholds their blame,
>   For Lucrece thought he blush'd to see her shame:
>
> When, silly groom! God wot, it was defect
> Of spirit, life and bold audacity;
> Such harmless creatures have a true respect
> To talk in deeds, while others saucily
> Promise more speed, but do it leisurely.
>   Even so this pattern of the worn-out age
>   Pawn'd honest looks, but us'd no words to gage. (1338–51)

Part of the groom's "silliness" is his gross, insensitive humility; part of Lucrece's nobility is her hypersensitivity to her own guilt and to how it might appear. The groom's "defect" is both a sign of his innate inferiority (with the irony that it is exactly Tarquin's aristocratic "spirit, life and bold audacity" that have caused the tragedy) and a sign of a "true respect" too little seen in the modern era when servants defraud their masters. The *defect-respect* rhyme catches neatly the whole syndrome of a class-based condescension which is able to praise a servant for living according to the lack that makes him a servant.

The narrator's phrase "sour-fac'd groom" recalls Tarquin's threat to murder Lucrece if she resists and bear her "unto the base bed of some rascal groom" (671). Lucrece echoes this phrasing when she recounts the threat later, speaking of "some hard-favour'd groom of thine" (1632).[18] The curious overemphasis of this threat in all its guises—not just a groom, a *rascal* groom, a *hard-favour'd* one at that, and not just to his bed but to his *base* bed—brings out the importance of rank to Lucrece's shame. Tarquin will make Lucrece appear not just unchaste but a class traitor who is so debauched that she has relations with inferiors. Given the emphatic redundancy of this contempt in the poem, it is tempting to read the phrase "sour-fac'd groom," not just as signifying unwillingness or from a different angle dour respectfulness,[19] but as a marker of social inferiority. The attitude toward the groom is the open expression of an aristocratic attitude that pervades the poem.[20]

Lucrece appeals to the same class assumptions when she pleads with Tarquin before the rape:

> So shall these slaves [i.e., passions] be king, and thou their slave:
> Thou nobly base, they basely dignified;
> Thou their fair life, and they thy fouler grave;
> Thou loathed in their shame, they in thy pride.
> The lesser thing should not the greater hide:
>   The cedar stoops not to the base shrub's foot,
>   But low shrubs wither at the cedar's root. (659–65)

The explicit social hierarchy of the opening lines of the stanza leads to a meditation on universal hierarchy. "Nobly base" might in another poem suggest redeeming qualities, but Lucrece clearly does not intend such, and it is a sign of the deep exclusions inherent in the categories of *noble* and *base* that their mixture does not open up new social possibilities but merely poses a paradox. Somewhat later, after Tarquin has left, Lucrece meditates further on the paradox, and again it leads to a reinforcement of ideas of social hierarchy:

> The baser is he, coming from a king,
> To shame his hope with deeds degenerate;
> The mightier man the mightier is the thing
> That makes him honour'd or begets him hate,
> For greatest scandal waits on greatest state.
>   The moon being clouded presently is miss'd,
>   But little stars may hide them when they list.
>
> The crow may bathe his coal-black wings in mire,
> And unperceiv'd fly with the filth away;

> But if the like the snow-white swan desire,
> The stain upon his silver down will stay.
> Poor grooms are sightless night, kings glorious day;
> Gnats are unnoted wheresoe'er they fly,
> But eagles gaz'd upon with every eye. (1002–15)

Lucrece experiences Tarquin's crime as a violation of her rank, and there is clearly in the second stanza a drift toward a meditation on her own polluted state: the swan is defiled by what is unperceived in the crow. She finds herself again thinking about grooms. Like Henry IV envying the sleep of the humble, Lucrece sees the lower ranks as living in a more tolerant social space, free from the moral obligations that define the aristocracy.

At the core of the aristocratic ideology is the presumption that the baseborn are not fully human and do not live by human standards. When, having despaired that Tarquin has "rifled" her of "that true type" (i.e., the chaste wife) which she before represented, she discovers a new type in Philomel, the type of the speechless rape victim, she resolves to "unfold / To creatures stern, sad tunes to change their kinds: / Since men prove beasts, let beasts bear gentle minds" (1146–48). The logic of this last turn equates humanity with gentility. Tarquin's crime jeopardizes the state,[21] but non-gentles may well feel their exclusion from this economy that identifies nobility with the state and humanity with gentility. The poem is concerned almost exclusively with the feelings and the morals of the class of Roman patricians. It is fitting to the poem's narrow interest in the very highest class that at the end, when Lucrece appeals to the lords around Collatine, it is a code of knighthood, the "noble disposition," that she and they invoke:

> "For 'tis a meritorious fair design
> To chase injustice with revengeful arms:
> Knights by their oaths should right poor ladies' harms."
>
> At this request, with noble disposition
> Each present lord began to promise aid,
> As bound in knighthood to her imposition. (1692–97)

Like knights at the court of the Faerie Queene, these Romans "right poor ladies' harms." "Poor ladies" cannot be impoverished women since Lucrece is referring to herself. The adjective *poor* refers only to her powerlessness and her suffering, not to her economic status. Once again we see how certain social presumptions restrict the possible readings of language that might otherwise have suggestive moral complications.

The contradiction of the richest woman in Rome being a "poor lady" is encompassed by Lucrece's suicide, which is essential to her elevation as a saint of virtue, an act at once fiercely aggressive and passive[22] and an intricate expression of dominant ideology. Suicide for honor has a long aristocratic tradition, and it also serves as a confirmation of the truth of her accusation against Tarquin.[23] She puts her word beyond doubt by this assertive act of absolute self-denial, and thereby reasserts her sense of being defined by her *honor,* a privilege hardly available to women from less powerful social spaces. My point is not that women of other social strata have a less powerful sense of honor but that the aristocrat is able to define herself almost entirely by her honor, and that the suicide beautifully locks in that definition and prevents any reading that might question Lucrece's virtue.[24]

Willobie, His Avisa, in explicit contrast to Shakespeare's depiction of an aristocratic female virtue, depicts a middle-class virtue. The author of *Avisa* has little patience with psychological complexity except to see through strategies of seduction. Unlike Lucrece, Avisa never thinks of her reputation. She acts rightly for the sake of righteousness itself, a righteousness defined by "the ever-living God." If Lucrece inhabits a shame culture,[25] Avisa, true to her Protestant training, inhabits a guilt culture in which her knowledge of her own virtue (and God's all-seeing wisdom) suffice.

The first "Trial" of Avisa, her resisting a "Noble man,"[26] is filled with intense consciousness of differences in rank. The section is subtitled, "under which is represented a warning to all young maids *of every degree* that they beware of the alluring intisements of *great* men" (137, emphasis added). This poem is not simply warning young women that "Young men will do't / if they come to't"; it emphasizes how differences in wealth and rank function in the attempted seduction. The nobleman is very conscious of his rank and of Avisa's inferiority. He can bitterly scoff: "A merry time, when countrie maides / Shall stand (forsooth) upon their garde; / And dare controll the Courtiers deedes" (140). He teaches her that "Thy betters far, if they were try'd, / Would faine accept my proffered love." After recalling the models of Joane of Naples, Messalina, and Cleopatra, he asks, "What need'st thou then to feare of shame, / When Queenes and Nobles use the same?" (141). Later he invokes his power to protect her as an argument for her cooperation: "doth not my mightie name, / Suffice to sheeld thy fact from shame?" (144). Toward the end of the episode it becomes purely a matter of birth when he denounces her as "thou beggers brat" and, relying entirely on his own birth, asks "Am I fit man to be abus'd?" (150).

Avisa begins her rejection by positing the social situation: "I am too base to be your wife," by which she means that she knows he will never be able to marry her, and "To be your whore, I flat disdaine" (138). She can express grief at finding "In Noble bloud so base a mind" (145). Since she has no social power, Avisa appeals to divine commandment: "My wisdome is the living Lord" (143), but even the religious argument for chastity has for her a social dimension.

> The roote of woe is fond desire,
> That never feeles her selfe content:
> But wanton wing'd, will needes aspire,
> To finde the thing, she may lament,
>   A courtly state, a Ladies place,
>   My former life will quite deface. (139)

"Courtly state" and "Ladies place" are tragic achievements for a commoner. But what needs to be understood is that from Avisa's social position the argument that one should be content with one's place is hardly contemptuous of the lower ranks but rather conveys an intense and unsympathetic anger at the dominant classes.[27] When the angry nobleman has cursed her, Avisa invokes contentment: "Though you may vaunt of happier fate, / I am content with my estate. / I rather chuse a quiet mind" (151). The quiet mind is attained by moral-religious correctness and by social humility. Avisa's humble birth and her virtue are intricately related, and conversely the nobleman's arrogant immorality and his deafness to the religious argument are functions of his privileged status.

It is a sign of the material social awareness informing this poem that the nobleman's seduction at one point engages in detailed economic argument:

> Here's fortie Angels to begin;
> A little pledge of great goodwill,
> To buy thee lace, to buy a pin;
> I will be carefull of thee still:
>   If youth be quaild, if I be old,
>   I can supply that with my gold.
>
> Silke gownes and velvet shalt thou have,
> With hoods and cauls, fit for thy head;
> Of goldsmithes worke a border brave,
> A chaine of golde ten double spread;
>   And all the rest shall answere this,
>   My purse shall see that nothing misse.
>
> Two wayting maides, attendant still,
> Two serving men, foure geldings prest,
> Go where you list, ride where you will,
> No jealous thought shal me molest;

> Two hundreth pounds I doe intend,
> To give thee yearely for to spend.

> Of this I will assurance make,
> To some good friend, whom thou wilt chuse
> That this in trust from me shall take,
> While thou dost live, unto thy use;
>   A thousand markes, to thee give I,
>   And all my Jewels when I die. (147–48)

The detail here is remarkable: forty angels now, two hundred pounds a year, and jewels and a thousand marks on the lover's death.[28] The poem at this point becomes almost a contract. One has only to recall the symbolic quality of Marlowe's pastoral temptation to appreciate how realistic this bargain is, and we seem to hear an echo of Ralegh's nymph's reply in Avisa's rejection of this economic temptation:[29]

> Your gownes of silke, your golden chaines,
> Your men, your maides, your hundreth pounds,
> Are nothing else but divelish traines,
> That fill fond eares with tickling sounds,
>   A bladder full of traiterous wind,
>   A fardest off from filthy mind. (149)

But if the rhythms echo the nymph's wry distrust of "every shepherd's tongue," Avisa's severe moral tone with its denunciation of the corruptor's "filthy mind" is very different.

Avisa is assured of her own position and her ability to maintain her virtue. She declares "I'le never yeeld, I'le rather die," and, far from threatening suicide, she offers to murder the nobleman: "Except you leave, and so depart, / This knife shall sticke within your hart" (148). Admittedly, this nobleman is not quite a Tarquin, but Avisa still shows an outlook quite different from that of Lucrece. Tarquin is able to manipulate Lucrece by threats to her reputation, but Avisa never worries about how she will appear to her husband or to history. Her pat last words to the nobleman tell it all:

> You were my friend, you were but dust,
> The Lord is he, whome I doe love,
> He hath my hart, in him I trust,
> And he doth gard me from above,
>   I waie not death, I feare not hell,
>   This is enough, and so farewell. (152)

With her knife at ready and after denouncing the nobleman's "Painted words" and "brave pretence," Avisa declares: "Then thus to yeeld by chaunted charmes, / I'le rather die within your armes" (149). It is a sign of the unambiguous earnestness of Avisa's position that a line which in a courtly poem would be filled with erotic suggestion is here spoken, apparently, without sexual implication. It may be impossible to prove the absence of irony, but irony in this context would make no sense. We are here in a sensibility and intelligence almost without ambiguity and implication; it speaks a language the very antithesis of the courtly subtlety that Javitch has praised in *Poetry and Courtliness.* And it is exactly this straightforwardness that defines the social situation of this poem.

The episode of the nobleman makes more of the tempter's social rank than do the other episodes, but economics and social stature are never entirely absent. Signs of a middle-class perspective hostile to aristocratic style and morality persist throughout the poem. The prose introducing the third suitor, "D.B. A French man," warns that "a long continued course of courtesie, at length prevaileth with many both maides and wives" (163), but Avisa's stern straightforwardness finds such "courtesie" incomprehensible. She is able to read the practical goals of courtly pretense, but she finds the behavior confusing.

> Your Ring and letter that you sent,
> I both returne from whence they came,
> As one that knowes not what is ment,
> To send or write to me the same,
> > You had your answere long before,
> > So that you need to send no more. (174)

The third line could refer equally well to D.B., who does not seem to understand Avisa's denial, and to Avisa herself, who cannot comprehend how solicitation can continue after her clear rejection. She then interprets the posie on the ring, "do but dally not":

> Your chosen posie seemes to show
> That all my deeds but dallings [*sic*] bee,
> I never dallyed that I know,
> And that I thinke, you partly see,
> > I shewde you first my meaning plaine,
> > The same is yet, and shall remaine. (175)

She is alert to the looser implications of "dally," and she asserts a strict code of behavior in its place. The third line can be read as a moment of self-doubt (I am not aware of ever having dallyed) that would match her sense of D.B.'s own "partial" understanding. But a more likely reading is a strong denial (I know I never dallyed).

Though the later tempters cannot offer the life of kept ease that the nobleman does, nevertheless they always return to a concrete sense of the economics of the situation. D.B. is careful to inform Avisa,

> I have a Farme that fell of late,
> Woorth fortie pound, at yearely rent,
> That will I give to mend your state,
> And prove my love is truely ment. (169)

And D.H., the Anglo-German merchant who finds Avisa on his travels, is aware that he cannot match the nobility:

> I will not bost me of my wealth,
> You shall no Gold nor Jewels want,
> You see I am in perfect health,
> And if you list to give your grant,
>   A hundreth pounds shall be your hire,
>   But onely doe that I require. (180)

He then offers as earnest deposit "a Bracelet to begin, / Worth twentie Angels to be sold."

A more subtle sign of the poem's belligerent uncourtliness is its occasional denunciation of non-Christian authors. To D.B.'s argument that there is precedent for a woman's surrendering, Avisa replies: "Your gravest men with all their schooles, / That taught you thus, were heath[en] fooles" (167).[30] And against Plato, who, she knows, "that freedom gave, / That men and women for delight, / Might both in common freely have," she declares that God threatens death "To them that breake their wedlocke faith." The author of the poem, always on Avisa's side, provides a gloss with citations of Exodus and Leviticus (181). Though the poem proper does not mention Lucrece and Roman history, it clearly finds that pagan world dangerous and immoral.

Avisa's world, sustained by an omnipotent God who punishes immorality, is very different from Lucrece's "wilderness where are no laws" (544). It is tempting to see the difference as simply that between a Christian and a pagan worldview, but I would suggest that the social difference is at the core. Avisa makes her virtue obedience (to God and to husband) and absolute resistance to wrong; Lucrece, more privileged, invents her own virtue by her suicide, which is rhetorically possible because she is surrounded by men in a position to play the "knights" who will enforce its moral imperative. Tarquin's crime has certainly violated the codes, but he has not reduced Roman society to a Hobbesian state of nature; finally, there is the threat of patrician power which her suicide, by its sacrifice, lets loose. To recent criticism's reminder that the story of Lucrece is the story of the founding of the Roman republic, one need only add that, as nonaristocrats will be aware, a republic is not a democracy; that this is the story of the triumph of nobility over tyrannic monarchs.

Willobie, His Avisa is in its way a poetic manifesto, originating in middle-class Protestant social space, which, in describing Avisa's rejection of her various suitors, attempts to define in opposition to Shakespearean art what this social faction would see as a truly moral poetry. If, as the introductory matter of *Avisa* suggests, this social faction believes that the rape has polluted Lucrece and robbed her of the "Gareland of her rarest fame," then Shakespeare has chosen the wrong heroine to make a moral point. According to this reading, Shakespeare has further erred by choosing to depict not just virtue in action but the commission of a crime. The line "And *Shake-speare,* paints poore *Lucrece* rape" does more than simply identify a famous contemporary poem; it points to the area of moral failure that *Avisa* sets out to correct. For such earnest moralists, Shakespeare's art, because it "paints" the "rape," seems to collaborate with Tarquin and thereby undermine the educational project of, to quote Sidney, "feigning notable images of virtues."[31]

Willobie's claim to know Avisa herself is part of this middle-class aesthetic project. In famous lines in the *Apology for Poetry,* just before making the argument that poetry is "that feigning notable images of virtues, vices, or what else" (21), Sidney invokes Lucretia herself as his exemplary "image of virtue." He distinguishes "right poets" by contrasting them to "the meaner sort of painters (who counterfeit only such faces as are set before them)" and holds up as the poets' model the "more excellent, who having no law but wit, bestow that in colors upon you which is fittest for the eye to see: as the constant though lamenting look of Lucretia when she punished in herself another's fault. Wherein he painteth not Lucretia whom he never saw, but painteth the outward beauty of such a virtue" (20). Sidney skillfully defends the game of fiction, but the earnest, religious, plebeian poet will sympathize with Gosson's distrust of an art that "makes up" its images of virtue. If the aristocratic Sidney can praise an artist who paints a Lucrece he never saw, Willobie fulfills the aesthetic of the "meaner sort" by claiming to depict a living woman. The more the poem makes readers think the persons described actually exist, the more successful it is. It is so convincing in this rhetorical ploy that Harrison was persuaded more than three centuries later to devote his energy to trying to identify the actual Avisa. I suspect the *Avisa* poet is a touch more sophisticated than Harrison allows; his "realism" is a rhetorical illusion in the service of moral education. Willobie is claiming to create an art that never lies because it tells of real people. This is a dangerous game, however, because if Avisa is real, then so are, supposedly, the men who attempt to seduce her. My point is not that we should try to identify these figures but that we should respect the social agenda behind such a realistic pose. This poem, coming from a social space that distrusts hegemonic claims to speak the "universal," consciously works with a rhetoric and an idea of morality that are in profound conflict with Shakespeare's rich rhetorical painting of imagined psychologies.

Though coming out of a fervent and strict religious space, *Avisa* is a poem aware of current cultural production and intent on inserting itself strongly as a critique of what it sees as the nobility's oversubtle and even evasive play on virtue. Hadrian Dorrell's modest defense of Willobie is, in fact, a subtle rejection of the courtly mode: "Although hee [i.e., Willobie] flye not alofte with the winges of *Astrophell,* nor dare to compare with the Arcadian shepheard, or any way match with the dainetie Fayry Queene; yet shall you find his wordes and phrases, neither Tryviall nor absurd etc." (126). Though couched in the tropes of humility, this apology may be read as a strong disavowal of the "lofty" and "dainty" art of Sidney and Spenser. In its downright, "just say no" morality *Avisa* reveals more than an ethical attitude; it stands for a social posture. We need to keep aware of such oppositional activity, for it shapes the cultural landscape even if it does not triumph. After all, Milton owes much to this tradition. Ambiguous language can conceal even slight challenges or taunts, and a strategy of playing at the edge of offense is invisible so long as it succeeds. We become aware of how daring and dangerous the game is only when the strategy of eluding censorship fails; it is the fact that the bishops thought fit to burn this morally unexceptionable poem that alerts us to its social challenge. The language of disadvantaged poets is always working in such a realm of ambiguity, appearing orthodox and supportive of established hierarchy while at the same time allowing for another understanding that sees the outrageous injustice of the status quo. Unless we appreciate the risk such a poem is taking, we will seriously misread it, just as we will be deaf to the offensiveness some contemporaries may feel at the aristocratic presumptions behind an art like Shakespeare's.

All common people do not begrudge the behavior of the nobility. Some admire it and try to emulate it. Barnabe Barnes attracts our interest because he, a second son of a bishop, a man who would have to make his own way, begins his career by publishing a sequence of erotic lyrics that at one level—in its range of forms and the sheer number of poems—outdoes Sidney and any of his imita-

tors. This curious book, *Parthenophil and Parthenophe* (1593), which to most
modern readers is just another rather long collection of lyrics ranging over fa-
miliar amorous situations, is distinguished by the remarkable hostility it gener-
ated among courtiers and courtly aspirers. In one of his epigrams Campion makes
fun of the sonnet in which Barnes hopes to be the wine that passes through his
beloved's lips and by becoming her urine passes "by pleasures part," and in an-
other develops a fantasy of Barnes and Harvey cuckolding each other.[32] Haring-
ton also writes an epigram, number 67, which with much double entendre mocks
Barnes's social aspirations.[33] To aristocrats and those who pretend to aristocratic
tastes, *Parthenophil and Parthenophe* is a grotesque set of poems; it slightly but
disastrously misreads the voice that gives courtly eroticism its exquisite tonality;
Nash calls it a "philistene" poem.[34] It is this pretension to the style of a rank which
he could not otherwise claim that has made Barnes's poem so hard for modern
criticism to evaluate.[35] To understand Barnes one must do more than simply read
a single strange book of poems, one must understand the whole project of amo-
rous poetry and its complex social meaning, which is not simply an argument
over sexual mores.

Barnes's most enthusiastic promoter was Gabriel Harvey. Though of humble
birth, Harvey wants to align himself with the courtly tradition of Sidney and
Spenser, but unlike Spenser his attitudes about literature are confused. In the
1590s, driven by Thomas Nash's relentless and ingenious teasings, he finds him-
self denouncing a phalanx of impoverished poets that includes, along with Nash
himself, Greene, Lyly, Marlowe, and some other more minor and more coded
figures. He is in the final analysis, despite his poor background, a deeply conser-
vative supporter of aristocratic traditions. "Better an hundred Ovids were ban-
ished, then the state of Augustus endangered, or a soveraign Empire infected."[36]
With perhaps an allusion to *Tamburlaine,* he warns "Take heed aspiring mindes,
you that deeme yourselves the Paragon wittes of the world; lesse your hilles of
jollity be converted into dales of obscurity."[37] He even takes his friend Spenser
to task for the satire in *Mother Hubberd's Tale.*[38]

Given Harvey's moralism and arrogant dismissal of poets outside the court, it
is surprising to find him championing Barnes's erotic collection. At the begin-
ning of *Pierces Supererogation* he declares to Barnes that "*Parthenophil* and *Par-
thenophe* embellished . . . . shall everlastingly testifie what you are." He bids Barnes
"go forward in maturity, as ye have begun in pregnancy, and behold *Parthenop-
oeus* the sonne of brave Meleager *Homer* himself, and of the swift Atalanta *Cal-
liope* herselfe: be thou Barnabe, the gallant Poet, like Spencer, or the valiant soul-
diour, like Baskervile; and ever remember *thy French service* under the brave Earle
of Essex" (sig. **3v).[39] Barnes returns Harvey's compliment in the same volume

by a fulsome commendatory letter "To the Right Worshipfull, his especiall deare frend, M. Gabriell Harvey, Doctour of Lawe" (sig. ***v) in which he urges Harvey to publish his "most praise-mooving works, full of gallantest discourse, and reason." "By this Publication of so rare, & rich Discourses, our English Ravens, the spitefull enemyes to all birdes of more bewtifull wing, and more harmonious note, then themselves, may shrowde themselves in their nests of basest obscurity, & keepe hospitality with battes, and owles, fit consorts for such vile carions" (sigs. ***v and ***2).[40] At this point, more important than any particular personalities depicted in these allusions is the sense we have of Barnes and Harvey allied in a defensive and yet self-congratulatory project to make their mark in the most fashionable genre then in vogue, the sequence of amorous lyrics. Barnes's poems can be seen as elements in a serious aesthetic program and the expression of an extraordinary social ambition. Harvey and he are involved in a social gamble not unlike (though also not as successful as) Jonson's: to fashion a position in the dominant class by a display of learning, taste, and contempt for mere aspirers.

In praising Barnes by linking him with Spenser, Harvey may be intending to recall his own earlier friendship with the great poet, but he is also identifying an important aspect of what identifies Spenser in 1593. By calling him a "gallant Poet, like Spencer" Harvey cannot be attributing to Barnes, the writer of sonnets, madrigals, and elegies, anything like laureate status. It is for his extraordinary and explicit eroticism, his Ovidianism if you will, that Barnes is being likened to Spenser. One can suppose that Harvey sees *Parthenophil and Parthenophe* as developing the Ovidian line begun in the last cantos of the 1590 *Faerie Queene*.[41] The cantos following the Garden of Adonis, that set piece of Platonic generation, explore erotic behavior stripped of cosmic justification. The presiding poet now is the Ovid of the *Amores*. Paridel's seduction of Hellinore transforms Homeric paradigms into Ovidian worldliness.[42] The "mystery of wine" through which Paridel speaks under the very eyes of the jealous husband is an analogue to the mode of communication that we have been studying.[43] But even more important is the comic freedom of the episode: here Spenser allows the Ovidian worldly voice to justify the verse. The episode is a scene of comic realism whose attention is psychological. Eros, liberated, becomes debauched and violent: Hellinore's cavorting with the virile satyrs leads to the deeply mysterious House of Busyrane wherein the sadism of courtly love is rendered. The liberation that Ovidian comic satire permits culminates in the famous, problematic (and later retracted) image of Amorette and Scudamore in hermaphroditic embrace.

Parthenophil and Parthenophe is an attempt to gain patronage and even perhaps to attain an aristocratic presence by the daring gesture of defining a new

genre that expresses Ovidian eroticism in the courtly forms—sonnets and mad-
rigals—and situations of traditional Petrarchism. In Barnes's poems the virginal
mistress thwarts the lover, not out of any question of his worth or out of affec-
tion for a rival, but simply because of the somewhat sadistic imperative of vir-
ginity. Parthenophil, "the lover of virginity," is by his very name complicit, but
the poems then, instead of elevating the beloved's purity, range over a variety of
erotic attitudes, from conventional praise of the beloved's red and white, to em-
bellished descriptions of her body, to unambiguous fantasies of rape. Put next to
Astrophel and Stella, which it clearly asks to be both by its dating (three years after
the first publication of Sidney's sequence) and by references within the sequence,
Barnes's book appears violent and crude. Astrophel's subtle negotiations with a
sophisticated, powerful, and not altogether uncooperative Stella become in
Barnes's hands a blunt expression of anger and a frustrated fantasy of revenge.
The misogyny that Hunter identifies with humanism is here untempered by the
courtly feminism that allows a Sidney to compliment his beloved.[44]

Repeatedly Barnes seems to miss the tonality that distinguishes aristocratic
eroticism. As Victor Doyno observes, Barnes's translation of Desportes, unlike
Spenser's "Ye tradeful merchants," cannot rest content with the conceit that the
beloved is of more value than the merchants' cargo, but he must include the blunt
hope "That I my sweet Parthenophe may get."[45] One cannot imagine a courtly
lover using the verb "get" in this way. Similarly, the triple sestina that concludes
the collection reads more like Busyrane's fantasy than a courtly lover's. The poet
acknowledges that "Her cruell loves in me such heate have kindled" that he must
invoke a charm that will bring him Parthenophe naked on a goat and "raging
woode," and he describes, with leering double entendre, the consummation of
his love:

> And cease (*Parthenophe*) sweet cease thy teares:
> Beare golden *Apples thornes* in every woode,
> Joyne heavens, for we conjoyne this heavenly night:
> Let *Alder* trees beare *Apricockes* (dye furies)
> And *Thistles Peares,* which prickles lately bare.
> Now both in one with equall flame be kindled. (130, lines 91–96)

The dream of mutual arousal is crudely deaf to Parthenophe's feelings, and the
imagery of crossbreeding seems less a logical argument (as in, say, Donne's "The
Extasie") than a contorted effort to introduce sexual puns.

We may tend to forget as we read Petrarchan imitations how much the con-
ventions of the social situation of the lover's discourse cushion the aggressions

implicit in the standard language. "Cruelty," for instance, is usually understood in a special way to mean simply coolness. But in Barnes's poems the beloved's rejection of the advances of the lover are treated as more than cool; they are sadistic. The barely controlled panic of the lover, and the haughty irony of the beloved are clear in sonnet 8:

> Then to Parthenophe (with all post hast)
>> As full assured of the pawne fore pledged
> I made, and with these wordes disordred plac'd,
>> Smooth, tho with furies sharp out-rages edged:
> Quoth I (fayre mistres) did I set mine hart
>> At libertie, and for that made him free,
> That you should arme him for another start
>> Whose certaine bale you promised to bee?
> Tush (quoth Parthenophe) before he goe
>> I'le be his bale at last, and doubt it not.
> Why then (said I) that morgage must I shoe
>> Of your true-love which at your hands I got?
>> Ay me, she was, and is his bale I wot,
> But when the morgage should have cur'd the soare:
>> She past it of, by deed of gift before. (7)

One does not hear a voice like that of Parthenophe in other sequences. The dismissive "Tush" is in itself startling, but more revealing about her relation to the lover is the almost brutal pun on "bale" (bail and pain) and the unsympathetic firmness of "and doubt it not." The woman's pleasure in the lover's suffering is confirmed later in sonnet 39: "in my bale she joyes to see me boyle." Such visions of women as tribulation may occur in drama and in poems explicitly in the misogynist tradition, and they may even from time to time occur in the more decorous sonnet sequences, but one does not expect them to define the general attitude toward women in a sequence. The exception to these generalizations may be Shakespeare, who can also pun on prick and render the tribulations of a love affair in comparatively crude terms. But Shakespeare's sonnets appear more than fifteen years later, and they clearly play on the by-then tired conventions of the courtly sonnet form. Barnes's poems show no sense of literary irony; they seem to be intended as exactly what Harvey describes, a contribution to the Spenserian erotic tradition.

The allusion is clear when, with a passing reference to Faustus and Helen, Barnes turns Spenser's hermaphrodite into a sensual and frustrating dream:

Soft lovely Roselike lippes, conjoyn'd with mine,
　　Breathing out pretious incense such,
　　Such as at Paphos smoake to Venus shrine,
　　Making my lippes immortall with their tuche:
　　My cheekes with tuch of thy soft cheekes devine,
Thy soft warme cheekes, which Venus favour much:
　　　　Those armes, such armes which me embrac'de,
　　　Me with immortall cyncture guirding rounde
　　　Of everlasting blisse, then bounde
　　With her enfolded thighes in mine entangled,
　　　And both in one selfe soule plac'de,
Made an Hermophrodite, with pleasures ravish't:
　　There heate for heats, soule for soules empyer wrangled,
　　Why dyed not I with love so largely lavish't?
For wake (not finding truth of dreames before)
　　　It secret vexeth, tentimes more. (38–39, madrigal 13)

If Barnes likes to allude, he does so with a blunt knowingness that seems to say that there is nothing beyond the sexual need. This poem is typical of Barnes's style: the padded wordiness ("Those armes, such armes"), the linking repetition of words ("such," "Lippes," "tuche"), the conventional, hyperbolic vocabulary (e.g., "immortall cyncture"), the loose grammar (what is the function of "Of everlasting blisse"?), the conventional sexual pun on "die." But such a style is not entirely alien to Spenser himself. Apart from the pun on "die," one could find all these qualities in the canceled final stanzas of book 3 of the *Faerie Queene*.

It is not the sexual behavior that is at issue here, but the style by which it is treated. After all, Wyatt in "They flee from me" could imply a sexual openness that matches that of Barnes, and Astrophel could admit that, after a long praise of Stella's "virtue," "Desire cries, Ah give me some food!" Barnes's material and erotic coloring of the Petrarchan conventions gives a tone to the tradition that transmutes the aristocratic postures into a simple, misogynistic sexism. Nash, in rejecting that tone as "philistene," leagues himself with easy aristocratic attitudes of condescension. Spenser can play the erotic game because he has a courtly ear for the delicate point at which courtly sophistication loses its wit and becomes crude and reads like comic satire. Barnes has no such delicacy; he describes the mind not of Astrophel but of Malbecco. Stoic postures of endurance are not valued by him. Suffering is simply pain. Yet Barnes seems to see this dream of copulation as appropriate to the tradition of Petrarchan lament. In the next poem in the sequence Parthenophil complains to Parthenophe:

Thou scorn'st my lynes, a sainct which make of thee,
Where true desiers of thine hard hart complaine:
        There thou bove stella plac'de,
Bove laura with ten thousand more install'd. (39, madrigal 14)

From Nash's perspective, the man knows no shame. He does not recognize the superior quality of his poetic or social betters. The Jonson of *Poetaster* administers a "purge" to just such pretenders to courtly style.

By voicing humanist misogyny in a courtly discourse, Barnes disrupts the genre's ideology, and while he is quite skillful at many formal difficulties—who else wrote a triple sestina?—he misses the delicacy that marks a true courtier. This is a "taste" difficult to elucidate without condescension. *Parthenophil and Parthenophe* is an attempt by the poet to sound like a member of a class whose real values he does not share. Like Gosson before him, Barnes makes a stab at a literary career, and when that fails he quickly redirects his ambitions to moralism with *A Century of Spiritual Sonnets* three years later.[46] It is exactly the element of clumsy ambition on which Nash, a man who understands "style" in a way that Harvey and Barnes cannot match, seizes. Nash is supporting a "courtly" aesthetic, while Harvey and Barnes, though they come from a roughly similar social level, have tried to use the opportunity offered by the popularity of Petrarchism and Ovidian openness to introduce what they would consider "classical" eroticism into the discourse of English verse. What makes our understanding of the situation particularly difficult is that the aristocratic values represented by Spenser are claimed by all participants in this debate.

Each of these texts requires us to "pick out" elements which, once isolated and understood, explain why the poem or tract should have offended authorities with licensed or cultural power. Stubbes's impassioned illogic is not as skewed as it might seem; for those who share his social perspective the gestures of denunciation ring even after they are retracted, and the gestures of humility and obedience carry less weight precisely because it is understood that they are forced. Stubbes's tract shares with *Willobie, His Avisa* a moral energy that masks the social hostility; yet for both texts the social meaning is intrinsic to the moral one. It is thanks to the haughty and spontaneous response of Peter Colse that we are able to begin to understand how such a seemingly unexceptional praise of the virtue of chastity could rouse official anger. Once we see it, however, the lengthy debate with the nobleman assumes a special significance: it is not a matter of simply denying his immoral solicitation; Avisa's heroic achievement is to resist the power of his social position, with all the insult and hegemonic persuasiveness that for most people would be seen to belong to it—to say nothing of the physical threats that such power inevitably implies.

Finally, Barnes's attempt to define a place for himself by his outrageous version of Ovidian eroticism expressed in elaborate and ingenious formality would be merely curious were it not for the contempt it immediately generated. In their mocking of Barnes, Campion, Harington, and Nash speak for what I am calling the aristocratic position. What is interesting for us is that, as we shall see in chapter 6, Chapman, too, derides Barnes, but not for the grotesqueness of his aspiration to aristocratic style. From Chapman's social perspective, *Parthenophil and Parthenophe* represents the epitome of a style that Chapman detests and is therefore linked, without irony, with Shakespeare's *Venus and Adonis* and with the work of most of the courtly sonneteers, all of whom Chapman sees as trivializing poetry and robbing it of its true social importance.

2

"Midas Brood Shall Sit in Honor's Chaire": Resentment and Poetry

> Agents shape their aspirations according to concrete indices of the
> accessible and the inaccessible, of what is and is not "for us," a division
> as fundamental and as fundamentally recognized as that between the
> sacred and the profane.
> —Bourdieu, *The Logic of Practice*, 64

Bourdieu's aphorism identifies the complex and partly internal dynamic that limits and shapes the aspirations of poets. It explains why in some cultures poets might never think of comparing themselves to people of rank; it is a principle of stability, and it alerts us to what an important historical event is entailed when agents try to reorganize these categories. The resentment that inspires aesthetic change has profound social consequences. Yet, the aphorism also poses a puzzle: if the class differences which define different accessibilities are as fundamental as the "sacred and the profane," how is it we have been able to ignore them? In Bourdieu's quotation it is the "agents" who "fundamentally recognize" the different accessibilities and therefore regulate their own aspirations; outsiders—whether social superiors who take their privilege for granted or later scholars who see the rarity of steeply ascending trajectories as simply a sign of the limits of talent—may well be unaware of any such aspiration altogether.[1]

Classical poets are not immune to such anger and aspiration, and one way more modern poets may find of expressing their disaffection is by drawing attention to such earlier expressions of a similar stance. Among Chapman's last published works is a translation of Juvenal's Fifth Satire (1629), a critique of the humiliations imposed by the patron-client relation, or as Chapman puts it, "a just reproofe of the Romane smell-Feast."[2] One can read the translation as a gesture of classical homage, but it is also an earnest and angry expression of resentment at the injustice of the patronage system. The Juvenal poem is not simply an attack on the arrogance of wealth but also an exploration of the cost, in dignity and credibility, of clientage.[3] Appealing to Trebius to abandon his servile attendance at Virro's table, the poet observes how the client's discourse is controlled by his poverty:

> Nor must your note faile, how huge difference
> There is 'twixt the unlacing of your hare,
> And Hens dissection: 'gainst which, if you dare
> But whisper, like a three-nam'd Noble man,
> Like *Cacus,* struck by hands—Herculean,
> Thou shalt bee, by the heeles, drag'd forth the place:
> But when doth *Virro* then vouchsafe the grace
> To drinke to thee? Or touch the Cup that thou
> Hast, with thy lippes prophan'd? Or which of you
> So desperate is? so lost? to bid the King
> Drink to me Sir? No: there is many a thing,
> That thred-bare coates care not for feare bring forth. (230–41)

The ambiguity of the Latin ("ut dicat regi bibe?"), where *rex* clearly refers to Virro, the "patron," nicely allows Chapman to suggest a special application to modern England. Similarly, by translating "tamquam habeas tria nomina" as "like a three-nam'd *Noble* man" Chapman introduces the issue of "nobility" while at the same time appropriately explicating the meaning of the text. In the last line and a half of this passage Juvenal is direct: "plurima sunt quae / non audent homines pertusa dicere laena." Chapman's more contorted "Care not for feare bring forth" adds to the threat in the original a sense of the abject and diplomatic position of the impoverished client. To complain or even speak truth is dangerous, but to be silent is to collaborate in your own humiliation.

Near the end of the satire, the poet talks explicitly about the pleasure the patron derives from the "comedy" of "a weeping-gut":

> All is then done: (if we must teach thine eares)
> To make thee purge thy choler by thy teares,
> And live still gnashing of thy great-eye-teeth,
> Thou think'st, he thinks thee free; & not beneath
> Guests for his love and Grace: but he knowes well
> Thee onely taken with his kitchins-smell:
> Nor thinks amisse. (284–90)

Juvenal simply says "tu tibi liber homo . . . videris" ("you think yourself a free man"); Chapman adds a layer of misperception: the client thinks that his obeisance at least fools the patron, but in fact the cynical patron is more in touch with the economic and theatrical reality than the client. In Chapman's version the position of the client is rendered particularly horrible because, thanks to the patron's crude understanding of the material economic situation, no gesture of independence can be convincing. Both the translation and the original conclude with ironic praise of the patron: "He's wise that serves thee so: for if thou can / Beare all, thou shouldst" (300–301). He who refuses to suit and serve his need deserves his load.

The Juvenal poem expresses the anger intrinsic in the poor client's situation and the stress his courtly ambitions would have incurred, but it does not account for the career that Chapman finally chose and the cultural reward of being a poet. The man we can picture seeking a loan in 1585 to follow Sir Ralph Sadler and somewhat later in 1591 spending his inheritance (of a silver spoon) to go to war[4] finally appears on our literary horizon in 1594 with poems announcing the importance of learned, coterie poetry, addressed not to a possible economic patron but to an obscure and impoverished poet, Matthew Roydon.[5] For Chapman Roydon is a source of inspiration in a cultural situation in which poetry is treated frivolously by influential people who pursue wealth and power rather than culture: "How . . . may a man stay his marvailing to see passion-driven men, reading but to curtoll a tedious houre, and altogether hidebownd with affection to great mens fancies, take upon them as killing censures as if they were judgements Butchers, or as if the life of truth lay tottering in their verdits." The rage at casual poetic judgments leads to a mounting irony: "Why then should our *Intonsi Catones* with their profit-ravisht gravitie esteeme her [i.e., poetry's] true favours such questionlesse vanities, as with what part soever thereof they seeme to be something delighted, they queimishlie commende it for a pretie toy. Good Lord how serious and eternall are their Idolatrous platts for riches! no marvaile sure they here do so much good with them. And heaven no doubt will grovill on the earth (as they do) to imbrace them."[6] The next year Chapman again writes a dedicatory letter to Roydon, expressing much the same outrage, announcing "The prophane multitude I hate, & onelie consecrate my strange Poems to these serching spirits, whom learning hath made noble, and nobility sacred."[7] Roydon inspires Chapman's high ambitions for his ability to counter the tyranny of patrons with an ideal of culture that will, if not earn him money, at least give him dignity and social authority. Before the modern social formation of the poor poet is in place Chapman seems to have imagined such a social category and set out to occupy it.

He is not alone in aspiring thus high. Thomas Lodge, at just this time in the middle 1590s, publishes a lament about the state of culture, and he, too, finds in Roydon intellectual support in the face of economic neglect. In his "Third Eclogue: To Rowland" in *A Fig for Momus* (1595) Lodge depicts in some detail the anxieties and angers involved in a poor poet's labor. The poem consists of a conversation between Golde (Lodge) and Wagrin (Guarin) about the difficulties Golde is having obtaining patrons.[8] Wagrin is optimistic that, though the audience for Golde's art be small, it is nevertheless discriminating and supportive. Golde is embittered that even his former readers fail to support him, and he declares that until patronage is more secure he will not write. Wagrin consoles Golde that such an elite verse, "hid" from "base-humor'd braines," will live "to after age," and he urges the disgruntled poet to "let thy fame, / Eternise thy deserts, and tell their shame." But Golde knows that the revenge of eternal fame will hardly sustain him or inspire him:

> Why should I make mine industrie a slave,
> To day, and night? why should I dwell on thought
> When as some scoffing ideot shall deprave
> That which with travaile learning forth hath brought. ([C4])

The "scoffing ideot," like Chapman's "Butchers," is certainly not just anybody: he must be someone with cultural power, a courtier probably, who can by a gesture ruin the "travaile" of "learning." Courtly criticism shapes the poetic market: "And though in furnace of true art I trie / My labor'd lines, yet scape not obloquie" (C4v). Lodge is not pretending to courtly *sprezzatura*. The "furnace of true art" produces something other than courtier verse. The phrase "labor'd lines" plays on both the difficulty of the poet's process of composition and the difficulty the lines present to the reader.

Lodge's poem explores the essential role of patronage for poetic creation. When Wagrin again urges the poet to attach himself (like ivy on oak) to "some fewe, (alas that they were more) / That honour poesie, and wit adore," Golde bitterly describes the failure of promised patronage and a general cultural decline. The patrons, who once seemed to offer "the sunne-shine of their grace," have become "niggard mindes," "worldlie, covetous, and base." In the absence of an enlightened class of patrons:

> Arts perish, wanting honour, and applause,
> And where imperious neede doth tyrannise,
> The holie heate, through worldly cares doeth pause,
> The minde, (with-drawne to studie for supplies)
> Is soyld with earthlie thoughts, and downward drawes;
> Hence come those dull conceits amongst the wise,
> > Which coy-eard readers censure to proceede,
> > From ignorance, whereas they grow by neede. (D–Dv)[9]

Patronage is not just a reward that comes after composition; it is intrinsic to the process. Golde complains that "The colde conceit of recompence doth lay / [Poets'] fierie furie when they should begin" (Dv). Financial insecurity stifles inspiration, and the quality of poetry itself declines. Need produces "dull conceits," which are then misread by "coy-eard readers" as "ignorance."[10]

Golde concludes by resolving that unless patronage is forthcoming he will leave the writing of poetry altogether: "I rest resolv'd, if bountie will, I wright, / If not, why then my muse shall flie the light" (D2).[11] He has been inspired to this resolve by Wagrin's urging him to "follow harvest, where thy *Donroy* gleanes." Donroy is Chapman's source of encouragement and strength, Matthew Roydon. For Lodge, as for Chapman, Roydon is a poor but charismatic figure who gives courage in an otherwise depressed situation. We here touch a mysterious source of social and poetic inspiration that somehow plays against the blunt economic realities of the patronage system but which is also, in its very opposition, concerned with that system.

We do not know much about Roydon, but in one of the few works of his that we have he shows himself attentive to the failure of patronage. In the poem he writes commending Thomas Watson's *Hekatompathia* in 1592, Roydon sketches a gloomy allegory of injustice:

> It's seldome seene that *Merite* hath his due,
> Or els *Dezerte* to find his just desire:
> For now *Reproofe* with his defacing crewe
> Treades underfoote that rightly should aspyre:
>   Milde *Industrie* discourag'd hides his face,
>   And shuns the light, in feare to meete *Disgrace*.[12]

Just as Lodge resolves to "flie the light," Watson, in Roydon's words, "shuns the light" in discouragement. Chapman will write a hymn to this mood, his first publication, "Hymnus in Noctem," in which he declares his own intention "to detest the light" (373), and fittingly he inscribes the poem to Roydon. In 1589 Nash praised Roydon's "immortal" elegy for Sidney, which was later printed both in *The Phoenix Nest* and *Colin Clouts Come Home Again*.[13] Roydon was also associated with Marlowe, such that on Marlowe's arrest it was reported that Roydon had fled to Scotland.[14] He is a mysterious but important man, connected with poor, intellectual poets, whom he inspires to an ideal of culture that is above and in some sense superior to the frivolous and undependable world of patronage.

It is Marlowe who most memorably declares the Roydonesque outrage at the economic plight of poor learned poets in the angry lines that conclude the Mercury episode in *Hero and Leander*. Mercury, at the request of a shepherd lass he is seducing, steals a cup of nectar from heaven. Jove punishes him. In revenge, Mercury with Cupid's aid woos the Fates and when, enamored, they hand over their power to him, he dethrones Jove and restores the golden age. But after Mercury slights their love, the Fates restore Jove and make scholars, whom Mercury patronizes, poor. The poet then comments:

> And but that Learning, in despight of Fate,
> Will mount aloft, and enter heaven gate,
> And to the seat of *Jove* it selfe advaunce,
> *Hermes* had slept in hell with ignoraunce,
> Yet as a punishment they added this,
> That he and Poverty should always kiss.
> And to this day is every scholar poore;
> Gross gold from them runs headlong to the boore.
> Likewise the angrie sisters thus deluded,
> To venge themselves on Hermes, have concluded
> That *Midas* brood shall sit in Honor's chaire,
> To which the *Muses* sonnes are only heire:
> And fruitful wits that in aspiring are
> Shall discontent run into regions farre.
> And few great lords in virtuous deeds shall joy,
> But be surprised with every garish toy[15]
> And still inrich the loftie servile clowne,
> Who with incroching guile keepes learning downe. (1.465–82)[16]

The reference to discontented wits who "run into regions far" may refer to Marlowe's own time in France, and uncannily anticipates Roydon's flight to Scotland. The importance to Marlowe himself of the social attitude expressed by these lines is impossible to question. Son of a cobbler, scholarship student at Canterbury and Cambridge, associate in London of Watson, Greene, and Nash, Marlowe represents for this period a triumph of self-fashioning, an achievement of will and intellect over rank and inheritance.[17]

The resentment, which the modern critic hears as "querelous," is a major element in the episode's thematic point.[18] Social ambition is at the core of the Mercury myth. What sets the story of divine rape in *Hero and Leander* apart from other similar tales is the shepherd lass's "thirst . . . after immortalitie" (427) that leads her to demand from Mercury "a draught of flowing Nectar" (451). At this point the narrator interjects one of his notorious aphorisms, "All women are ambitious naturallie" (428). While this remark can be given a misogynist slant, it can also be seen in more positive terms. It declares that this shepherd lass has the same "aspiring mind" that causes another of Marlowe's shepherds to seek "the sweet fruition of an earthly crowne" (*Tamburlaine* 880). Faustus, too, in famous lines seeks immortality from Helen's kiss and then envisions himself, parallel to the ambitious shepherd lass, as the masculine Semele to Helen's Jupiter: "Brighter art thou then flaming *Jupiter*, / When he appeard to haplesse *Semele*" (A, 1372–73).[19] While the logic of misogyny will denounce in women what is admired in men, that very inconsistency then allows Marlowe to think about ambition without being accused of sanctioning it.

A similarly deceptive illogic rules when the lowly lass is described as proud. She is innocent and without guile, "Yet proud she was, (for loftie pride that dwels / In tow'red courts, is oft in sheapheards cels)" (393–94). A socially biased reading would condemn her for pride while approving an identical pride in her social superiors. And when Mercury "boast[s] of his parentage" (409) she knows how to market her chastity, which is her "only dower" (412). In the economy adumbrated here, her "thirsting after immortality" is a code for a social ambition. What is remarkable, but makes perfect sense in this reading, is that, unlike Semele, who was destroyed for her ambitions, the country lass does not suffer for her request. Mercury is punished for giving away to her that which belongs to the gods. What we have here is a parable not just of the disruptions of love but of social ambition and of the way rank is protected. The "ambitious" woman here stands for all "aspirers," including the poet.

From the social perspective of the disadvantaged poet the great Marlowian theme of "The overreacher" has a more practical goal than is commonly realized. One of the elementary pleasures of *Tamburlaine* is watching a brazen upstart triumph and thinking through some of the easier ironies the inversion of rank creates. The entertainment might be considered extremely insulting not just to the queen but to all inherited ranks, but Marlowe can always disclaim authorial responsibility.[20] A representation of historical truth can hardly be blamed on Marlowe; and even if it were, the play is set in such an exotic and alien space that, were offense to be taken, it could easily be claimed that barbarian Scythian customs are irrelevant to civilized England. But, of course, for those of us alert to critique, the work is fraught with ironic analysis. Out of mysterious, piratical beginnings Tamburlaine by sheer force of will establishes a meritocracy, a world of elementary masculine justice wherein heroic leaders are rewarded: "I am a Lord, for so my deeds shall proove, / And yet a shepheard by my Parentage" (230–31). His men are "friends" (225) who, though they need spoils, are not mercenaries. By contrast, Cosroe, a king who temporarily allies with Tamburlaine, though he can sharply criticize his brother Mycetes' complete dependence on rank, can never

accept the true egalitarian implications of Tamburlaine's triumph. He agrees with
Ceneus, whose class presumptions are clear:

> He that with Shepheards and a litle spoile,
> Durst in disdaine of wrong and tyrannie,
> Defend his freedome gainst a Monarchie:
> What will he doe supported by a king?
> Leading a trope of Gentlemen and Lords,
> And stuft with treasure for his highest thoughts? (508–13)[21]

The irony is, of course, that the king, gentlemen, and lords are no match for the
Scythian shepherd when he turns on them. He and his men become kings by
their deeds and for the fun of it, for the insult to kings.[22] When in act 3 Zabina
demands "How dare you thus abuse my Maiesty," she is answered: "Her time is
past: / The pillers that have bolstered up those termes, / Are falne in clusters at
my conquering feet" (1324, 1326–28). These are lines that, for anyone attuned to
hear criticism of the entitled aristocracy and its privileges, reverberate with pow-
erful meaning through the 1590s. A sign that they struck home is that at the end
of the decade Joseph Hall (who was, we may recall, included in the bishops' list
but then removed) attacked poets who "with some Pot-fury ravisht" dare to de-
pict royalty on stage, and he found particularly offensive the sight of "some up-
reared, high-aspiring swaine / As it might be the Turkish *Tamberlaine.*"[23]

Doctor Faustus shows Marlowe's linking of learning, eroticism, and social as-
piration most intricately. As the criticism frequently notes without elaboration,
Faustus comes from "parents base of stocke" (A, 12). As in *Tamburlaine,* part of
the audience's pleasure in *Doctor Faustus* is watching a social upstart move among
his "betters" and even at times humiliate them. In *Faustus* we see a series of dis-
placements by which material social ambition is blurred with cultural ambition,
and that is in its turn blurred with erotic ambition. Early in the play Faustus is
dissuaded from suicide because of an erotic literary experience:

> And long ere this I should have slaine my selfe,
> Had not sweete pleasure conquerd deepe dispaire.
> Have not I made blinde *Homer* sing to me,
> Of *Alexanders* love, and *Enons* death?
> And hath not he that built the walles of *Thebes,*
> With ravishing sound of his melodious harp
> Made musicke with my *Mephastophilis,*
> Why should I dye then, or basely dispaire? (A, 653–60)

What needs emphasis here is that "sweete pleasure," while pervasively erotic, is also explicitly literary. It is Homer who makes life meaningful, and he is an erotic poet, an Ovid in disguise, if you will. It is not surprising, then, that at the end of the play Faustus should generate such a cluster when he invokes Helen, a literary as much as an erotic figure: "Was this the face that lancht a thousand shippes? / And burnt the toplesse Towres of *Ilium*? / Sweete *Helen,* make me immortall with a kisse" (A, 1357–59). In these famous lines we hear again the mixture of Homeric and Ovidian allusion. Another moment in *Doctor Faustus* returns us explicitly to *Hero and Leander.* Early in the play Faustus boasts that his skill in "concise syllogisms" has "made the flowring pride of *Wertenberge* / Swarme to my Problemes as the infernall spirits / On sweet *Musaeus* when he came to hell" (A, 147–49). A powerful idea of literary culture is being invoked. The allusion (*Aeneid* 6.667) is to the Musaeus whom Aeneas sees in the underworld as the foremost of those "qui vitam excoluere per artes [inventas]" (663) and whom the poet and his audience would have believed to be the author of *Hero and Leander.* Though syllogisms and the magic of Agrippa are also a part of the vision in the *Faustus* passage, at its heart is the erotic literary tradition which is seen as both a redeeming source of pleasure and the motive for civilization.

Faustus and Tamburlaine represent quite different approaches to the questions of what is to be desired in life. Tamburlaine sees something like the Homeric heroic as sufficient, and his greatest pleasure seems to be in disrupting the artificial hierarchies that impose on humankind. Faustus, while in some sense he has more "power" than Tamburlaine, never actually takes power. He remains always a member of the "dominated fraction of the dominant class." If Tamburlaine seems unsubtle and direct in realizing his desires, Faustus seems confused. Echoing Freud's famous question about women, we might ask, what does Faustus want? Power? renown? wealth? status? knowledge? sensual pleasure? The play never concludes on any one version of success.[24] The prologue tells us "Nothing so sweet as magicke is to him" (26), and in the first scene Faustus himself, after dismissing logic, medicine, law, and divinity, exclaims:

> These Metaphysickes of Magicians
> And Negromantike bookes are heavenly;
> Lines, circles, sceanes, letters and characters:
> I, these are those that *Faustus* most desires.
> O, what a world of profit and delight,
> Of power, of honor, of omnipotence,
> Is promised to the studious Artizan! (A, 79–85)

But what is the "omnipotence" magic offers? In this idea of magic we see Marlowe identifying something like the power and the difficulty of what Bourdieu would much later formulate as cultural capital. The confusion that surrounds Faustus's desires is essential to the misrecognition that is endemic to cultural production: "art" is more important than material wealth, says the artist, though he also complains about poverty. Bourdieu has many insights into the rhetorical complexity of this stance: the purity of the aesthetic commitment is crucial to the appeal for material support.

Later in the play, when agreeing on the terms of the contract for his soul, Faustus asks that he "live in all voluptuousness" (A, 335), a formulation that at this point seems to mean little more than getting what he wants, but as the play progresses becomes increasingly associated with sensual pleasure. But the route is not a straight one; "pleasure" for Faustus is always involved with knowledge and culture. Mephostophilis, on the signing of the contract, says "Now, Faustus, ask what thou wilt" (A, 560), a line that could be understood as an offer of any kind of material wealth or pleasure, but Faustus proceeds to "ask" questions about hell and the cosmos. At another time Faustus finds sceptic pleasure in the pageant of the seven deadly sins (and the duke of Vanholt takes a similar pleasure in the view of Helen and her mole). These pleasures are not mere sensual gratification or satisfaction; they are pleasurable because they grant a sense of cultural wealth and therefore social superiority. Only the pregnant duchess of Vanholt, who Faustus fears may "take no delight in this" (A, 1233), asks for a purely sensual gratification: ripe grapes out of season. The male (and therefore, superior) pleasure is mental, the pleasure of culture.

In his last days, as in despair he seeks a pleasure that will somehow compensate for or at least assuage the damnation he now dreads, Faustus finally asks Mephostophilis "To glut the longing of my hearts desire" and grant him Helen "unto my paramour" (A, 1349–50). He seeks this indulgence in erotic pleasure, however, not as a goal or justification for the contract but as a narcotic, "Whose sweet imbracings may extinguish cleane / These thoughts that do disswade me from my vow" to Lucifer (A, 1353–54). But Faustus, a creature of culture, can never get outside of literature, and even his passionate dissipation quickly becomes a participation in the *Iliad*.

> I will be *Pa[r]is*, and for love of thee
> Instead of *Troy* shall *Wertenberge* be sackt,
> And I wil combate with weake *Menelaus*,
> And weare thy colours on my plumed Crest,
> Yea, I will wound *Achillis* in the heele,
> And then returne to *Helen* for a kisse. (A, 1364–69)

There is no pure "experience" for him; there is only the accumulation of cultural capital by participating in canonic art. The literariness of Faustus's pleasure has been evident from the start.

What I am describing is not the psychology of the character, Faustus but the expression of Marlowe's *habitus*. Both the greatness and the limits of his imagination derive from his poor upbringing in Canterbury when the shape of pleasure and success was defined for him. Faustus's late confession to the other scholars, "Ah Gentlemen! I gave them [i.e., Lucifer and Mephostophilis] my soule for my cunning" (A, 1423) is tellingly Marlowe's own. "Cunning" is the highest virtue to which a man from his background can aspire. The wealthy and powerful would not ask the devil for cunning, but the poor, who suspect in their hearts that they will never be "noble" and that at best they can hope to patch together a livelihood, and especially poor scholars who know that wit is the key to any kind of realistic social success, ask for a *practical* talent which will gain access to an accessible (in Bourdieu's sense) social space.

The play such a man writes is both an expression of this *habitus* and also a (probably unintentional) argument for the very values that limit it. Put another way, *Doctor Faustus* is an important moment in the development of the modern idea of culture because, while never formulating the idea of cultural capital in a pure sense (i.e., wealth, power, etc. contaminate Faustus's cunning), it lays claim to the idea that the "cunning" "artizan" is the most successful man. This is an idea which is quietly but significantly developed in the strange set of comic scenes with Benvolio that appear in the 1616 text. The awareness of rank that motivates these scenes was probably more evident in the Renaissance than it is today. Benvolio is an ambitious and rank-conscious man who is eager to attend on the emperor and is embarrassed by the trick Faustus plays on him because "every servile groom jests at my wrongs" (B, 1377). His lack of interest in the "conjurer" (the term occurs often in the conversations of Benvolio, his friends, and the soldiers he has hired) seems to be occasioned by Faustus's low social ranking. When Benvolio and his friends ambush Faustus, Frederick, one of the attackers, calls out: "Close, close! the Conjurer is at hand / And all alone, comes walking in his gowne; / Be ready then, and strike the Peasant down" (B, 1407–9). To these men Faustus, whatever his accomplishments, is a man of no standing. Faustus returns the compliment when he counterattacks the soldiers with the cry, "Base peasants stand" (B, 1479). What is important here is that Faustus through cultural achievement, that is magic, though a "peasant" himself, is able to term others "peasants." Marlowe's low-born Faustus, the peasant conjurer, can nevertheless assume the language and stance of the very haughty and arrogant nobility that condescends to him. At one level the exchange seems socially muddled, but in a social structure that claims clear ranks and degrees muddle itself is a disconcertingly potent challenge.

To return to *Hero and Leander,* we can now see that at the heart of Marlowe's "querelous" digression is a high sense of the importance of poetry itself to the meaningfulness of life, and therefore of the importance of the ambitions and value of the poet himself. But this awareness is also a source of frustration because the world does not reward poets: the line "Gross gold from them runs headlong to the boore" catches the elaborate and contradictory social feeling at work. It expresses the basic chiasmus at the heart of Bourdieu's vision of power with its rival markets of economic and cultural capital.[25] Gold is gross and contemptible, but it is an insult and a sign of cosmic injustice that scholars lack it while boors become rich. This is not a surprising complex of attitudes; in fact one might argue that it is central to all declarations of the value of cultural capital. By devaluing gold scholars and poets hope to increase the market for cultural capital, and by improving the exchange rate they hope to improve their material conditions.

The insult to "Midas' brood" is broad enough to be inoffensive to possible patrons, who can exempt themselves from the charge of boorishness by reasoning that they are rich *and* cultured and therefore represent the best of both conditions. But the lines near the end of Marlowe's passage play a tricky game. The ambiguous address to "few great lords" sets up two possible lines of argument: (a) hardly any lords reward virtue, and (b) yet there are a few lords who reward virtue. The next lines, however, catch the lord who has identified himself with the second meaning and make him gullible and undiscriminating. This is a rhetorical ambush of the very lords who will so disappoint Lodge. Finally, the enemy of learning and art is the oxymoronic "loftie servile clowne": "loftie," because of high rank; "servile," because, as Chapman will put it a year or two later, he "strives to be of kings / The abject slave of drudgery";[26] and "clowne," because he is, despite his rank, unlearned and without dignity.

The issue of resentment posed by Marlowe does not go unheard, and it is a sign of the remarkable resonance such a stand had that just a few years later it is the central theme of the student plays being put on at Cambridge, "The Pilgrimage to Parnassas" and the two parts of "The Return to Parnassas." In the space of less than a decade the thematics of culture could change so that the complaint about the imbalance of reward is a commonplace: "We have the wordes, they the possession have" (403).[27] The "Second Return" knows something about how "a little vermine poverty altereth a whole milkie disposition" (437–38), and it shows some vigorous anger at the humiliations of patronage.[28] It is, surely, appropriate that Juvenal, whom Chapman is translating at the end of his career, is the text that opens the play. The centrality of Marlowe's complaint becomes evident when the "Pilgrimage" begins with allusions to *Hero and Leander.* Consiliodorus, entrusting Studioso and Philomusus to the academic life, bids them "wash youre tounge in Aganippes well" (42)[29] and

> There may youe sit in softe greene lauriate shade
> And heare the muses warble out a laye,
> And, mountinge, singe like larke in somers daye.
> There may youe scorne *each Mydas of this age,*
> Eache earthlie peasant and each *drossie clowne*
> That knoweth not howe to weighe youre worthiness,
> But feedeth on beste corne like a stall fedd ass
> Whose statelie mouth in scorne by wheate doth pass.
> I doe com[m]ende youre studious intent
> In that youe make soe faire a pilgrimage.
> If I were younge, who nowe am waxen oulde,
> Whose yontes [i.e., joints] youe see are dryde, benumd, and coulde,
> Though I foreknewe that *gold runns to the boore,*
> Ile be a scholler though I live but poore. (51–64)

He warns them that "Learninge and povertie will ever kiss" (76). And at the end of the "First Return" Studioso again recalls the Marlowe passage when he acknowledges: "Yea *Midas brood* fore eare must honored be, / Whils Phoebus followers live in miserie" (1553–54). The spirit of resentment as both subject and motive for poetry is central to the set of plays.

The population of St. John's mirrors the struggles I have been explicating within the dominant fraction of the society. Over the course of the sixteenth century the universities, which at the beginning of the century had been schooling primarily men beneath the rank of gentleman, had become increasingly important to the upper classes. By 1600 about half the college enrollment was gentry and nobility.[30] Moreover, though most of these students will not become poets themselves, they recognize the feelings of resentment that serious but needy poets must feel, and they understand how that resentment reveals itself in the form and style of the poetry. Thus, Hazlitt may be wrong about the primacy of this particular expression of disgruntlement[31]—Lodge, Roydon, Marlowe, and Chapman, to name the principal poets I have been concerned with, have been voicing this anger for almost a decade—but he is correct that this is a remarkable moment when such a feeling becomes part of the dominant class's sense of the situation of poetry. It may not be fanciful to imagine that twenty-five years later Cambridge undergraduates, among whom would be John Milton, would continue to encourage this spirit.

❉

It has been traditional to try to explain Chapman's taking up *Hero and Leander* by seeing both him and Marlowe as serving Sir Walter Ralegh. Marlowe was reputed to have read his "atheist lecture" to Ralegh and to have spent some time in his household. Both poets were friends of Thomas Harriot, "Ralegh's man," a kind of MacArthur fellow whom Ralegh supported. And in 1596 Chapman had printed his "Guiana Ode" in the narrative of the second voyage to Guiana by Ralegh's lieutenant, Lawrence Keymis. I am, however, skeptical of the argument that Chapman was Ralegh's client. In the same year (1598) that Chapman completed *Hero and Leander* and wrote a poem to Harriot, he also dedicated his first translations of Homer to the earl of Essex, Ralegh's political and courtly rival. Whatever Marlowe's connection with Ralegh, Chapman seems to have at best been at the outskirts of this circle. His "Guiana Ode" and the dedications to Essex were probably attempts to get attention and patronage.

Chapman has more essential reasons for wanting to finish Marlowe's poem: he shares Marlowe's sense of outrage at the economics of learning and poetry.[32] In Chapman's portion of *Hero and Leander* the court becomes the prime image of false values and undependable expectations. Hero is complimented by the poet for being "uncourtly" (3.251). In his dedication to Lady Walsingham Chapman also identifies himself as "uncourtly," claiming to be "glad simply for the naked merit of vertue." This can be taken as a gesture of humility, but we should also consider it as a boast. Although the language of social critique might not seem appropriate for flattering a patron, Chapman uses the occasion to praise Lady Walsingham for encouraging "men of desert" out of "absolute respect to their meere good parts." This he says, is the consequence of her "Noblesse,"[33] which he explicitly distinguishes from "others" who "displaied Ensignes of state and sowreness in [their] forehead[s]; made smooth with nothing but sensualitie and presents." One way of translating this perhaps intentionally enigmatic insult is to see "Ensignes of state and sowreness" as reference to the pride and condescension of the powerful, and "sensualitie and presents" as reference to the flattery that such powerful people usually demand. Chapman here is recalling the boors and the "lofty servile clown[s]" who aroused Marlowe's anger.

Chapman's poem conceals the disruption of established social ranks within the very myths of order. The fifth sestiad's "Tale of Teras," depicting the archetypal marriage between Hymen, who would become the god of marriage, and the maid Eucharis, has generally been treated as a kind of praise of order and ceremony and therefore as in moral contrast to the hectic, consuming love of Marlowe's poem.[34] But looked at from the angle of social aspiration, this tale is, like the story of the shepherd lass with Mercury, a covert model of the overriding of social distinctions. Hymen is frequently identified as the noble Eucharis's social inferior, her parents "exceeding *Hymens* so" (5.267), and it is this social inequality that drives the plot:

> her estate
> In passing his, was so interminate
> For wealth and honor, that his love durst feede
> On nought but sight and hearing, nor could breede
> Hope of requitall, the grand prise of love. (5.123–27)

As we shall see later, when Corynna raises this issue in similar terms Ovid has an answer for her. Eucharis, however, is more conventional than Corynna:

> Coynesse and Love striv'd which had greatest grace,
> Virginitie did fight on Coynesse side;
> Feare of her parents frownes, and femall pride,
> Lothing the lower place, more than it loves
> The high contents, desert and vertue moves. (5.242–46)

"Femall pride," which also motivated the ambitious shepherd lass, can be a reactionary force. After Hymen rescues Eucharis and the other maidens from pirates, it is agreed that he alone will bring the news of the maids' rescue back to the city to convince her parents that he is a worthy husband despite his lowly birth. Adolesche, a "Nymph borne hie" (287), attempts to protect the distinctions of inherited rank by returning before him and thus spoiling his triumph, but she fails, and the archetypal marriage bridges social inequality. The tale of Teras, therefore, is not just a myth of proper ceremony; it is a fantasy of a meritocratic world in which inheritance and rank acknowledge accomplishment.

The tone of the sixth sestiad is defined by a series of extended similes that equate fate to the falsity of the courtly world. This strange comparison, however it accounts for the lovers' tragedy, reflects on the social conditions of the poem itself. The similes of the main narration ring with anger and suggest that it is not only "fate" that causes the problems of the world but the system of social rank. As Chapman strikingly poses the case early in the sestiad, fate is a fop. Describing the fates who calm the seas to lure Leander on, Chapman compares them to "a fleering slavish Parasite" who,

> In warping profit or a traiterous sleight,
> Hoopes round his rotten bodie with devotes,
> And pricks his descant face full of false notes,
> Praysing with open throte (and othes as fowle

As his false hear) the beautie of an Owle,
Kissing his skipping hand with charmed skips,
That cannot leave, but leapes upon his lips
Like a cock-sparrow, or a shameles queane
Sharpe at a red-lipt youth, and nought doth meane
Of all his antick shewes, but doth repayre
More tender fawnes, and takes a scattred hayre
From his tame subiects shoulder; whips, and cals
For every thing he lacks; creepes gainst the wals
With backward humblesse, to give needles way:
Thus his false fate did with *Leander* play. (6.20–34)

The extraordinary imaginative energy of this long simile describing the "antick shewes" of the fop with his gestures of blowing kisses and brushing off loose hairs seems particularly startling when applied to the perversity of fate. But it is exactly this misdirection that contributes a new dimension to Chapman's poem and echoes Marlowe's digression on why the Fates hate love and learning.

A similar obsession with social falsehood overcomes the poem some thirty lines later when Hero's torch is described, and the poet sets up a long and quite difficult simile of the torch as the "true Glasse of our societie":

What man does good, but he consumes thereby?
But thou wert lov'd for good, held high, given show:
Poore vertue loth'd for good, obscur'd, held low.
Doe good, be pinde; be deedles good, disgrast:
Unles we feede on men, we let them fast. (6.61–65)

I want to emphasize how complex Chapman's thought is here. The torch shows that we must be "used," but the present social structure wastes people. The torch in being consumed serves a purpose, but a virtuous person is "pinde," while the good person who tries not to be consumed, who is "deedles good," does not come to any better end; he is "disgrast." A society that does not "feede on men" starves them. The last very problematic line then leads Hero to meditate on the "use" of chastity, which in turn leads the poet to dread the forthcoming tragedy ("Would God she were not dead, or my verse ended" [79]). He then returns to the initial simile:

Leander did not through such tempests swim
To kisse the Torch, although it lighted him:
But all his powres in her desire awaked,
Her love and vertues cloth'd him richly naked.

> Men kisse but fire that only shewes pursue,
> Her Torch and *Hero,* figure shew and vertue. (6.84–89)

This is extraordinarily intricate, and part of its purpose seems to be to confuse the focus so that the sign of the torch becomes an emblem both of social mis-evaluation and of a deeper truth, that it is only through the signs that one finds virtue. At one level, the torch becomes an emblem of the deceptive show of so-cial form, loved as if it were good, elevated, just as Hero lifts it, and admired for itself rather than for what it identifies.[35] But the poem and the poet also know that this is the nature of signification and that the wise person attends to the "shew" in order to find the virtue behind it.

All this is preparation for the strangest simile in the poem, the long—and apparently misleading—simile comparing Leander to "an emptie Gallant full of forme":

> That thinks each looke an act, each drop a storme,
> That fals from his brave breathings; most brought up
> In our *Metropolis,* and hath his cup
> Brought after him to feasts; and much Palme beares,
> For his rare judgement in th'atire he weares,
> Hath seene the hot Low Countries, not their heat,
> Observes their rampires and their buildings yet.
> And for your sweet discourse with mouthes is heard,
> Giving instructions with his very beard.
> Hath gone with an Ambassadour, and been
> A great mans mate in travailing, even to *Rhene,*
> And then puts all his worth in such a face,
> As he saw brave men make, and strives for grace
> To get his newes forth;[36] . . . .
> . . . .
> So serious is his trifling companie,
> In all his swelling ship of vacantrie.
> And so short of himselfe in his high thought,
> Was our *Leander* in his fortunes brought,
> And in his fort of love that he thought won,
> But otherwise, he skorns comparison. (6.110–23, 131–36)

As in the simile of the Fates as fops, the enormous imaginative energy spent on the tenor of this simile hardly seems commensurate with the point that Leander counted his chickens too soon. As Leander's death occurs—by the accident of

Neptune's mace, hurled at the Fates in anger, itself cutting Leander's thread—the poet, in what might be read as a universal expression of Stoic wisdom, warns against anger. But these lines read somewhat differently if we acknowledge the social anger that has permeated this part of the poem:

> The more kinde *Neptune* rag'd, the more he raste
> His loves lives fort, and kild as he embraste.
> Anger doth still his owne mishap encrease;
> If any comfort live, it is in peace.
> O theevish Fates, to let Blood, Flesh, and Sence,
> Build two fayre Temples for their Excellence,
> To rob it with a poysoned influence.
> Though soules gifts starve, the bodies are held dear
> In ugliest things; Sence-sport preserves a Beare.
> But here nought serves our turnes; O heaven & earth,
> How most most wretched is our humane birth? (6.230–40)

We are at one of those points which will become more familiar as we develop Chapman's stance when a powerful moral and existential language hides an observation critical of the plight of the poet himself. The praise of "soules gifts" and the contempt for "Sence-sport" will show up repeatedly as a structure of social critique in Chapman's early work, with its contempt for "passion-driven men"[37] and its idealization of the literary tradition and the high value of poetry itself. If "fate" is to be complained against, it is a pathetic theme. Underneath rides a more concrete anger, not at accidents, but at the misjudgments of society and its failure to reward virtue, an injustice that is just as wasteful as "fate," but which is of human doing.

The ceremony that Leander has neglected and now tries to salvage is, it must be emphasized, not the civic spectacle of "fortune glossed pompists." It is, as D. J. Gordon explicated many years ago, an order that has a place for individual passion and disregards, even disrupts, that other order that sorts people by rank. If Marlowe's fragment famously depicts passion, Chapman's completion understands the complexities of passion in a social setting, and in doing so it elaborates the implications of Marlowe's digression. The "lofty servile clown" recurs in Chapman's portion as a metaphor of cosmic injustice and of fate itself.

The issue of the proper "use" of men, as emblematized by Hero's torch, was very much on Chapman's mind in 1598 as he began to make a name for himself on the stage and to publish the first Homeric translations.

> For though I now consume in poesie,
> Yet *Homer* being my roote I can not die.
> But lest to use all Poesie in the sight
> Of grave philosophie shew braines too light
> To comprehend her depth of misterie,
> I vow t'is onely strong necessitie
> Governes my paines herein, which yet may use
> A mans whole life without the least abuse. ("To M. Harriot," 125–32)[38]

Now Chapman envisions a utopian space in which a proper necessity, poetry and philosophy, may "use / A mans whole life without the least abuse." These lines come from Chapman's clearest, most concentrated, and strongest statement of his ideal of cultural capital: his 164–line poem to M. Harriot with *Achilles Shield* (1598).

Bartlett tells us that the poem comes at the end of the volume in which it appears (*Poems,* 478), but even with that knowledge one may miss the dignity Chapman gives this poem; it may not be announced on the title page, but it is an equal partner to the only other poem in the well-printed little book, the translation of "Achilles Shield." Harriot, a scientist and philosopher whom Ralegh supported in a house on the grounds of his London residence, is here addressed as the ideal audience and the model of intellectual aspiration. Lines bewailing the necessity of clientage appear early in the poem:

> Thus as the soule upon the flesh depends,
> Virtue must wait on wealth, we must make friends
> Of the unrighteous Mammon, and our sleights,
> Must beare the formes of fooles or Parasites. (27–30)

The soul/body opposition becomes the analogue of virtue/wealth and of fire/earth. Harriot is in touch with the same spirit of "strangely intellectual fire" (*Hero and Leander* 3.183) that communicates with Marlowe, Harriot's "whole Sphere of fire" being the poet's aspiration (34).

While he is realistic about the relations of culture and economics, Chapman makes a place for a purely intellectual social power in the band of like-minded thinkers. Understanding both the plight of the economically dependent poet and the difficulty of expression itself, he laments that

> what zeale or power soever
> My free soule hath, my body will be never
> Able t'attend: never shal I enjoy
> Th'end of my happles birth: never employ

That smotherd fervour that in lothed embers,
Lyes swept from light, and no cleare howre remembers. (35–40)[39]

But he also takes hope in readers like Harriot:

O had your perfect eye Organs to pierce
Into that Chaos whence this stiffled verse
By violence breakes: where Gloweworme like doth shine
In nights of sorrow, this hid soule of mine:
And how her genuine formes struggle for birth,
Under the clawes of this fowle Panther earth;
Then under all those formes you should discerne
My love to you, in my desire to learne. (41–48)

Chapman puts himself in the position of the Platonic disciple to Harriot's master. Harriot represents not simply intellectual accomplishment but a relation with the world which can transform cultural capital into social dignity.

No sooner has Chapman's energetic and dialectical mind established this system of pure spirit and foul earth than, in a pattern of revision that will characterize much of his early verse, he transcends it. "Most students, . . . / Leaning like rotten howses, on out beames, / . . . . with true light fade in themselves like dreames" (59–62). For

True learning hath a body absolute,
That in apparant sence it selfe can suite
Not hid in ayrie termes as if it were
Like spirits fantasticke that put men in feare. (63–66)

The polarity of the symbolism has reversed: trivial learning is "ayrie," and a "body absolute" identifies "true learning," a kind of Platonic ideal.[40] We may also hear in this praise of the materiality of Harriot's learning a compliment to the skepticism which caused Baines to link Harriot with Marlowe.[41] Then with a clarity rare for him Chapman describes the difficult situation of culture itself, whereby the learned man, despised and treated with contempt by the powerful, can claim superiority:

When thy true wisedome by thy learning wonne
Shall honour learning while there shines a Sunne;
And thine owne name in merite; farre above,
Their Timpanies of state that armes of love,
Fortune or blood shall lift to dignitie;
Whome though you reverence, and your emperie

> Of spirit and soule, be servitude they thinke
> And but a beame of light broke through a chink
> To all their watrish splendor: and much more
> To the great Sunne, and all thinges they adore,
> In staring ignorance: yet your selfe shall shine
> Above all this in knowledge most divine,
> And all shall homage to your true-worth owe,
> You comprehending all, that all, not you. (75–88)

This is hard to track, but it makes clear sense. To paraphrase: "Your name is in merit far above that of powerful personages ("Timpanies of state") dignified by love, fortune, or blood. You give them reverence (i.e., the mannerly obeisance due them) and they think your superior intellect at their service and merely a sliver of light compared to their grandness ("watrish splendor"), to the sun (the monarch?), and to all the things they in their ignorance admire. But you shall triumph by knowledge, encompassing and understanding ("comprehending") everything, including the powerful ("that all") who will not understand or encompass you." The verb "comprehend" at the end has a rich play of understanding and power. Harriot somehow does the proper "reverence" while still maintaining his integrity.

In the final section of the poem Chapman scoffs at versifiers who "rime and give a verse smooth feet, / Uttering to vulgar pallattes passions sweet" (133–34), and he holds up a higher idea of "serious poetry,"

> Yet where high *Poesies* native habite shines,
> From whose reflections flow eternall lines:
> *Philosophy* retirde to darkest caves
> She can discover: and the proud worldes braves
> Answere in any thing but impudence,
> With circle of her general excellence. (137–42)

To answer "the proud worldes braves" with poetry is an intricate feat, perhaps unheard of before in English culture. In denying "impudence" Chapman shows an awareness of the delicate social implications of such a cultural claim. Earlier in the poem he accused poetry's enemies of impudence: "how like gnats appeare: / O fortune-glossed Pompists, and proud Misers, / That are of Arts such impudent despisers" (98–100). Chapman's poem represents a very special moment, for while it appeals to the archaic tradition of dark meaning, it also gives glimmers of a more modern idea of the mysterious value of poetry itself as cultural capital, as a weapon against the "proud worldes braves." Out of resentment Chapman is inventing a stance that will become conventional three centuries later.

3

Virtue and the Critique of Nobility

Tamburlaine announces to his men the end of arbitrary, inherited rank: "Your byrthes shall be no blemish to your fame, / For vertue is the fount whence honor springs" (1768–69). Virtue as the source of honor is a standard stoic idea, but its revolutionary implications—that peasants can by their virtue attain honor— are posed here in a deceptively casual way. Later Tamburlaine closes his speech wooing Zenocrate with very similar sentiments and language: "[I] shal give the world to note for all my byrth, / That Vertue solely is the sum of glorie, / And fashions men with true nobility" (1969–71). "True nobility" fashioned by "virtue" will become in the next few years a code phrase identifying a broad understanding that claims recognition for the accomplishments, especially literary ones, of people unable to claim the "birth" and "blood" that conventionally identify the nobility.

In "A Coronet for His Mistresse, Philosophie" Chapman can allude to the same line of thought when he criticizes "false nobility." Speaking of Philosophy, he says,

> titles of primacy,
> Courtship of antick gestures, braineles jests,
> Bloud without soule of false nobilitie,
> Nor any folly that the world infests
> Can alter her who with her constant guises
> To living vertues turns the deadly vices (6.9–14)[1]

Courtship here may be read narrowly as erotic wooing and more broadly as the whole political art of the courtier. Courtship's "gestures" become by a homonym "jests." In the context of the previous two lines, with their attack on titles and the court, the line "Bloud without soule of false nobility," while it never denies the possibility of a reading that might allow a "true" nobility of blood, criticizes the very idea of blood as a criterion for nobility. The paradox of the last line offers the possibility of a discourse, based on a disguised ("constant guises") inversion of the moral language of the court, that will criticize and restructure social values.

It has been common to treat such a moment as an assertion of Chapman's own learning and accomplishment without considering the threat to conventional social rankings that such praise of "Philosophie" implies.[2] The "ignorants" whom he often denounces are not the mob (though he has no use for the "vulgar" either) but his blooded but ignorant social superiors, the "false nobility" with the leisure and education "to read to curtail a tedious hour" who pass judgment without any real knowledge. For Chapman—and for the other ambitious but disadvantaged poets—learning and poetry identify an intellectual hierarchy, a "true nobility," that poses an alternative to, and therefore always entails a criticism of, the actual social structure, dominated by a "false nobility" of "blood."

The humanist debate on "Nobility," which has a rich tradition going back at least to Dante, has always honored learning and virtue but does not seem to have entailed a critique of the social system. One often finds criticism of lineage and wealth as the sole criteria for nobility, but seldom denunciations of them. Typical of humanist neutrality on the issue is Flaminius in Buonaccorso's dialogue *Disputatio de Nobilitate,* who asserts, "The size of one's fortune or the grandeur of one's family can neither bestow nor remove nobility."[3] Fifteenth-century Italian humanists are economically comfortable, and if they display what Charles Trinkaus calls "insecurity" it is "moral and psychological rather than economic or political."[4] In the sixteenth century most of the English treatises on nobility lack the intellectual dimension of the earlier Italian models and are comfortable explaining to the world the characteristics of courtesy and generosity that distinguish the traditional nobility defined by family and wealth. As books on nobility shade easily into advice to the courtier, and treatises on courtiership often include an analysis of the nature of nobility, a circular reinforcement of established social structures takes place. The subtitle of Lawrence Humphrey's *The Nobles, or of Nobilitye* is typical: *The Original Nature, dutyes, right, and Christian Institucion Thereof.*[5] Commonly, these books take the existence of a noble class for granted and spend their attention describing how such a class should behave. Annibale Romei's *The Courtier's Academie* (English translation by John Kepers, 1598) includes a chapter on nobility arguing against the stoic idea that virtue should be the sole basis of nobility and requiring that a noble person be able to show three generations of illustrious forebears.[6] John Ferne's *The Blazon of Gentrie* begins by proving that plebeians are incapable of nobility before it concentrates on how the gentry should bear themselves.[7] One approaches the genre expecting aristocratic propaganda. The difficult social dynamics of the court are certainly a central concern of a book like *The Courtier*,[8] but finally the courtier is always the system's ally.

In their analyses of the link between wealth and nobility, all of these treatises invoke versions of the classical stoic commonplace "that only the wise man is rich." Such an assertion has always offered an opening for a criticism of material wealth, but, remarkably, the political consequences do not seem to have been drawn. Cicero, an immensely rich man, has no trouble explaining the wealth of wisdom as one of his *Paradoxa stoicorum*.[9] The humanists, despite the advantage of their Christian upbringing, tend not to consider the difficulty the rich man will have entering heaven when they invoke Cicero's text. The argument has been that others may pursue false riches, but you and I will pursue the authentic wealth of wisdom. This moral reading of the idea persuades wealthy people away from material interests to a life of learning, which is, as we might observe in the spirit of Bourdieu, a renunciation easily available to the wealthy and, more narrowly, only to the wealthy who are so secure in their economic and social position that they can play the trump card of denying that such position matters. The circle of privilege reinforces itself redundantly.

When it is given a political inflection, the discussion of nobility tends to reinforce the status quo. If Thomas Elyot can argue that virtue is prior to "nobility," he can at the same time assure his readers that in general the nobility are more virtuous than other ranks.[10] Quentin Skinner argues that a "deeply conservative" message is derived by most northern humanists of the Renaissance: "Having admitted that government ought to be placed in the hands of those with the greatest virtue, and having affirmed that those with the greatest virtue happen to be the nobility and gentry, they proceed to draw the pleasingly obvious conclusion: that in order to maintain the best-ordered form of political society, we ought not to tamper with any existing social distinctions, but ought on the contrary to preserve them as far as possible."[11] Given this circular logic it is not surprising that as long as aristocrats and writers entirely dependent on aristocrats are doing the arguing, there will be little challenge to the present social arrangements. What is perhaps most important is to understand how subtle and how similarly infinite must be the operations by which people—poor poets, for instance—fight the web of assumptions and definitions that everywhere put them in their place. Only when the social distribution is a source of offense will different meanings begin to be drawn from such commonplaces, and even then, thanks to the enormous power of the aristocracy and the continuing domination of the patronage system, any element of critique will in all likelihood be modest, muted, and veiled.[12]

The essential logic and language Marlowe and Chapman invoke in their appeals to "true nobility" come from a book written in Italian in 1542 and published in an English translation by William Jones in 1595: *Nennio, or a treatise of Nobility: Wherein is discoursed what true Nobility is, with such qualities as are required in a perfect Gentleman.*[13] Jones's translation was dedicated to the earl of Essex and was escorted by complimentary sonnets from a quartet of unprivileged but ambitious authors: Chapman, Spenser, Daniel, and Day.[14] Superficially it appears to be yet another conventional, stoically inclined praise of nobility, with some special attention to the importance of learning and virtue.[15] But *Nennio* differs pointedly from the many other works in the tradition, and Chapman's complimentary poem in particular brings into focus the way it redefines nobility.

The original *Nennio* had been written in Italian by "that famous Doctor and worthy knight Sir John Baptista Nenna of Bari." Just as the English edition is dedicated to a prominent nobleman, the Italian had been dedicated to Aragonia Sforza, queen of Poland and grand duchess of Lithuania and Bari.[16] The book claims to recount a discussion of nobility among a group of Italians who, in the common situation of avoiding the plague and the French armies, have retired to the country. After some sport they entertain a noble lady, Virginia, who as she leaves bestows upon Possidonio and Fabricio, her escorts, a ring for "him who is the most noble of you two." "*Possidonio,* as one descending of an ancient & noble family, being beside indued with great riches, claimed the gift; but *Fabricio,* who reckoned himself nothing inferior to the other in nobility (albeit that his ancestors were not of so noble blood, nor himself blessed with so great wealth) he pretended with great vehemencie, that the ring belonged to him because that from his youth, he had been vertuously raised to that substance he possessed, and thereby became wise, prudent and well conditioned" (B3–B3v).[17] For the rest of book 1, Possidonio makes the case for nobility by "blood." In book 2 Fabricio rebuts Possidonio and argues for the superior nobility of "the vertues of the mind." In book 3 Nennio, a member of the company who has been selected at the beginning to be judge, reviews and evaluates the two arguments and after a number of gestures toward false closure rules for Fabricio, who then graciously bestows the ring on Possidonio.

Though its title and the debate format might lead one to try to read *Nennio* in the tradition of *The Courtier* and the various treatises on nobility, the issue here is not how to succeed as a courtier. *Nennio* disregards the practical issues and poses bluntly and at length the radical and socially basic question in any aristocracy, what is nobility? The book allows that the conventional inherited nobility, that is, the class that the courtier aspires to and serves, may not deserve that title. If such a conclusion cannot be stated explicitly nor be openly approved by writers and poets expecting patronage, neither can it be entirely hidden lest the text simply reinforce the position it is critiquing. What is remarkable about *Nennio* is that it achieves a style which constantly voices ideas critical of a nobility of blood and riches but never authorizes them.[18] What Jones, the translator, calls "This ticklish title of Nobilitie" (A3v) remains teasingly evasive. The text knows more than it can say. Jones collaborates in this deception by concealing the fact that the book depicts the two kinds of nobility as antithetical. "In the first [book] is spoken in the behalfe of Nobility of bloud, conjoyned with riches: In the second, of Nobilitie purchased by vertue: in the Third, whether of the two is to be preferred: and what true and perfect Nobilitie is, whence it proceedeth, how it is gotten, maintained and preserved" (A4). From this description one would not know that the second book is a refutation of the first or that the conclusion is an ambiguous, even contradictory, negotiation of the mutually exclusive arguments and values.[19]

The treatise poses a hierarchical problem: which is more noble, blood or learning? But it repeatedly answers this question in terms of one special and extreme version of the question: is a virtuously learned commoner more noble than a depraved aristocrat? Let us grant that in the sixteenth century even this extreme version of the question does not lead to an easy answer.[20] It is a testament to the treatise's air of moral integrity that it can answer this version of the question unambiguously. As Jones strongly and clearly states in his introduction: "it were more praise worthy, to be born the sonne of a common Crier, with Horace; or of a Mason, with Socrates; or of uncertain parents with Euripides, and to be vertuous and learned: then the sonne of Nero or of Domitian and to be vitious" [A3v]. Yet, clear as this is, there is an element of evasion in it. In the competition between Possidonio and Fabricio it is never claimed that Possidonio is immoral, criminal, or tyrannical or the child of such parents. Nor, for that matter, is it ever claimed that Fabricio has the learned stature of a Horace, Socrates, or Euripides. Whatever importance this formulation of the meanings and values of nobility may have, it evades the deep issue that Virginia's challenge raises. The issue in question is the relative values of blood and learning, not the moral status of the specific disputants.

Nennio conceals the radical questions that it raises about nobility by at one point prominently disavowing any criticism of the aristocracy. In the third book Nennio assures the company that the discussion does not apply to anyone of the rank of baron or above. Since in common and technical usage the term *nobility* applies only to people of those ranks, this caveat would seem to deny the space of inquiry altogether.[21] Like Stubbes's criticism of pride, this is a social meditation which opens a space for thought by exempting the powerful people for whom the meditation is most obviously relevant. Also, despite the fact that it is the meaning of *nobility* that is being investigated, the treatise casually and repeatedly uses the term as if its meaning were already understood. When she first appears Virginia is called a "noble lady." It is unobtrusively announced that Possidonio comes from a "noble family."[22] Such looseness would seem to reassure that the inquiry, whatever its fictional claims, does not mean to challenge conventional usage and, therefore, will support the status quo.

Fabricio's argument that "the virtues of the mind" are the highest, perhaps the only, nobility traverses territory familiar to Christian stoicism. But within the conventional justification for moral learning Fabricio poses devastating arguments against the concept of the inherited nobility. He begins with the simple logical argument that if your nobility depends on your parentage, then their nobility also depended on their parents, and so forth back to Adam. "I say it is a foolish thing to hold, that nobility is left us by our ancestors, for if that were true, it should necessarily followe, either that we should all be noble, or else not one at all" (I2).[23] In *Nennio* the logic of this argument is never answered.

In Book 3 another man, Dominico, elaborates the implications of Fabricio's argument by developing a negative genealogy of nobility. God, Dominico argues, made men equal. "Man then himself was the inventor and beginner of this Nobility" (Y3). Cain was the first noble. A history of biblical tyrannies is sketched wherein men "either by force or fraude did surmount others" and came to be called noble. As kings granted special privileges, flatterers and criminals became the nobility until, as in the case of nature, the most savage (e.g., eagles and lions) or fruitless (e.g., oak and laurel) are deemed the most noble (Y4v).[24] Nennio acknowledges the force of the tirade and does not disprove it. He merely poses an alternate genealogy wherein "men did join together and did choose their Prince, amongst those that were good, the most wise, the most prudent, the most just, and the most understanding, to whom they did submit themselves" (Aa1v). Nobility was conferred on these heroes' children as a way of urging them to "strive to follow their steps and vertue." The strong negative arguments against the nobility of blood are left standing, though unauthorized, and the union of these two versions that Nennio finally proposes results in a profound ambiguity about the origins, meaning, and value of nobility: "You see three mighty causes, from the which nobility did spring, by the which doth clearly appeare, that it descendeth from the vertues of the minde, riches likewise hath beene the cause to make men noble. Moreover many in becoming tyrantes, and violently bringing others into subjection, have made that the originall of their nobility, as by you M. *Dominico* hath beene said. These are the principall beginnings of nobility, from hence noblemen first did spring: so that the vertues of the minde, tyrannie, and riches, were the first meanes and way to attain nobility" (Aa2). The cadences of a conclusion belie the difficulties this strangely neutral yet contradictory summation raises for any judgment. It is revealing of the provocative mode of the treatise that at this moment the discourse is interrupted by a visiting hunting party, and when Nennio resumes he has shifted to a discussion of nobles who perform crimes and who "are not worthy of life."

Parallel to the line which questions the origins of nobility is one which finds in inherited nobility the source of civil woe. "How grevious the hatred is which groweth by wicked oppressions made by the nobility against the comminality, they only know who have made tryall thereof"—a nicely and bitterly evasive assertion. But on the next page for a moment ambiguity falls away, and we have the following assertion, a whole paragraph in itself: "By this you see, that the nobilitie of blood, is not onely cause of pride and ignorance, but of the most cruell slaughters and mortall hatred" (Y1v). Nennio pauses, but then proceeds to argue that the blooded nobility's rivalry with the "comminality" leads to "hatred, persecution, envy, ambition, ignorance, and pride. These are the fruits which nobilitie of blood do give to the mind" (Y2v). Though its consequences are not followed out in the reasoning of the final judgment, this denunciation of the social and moral effects of inherited nobility occupies the center of Nennio's discussion.

Nennio's judgment begins with an analysis that raises doubts about the very possibility of an essential nobility. Though all nations define a "difference between noblemen and those of the baser sort" (T1), they do not at all agree on the terms of that distinction. Naples forbids nobles to hold public office. Venice allows merchants to be noble. In France nobles "live upon their lands, and hold it for rusticitie to dwell in townes, and contrarily in Italie, we leave the countrie for clowns to inhabite, and gentlemen dwell in townes" (S4v). Implicit in this argument is an anthropology which would treat the definition, privileges, and obligations of nobility as culturally relative.[25]

Later in his analysis Nennio introduces a variation on this line of argument by invoking "custom" as a way of defining nobility. Insofar as "custom" argues for inherited nobility, this line of argument tends to counter Fabricio's logic which would expose the fallacies of traditions of nobility.[26] Nennio plays a complex game whereby in arguing for the custom of inherited nobility he casts doubt on its status as anything but a corrupt and unjust tradition. The vulgar, he asserts, "understand not nobility of mind, but nobility of blood. Which maketh great in favor of Possidonio, for this word Noble, being simplie spoken by the courteous Lady, seeing that we are in doubt thereof, we ought to take it as it is received by the common voice" (V1v). This appeal to custom can go both ways. "Custom" is essential to the case Nennio develops for a "compound nobility," that is both well-born and learned. When a minor participant raises the objection that an "imperfection," that is, the vulgar conception of inherited nobility, cannot be a part of a perfect compound vertue, Nennio responds evasively that, though nobility of blood "was a kind of nobility exalted by the vulgar sort," the man of compound nobility will be considered noble by "both the vulgar sort and the men of wisdom." We must appreciate the art of this ambiguity which, while allowing for a reading that would severely devalue nobility of blood, never quite makes the argument and falls back on a Machiavellian practicality.

Somewhat later this same ambiguity is repeated in connection with the question of whether a prince can confer nobility:

> Understanding that nobility consisteth in the vertues of the mind, as you doe, it may easily be yielded unto, that an Emperour or a Prince cannot make another man noble: but taking it in that sort as I did give it you, it were surely no small fault to say, that unto him to who[m] so large authority is graunted in this world, to establish and abrogate lawes at his pleasure, this farre lesse power should be denied. Doeth not hee create Earles, Marquesses, Dukes, & such like, who by such dignities are made most noble? Yes surely, He may then farre more easily make one noble: not that he is able to endow him with justice, with prudence, with wisdome, and other vertues of the minde: but yet this he may do, that he shall be esteemed and reputed in the ranke of gentlemen, & be numbered amongst them. (Bb3v)

The circularity of this argument is rendered succinctly on the next page when Nennio points out that many are made noble by kings. "Who is there then that doth not judge them noble sith the king will have it so?" (Bb4). The realities of royal prerogative here explicitly skew the intellectual argument, thus revealing the conditions under which the argument takes place.

Nennio's conception of compound nobility would seem to deny the radical possibilities of Fabricio's argument, for as long as compound nobility is allowed and overrides the single emphasis on learning and vertue, the blooded nobility will always have the advantage, the other accomplishments being equal. If compound nobility were to carry the day, then, since no one makes the case that Fabricio significantly surpasses Possidonio in virtue (though Possidonio *shows* himself to be arrogant and ignorant of the complexities of the issue), we would expect Possidonio, who has the advantage of birth, to win the ring. But, as he is rendering his final judgment in favor of Fabricio, Nennio allows for the revolutionary possibility that a virtuous commoner may be superior to a virtuous aristocrat: "he is worthy of far greater glorie who of himself becommeth noble, then he who is simply born noble." This statement appears in the context of an anecdote about Gismond, "who being reprehended by some of his familiar friends, because he did advance men of base birth, yet adorned with vertue . . . answered.

As for me, I will exalt such as ought to be preferred before any men living, and those from whom true nobilitie proceedeth" (Cc4v).[27] As we have just seen, that very power leads to ambiguities, for who would challenge the king's power? Here at the end that ambiguous power has been reemployed, not to support custom, but to support virtue. But the defense of the nobility of virtue is still carefully imprecise, for finally it is not "nobility" that the virtuous attain but "glory." The social implications of the final judgment bleed off into a more indistinct realm: the self-made man has reason to be proud in a way that is impossible for the born noble, but the hierarchy of nobility may still not have sustained a challenge.

Fabricio's final gesture of giving the ring, which Nennio has turned into a symbol of learning and virtue, to the man of noble blood shows that thought and action are in an ironic relation in *Nennio*. The reading I am proposing treats such ironies, as well as the numerous moments in the text of blatant contradiction and pointed hiatus, as expressive devices, not as evidence of confusion. "The Courteous Reader" addressed in the preface will fill in the gaps and ignore the discrepancies, but a more discourteous reader will see all the flaws, appreciate the insults embedded in the compliments, and enjoy the game of communicating radical criticisms of domination under the innocent eyes of those criticized.[28] Put another way, this is a text that seems intent on voicing a critique but at the same time achieving deniability; an attentive reading raises many radical questions about the source and justice of the social structure, but the response within the text is always to a less radical, more conventionally moral issue.

The polyvocality of *Nennio* is evidenced in the apparatus of dedication and commendation that accompanies Jones's translation of the treatise.[29] The textual ambiguity is both ignored and enhanced by the dedication of the translation to Essex. "A more fit Patron I could not well chuse, considering the argument and substance of the discourse. It treateth of Nobilitie by descent. . . . It speaketh of Nobilitie, purchased by virtue . . . that both these conjoined together in your L. do make you perfectly Noble" (A2). This is exactly the crux that *Nennio* leaves problematic. A reader sensitive to subversive meanings may even find a double meaning in the first sentence of this quotation praising Essex: it may say only that under the limitations the patronage system enforces, Essex is the best one can find.

The range of interpretations the treatise allows is reflected precisely in the complimentary sonnets that accompany it. Poets with different social agendas can find different social uses for the text. Day's sonnet praising Jones avoids the issue of nobility almost completely. More interesting is Daniel, closely linked with the countess of Pembroke and apparently uninterested in challenging the system that supports him, who is able to use the occasion of this ticklish treatise to praise Essex:[30]

He here shal glasse himself, himselfe shal reed:
The modell of his owne perfections lies
Here plaine describ'd, which he presents in deed:
So that if men can not true worth discerne
By this discourse, looke they on him and learne.[31]

Spenser is engaged in a more complex relation with patronage. His sonnet depicts the argument of the treatise as a debate, and while observing openly that the book sets up a "true Nobility" "not by painted shewes and titles vaine, / Derived farre from famous Auncestrie," leaves the terms of the critique vague and manages to suggest that the conflict is simply a moral one:

Who so wil seeke by right deserts t'attaine
        Unto the type of true Nobility,
        And not by painted shewes and titles vaine,
        Derived farre from famous Auncestrie,
Behold them both in their right visnomy
        Here truly pourtray'd, as they ought to be,
        And striving both for termes of dignitie,
        To be advanced highest in degree.
And when thou doost with equall insight see
        The ods twixt both, of both them deem aright
        And chuse the better of them both to thee,
        But thanks to him that it deserves, behight:
To *Nenna* first, that first this worke created,
        And next to *Jones,* that truely it translated.

The social implications of the argument are ignored in such a way as to leave us with the impression that there is no social dilemma involved and that, simply, moral people will learn to choose rightly from this text. The ambiguous phrase, "chuse the better of them both," might convey a sympathy with Fabricio, though it might just as well be made to allude to Nennio's compromise of compound nobility.

Chapman's sonnet suggests more difficult consequences.

Accept thrice Noble *Nennio* at his hand
That cannot bid himselfe welcome at home,
A thrice due welcome to our native strand,
Italian, French, and *English* now become.
Thrice Noble, not in that usde Epethite,
But Noble first, to know whence Noblesse sprung,

Then in thy labour bringing it to light,
Thirdly, in being adorned with our tung.
And since so (like it selfe) thy Land affoords
The right of Noblesse to all noble parts,
I wish our friend, giving thee English words,
With much desert of Love in English harts,
　　As he hath made one strange an Englishman,
　　May make our mindes in this, *Italian.*
　　　Ex tenebris.

Though three years later Chapman will dedicate his first Homeric translations to Essex, here he pointedly refrains from using the occasion to curry favor. Dissatisfaction speaks strongly in this poem. The second line expresses the learned poet's own sense of powerlessness and of being excluded in his own land. By rejecting "that usde Epethite," and finding nobility in the idea, the writing, and the translating, Chapman sides with the voices in *Nennio* that attack the customary ideas of inherited nobility. The outrageousness of the hope expressed in the last line of the sonnet needs to be emphasized. Gabriel Harvey had attacked Italianate Englishmen in *Speculum Tuscanismi* and had reiterated the position in his feud with Nash. Anti-Italian references recur throughout the period;[32] typical is Whetstone who, in his elegy for Sidney, could assert: "An English-man that is Italianate: / Doth lightly prove a Devell incarnate."[33] Chapman turns these common prejudices on their head; Nennio's Italy is seen as a land of justice in which the true nobleness of intellect is honored; the hope that the book "may make our mindes in this, *Italian*" is a veiled wish for a transformation of social values.

When in the letter to Roydon before *The Shadow of Night* Chapman singles out three noblemen for special praise, we are at one of those points about which Bourdieu has alerted us when social distinctions are being signaled in what might appear as a typical and unproblematic locution: "But I stay this spleene when I remember my good *Mat[thew]* how joyfully oftentimes you reported unto me, that most ingenious *Darbie,* deepe searching *Northumberland,* and skill-imbracing *heire of Hunsdon* had most profitably entertained learning in themselves to the vitall warmth of freezing science, & to the admirable luster of their *true Nobilitie,* whose high deserving *vertues* may cause me hereafter strike that fire out of darknesse, which the brightest Day shall envie for beautie" (*Poems,* 19, emphasis added). In declaring these men's learning, rather than their wealth, lineage, or power, as the source of their "vertue" and "true Nobilitie," Chapman is again echoing *Nennio's* definition of "true nobility" as "the virtues of the mind," in opposition to the claims of "nobility of blood." These may be noblemen in the common sense, but they are more importantly men of "light-bearing intellect" who will, along with Roydon, make an appropriate audience for the difficult poems that follow.[34]

The linking of "virtue" and "true nobility" becomes a coded signal. Almost twenty years later we can still hear this double entendre embedded in "virtue" so that it signifies not a moral praise but a social distinction. In the dedication of *The Revenge of Bussy D'Ambois* to Sir Thomas Howard in 1613, Chapman responds to the "maligners" of the play who, objecting that there never was such a person as Clermont D'Ambois, "cavil at truth's want in these natural fictions." He asserts that "material instruction, elegant and sententious excitation to virtue, and deflection from her contrary, [are] the soul, limbs, and limits of an autentical tragedy." The moral language is misleading here. Chapman is fending off a pedantic insistence on actual fact and invoking a commonplace from poetic theory to argue that it is moral effect that defines tragedy. Chapman's dedication neatly speaks in a way that seems a conventional and close echo of Sidney's "notable images of virtue, vices or what else." But elsewhere in the short dedication the language, by repeated Nennian couplings, insinuates a special understanding. Twice Chapman links "virtue" and "nobility" and includes the telltale adjective "true": he entitles the dedication "To the right virtuous and truly noble knight," and in the first sentence he refers to "your undoubted virtue and exceeding true noblesse." Such locutions, without insisting on anything dangerous, allow for the understanding that there is a "true nobility" identified by a social and intellectual virtue that can be distinguished from that debased "blood without soul of false nobility" by its engagement in enlightened patronage. The next paragraph separates Sir Thomas from those "ignoble and sour-browd worldlings" (i.e., ignorant men of power who fail to patronize learning). Unlike many of his rank, Sir Thomas Howard by his patronage of "virtuous and divine expression" preserves his name to posterity and sets himself above his class equals.

In his enthusiasm for the ideal of "true nobility" Chapman clearly aligns himself with Fabricio's "virtues of the mind" against the privileges of birth. This is an important structuring identification that should cause us to question the direction of much Chapman criticism. Because it belongs to the conventional lexicons of sexual morality and courtesy, the term *virtue* which Chapman frequently invokes has caused his work to be interpreted in a narrow and moralistic way. Much attention has been devoted to such issues as the morality of Hero's sexual behavior and the legitimacy of Ovid's rhapsodies at the sound of Corynna's song. Bussy D'Ambois's affair with Tamyra has been treated as a sign of his lack of vir-

tue. But such precise distinctions miss the point: *virtue* in Chapman's vocabu-
lary stands for those individual qualities and accomplishments by which men and
women make themselves, achieve competency, merit their place, and it is defined
by its opposition not to *vice* but to all the unearned privileges of wealth and blood.
It is the key to a world of merit rather than inheritance.

In the "Coronet for His Mistress, Philosophy," Philosophy, like the "virtues
of the mind" which define Fabricio's idea of true nobility, is not just abstemious;
she is a principle of social value: worldly "riches" cannot compare "to the vertues
of my love" (7.14) or to "The maiestie and riches of the minde" (1.13). The poet,
assured that she will assuage "the wrongs [his] fortunes show" (9.7), sees Philos-
ophy as offering an alternative social success:

> Her selfe shall be my comfort and my riches,
>   And all my thoughts I will on her convert,
>   Honor, and Error, which the world bewitches,
>   Shall still crowne fooles, and tread upon desert,
> And never shall my friendlesse verse envie
> Muses that Fames loose feathers beautifie. (9.9–14)

"My love" (i.e., Philosophy) is an anti-courtly intelligence that, rather than in-
dulging in the conventional sonneteer's "exstasies" that eat out the lover's entrails
(2.4), offers an alternate rapture that "teach[es] by passion what perfection is"
(2.10). Her virtue short-circuits the normal systems of desert and rank: "Vertue
is both the merit and reward / Of her remov'd, and soule-infusde regard" (4.13–
14). The issue here is not moral purity or abstention but social recognition.

The revision of the criteria of rank implied by the word "virtue" is most pointed
in Chapman's understanding of Achilles as the exemplary hero of the *Iliad*. Un-
like Shakespeare's Ulysses, who criticizes Achilles for violating degree and there-
by unleashing disorder, Chapman finds in Achilles a "virtue" that speaks to true
nobility rather than the de facto rankings that distort merit. In 1598, three years
after *Ovids Banquet of Sence,* Chapman dedicates his first two translations of
Homer to Essex. He addresses *Seaven Bookes of The Iliades,* "To The Most Hon-
ored now living Instance of the Achilleian vertues eternized by divine HOMERE,
the Earle of ESSEXE, Earle Marshall &c." The dedication of *Achilles Shield* later
that same year to Essex ends, "presenting your Achilleian vertues with Achilles'
Shield."[35] To the modern understanding, for whom Achilles is, in Simone Weil's
reading, a terrifying, raw "force," the idea of "Achilleian vertues" may seem an
oxymoron.[36] And interpreters of Chapman have found Chapman's enthusiasm

for Achilles a problem. A common reading sees him as becoming disillusioned with Achilles and finding relief in Odysseus, whose mental prowess fits more neatly into the intellectual world Chapman is supposed to have advocated.[37] Chapman is not confused here; he sees Achilles as the man of worth who defends his integrity against powerful, aristocratic figures who misuse their power.

Chapman's dedication to Essex posits an analogy between the situation in the Greek camp and the plight of the obscure poet. "Helpe then, renown'de Achilles [i.e., Essex], to preferre and defend your grave and blamelesse Prophet of Phoebus [i.e., Homer or Chapman] from the doting and vitious furie of the two Atrides—Arrogancie and Detraction" (505). It is Achilles' defense of Calchas, who himself has been inspired by "prophetic force / Given by Apollo,"[38] against the arbitrary and selfish powers of Agamemnon and Menelaus, that rouses Chapman's admiration.[39] Achillean virtue is not strictly a warrior's excellence; it is integrity in the service of culture, a willingness to risk one's own power for the truth. Essex "then, most abundant President of *true Noblesse*" (504), is a Nennian figure for Chapman, whose authority derives not from his blood or the wealth of his family but from "the virtues of the mind." It is as champions of unregarded merit that Achilles and Essex are figures of "virtue."

A late explication of this ideal is Sarpedon's speech urging Glaucus to join him in assaulting the Greek bulwark in *Iliad 12* (Chapman's translation of this speech would appear in print a decade after the first Homeric translations). Chapman enthusiastically glosses the speech in the margin, "Sarpedon's speech to Glaucus, never equalled by any (in this kind) of all that have written" (*Homer* 1.247). Sarpedon explains that the luxury and benefits princes enjoy should be earned by accomplishment and not simply granted by arbitrary privilege. The argument is not difficult and may seem obvious, but in an aristocratic situation, in which powerful people claim privilege by birth, it is problematic. Sarpedon first links honor with merit:

> Glaucus, say why are we honord more
> Than other men of Lycia in place—with greater store
> Of meates and cups, with goodlier roofes, delightsome gardens, walks,
> More lands and better, so much wealth that Court and countrie talks
> Of us and our possessions and every way we go
> Gaze on us as we were their Gods? This where we dwell is so:
> The shores of Xanthus ring of this: and shall not we exceed
> As much in merit as in noise? Come, be we great in deed
> As well as looke, shine not in gold but in the flames of fight,
> That so our neat-arm'd Lycians may say: "See, these are right

Our kings, our Rulers: these deserve to eate and drinke the best;
These governe not ingloriously; these thus exceed the rest,
Do more than they command to do." (12.311–23)

This utopian vision of leaders who "Do more than they command to do," who neither buy nor inherit their privilege, echoes the line of reasoning of Achilles in book 1 when he accuses Agamemnon of taking more than his share of the spoils and conforms to the Nennian critique.

Sarpedon's second argument abruptly and surprisingly changes the terms of the discussion; by stripping military glory of its mystique it emphasizes the social basis of honor and reward:

O friend, if keeping backe
Would keepe backe age from us, and death, and that we might not wracke
In this life's humane sea at all, but that deferring now
We shund death ever—nor would I halfe this vaine valour show,
Nor glorifie a folly so, to wish thee to advance:
But since we must go though not here, and that, besides the chance
Proposd now, there are infinite fates of other sort in death
Which (neither to be fled nor scap't) a man must sinke beneath—
Come, trie we if this sort be ours and either render thus
Glorie to others or make them resigne the like to us. (1.323–32)

Spondanus points to the difference between Sarpedon's argument and Achilles' choice of glory over long life.[40] Sarpedon says with Hamlet that, since it will come when it will come, it might as well come now. The word "sort" twice in the last lines emphasizes this recognition of chance. But, as is his habit, Chapman has expanded on Homer at this point. In Chapman's rendering, battle is seen as "vaine valour" and "folly," words that have no basis in the Greek. Homer's Sarpedon in the midst of the meditation on chance and death still talks of "battle where men win glory."[41] Spondanus translates this as "pugnam ad illustrem." In Homer it remains somewhat muddled why one goes to battle: glory or chance alone might each be a sufficient argument, but the two together leave one uneasy. What is remarkable about Chapman's darker Sarpedon is that he sees through the mystique of glory as an end in itself. Like Hal trading glories with Hotspur, Chapman's Sarpedon is a realist who fights without illusions. He strips the argument of the transcendental motive of glory, leaving either a stoic fatalism or the social argument for merit as the justification for action.

Achillean virtue stands for just this unmystical motive, aware of mortality and yet demanding a just practice, hating those Agamemnons who take advantage of title or position to oppress others. It is a powerful individual resistance to established privileges. With Sarpedon, such virtue risks itself in battle, but the battle is with superiors as much as with rival equals. It is, finally, an ideal of moral integrity that dares disrupt the conventional hierarchies in the name of justice and truth. All of which is easy to grasp, but in the face of actual social power relations dangerous to propose and difficult to bring about. And, since such virtue is being invoked to protect Homer, Achillean virtue is, finally, in service to an independent cultural ideal, an idea of a serious poetry that speaks about difficult issues in opposition to the realities of power that will punish home.

Jonson speaks from a social position close to Chapman's, but without the element of social critique that distinguishes Chapman. As McCandles argues, Jonson has a nice sense of the intricacies of the nobility argument, and he is able to criticize and praise in the same gesture. In the late poem, "A Speech Acording to Horace," he can savagely mock the rich for their ignorance of virtue, while being acutely aware of the difficulty and danger in attempting to teach them better. Late in the poem the voice of the "Grandlings" (that is, as Hunter notes, "little grand ones")[42] parodies Sarpedon:

> Why are we rich, or great, except to show
>> All licence in our lives? What need we know?
> More than to praise a Dog? or Horse? or speake
>> The Hawking language? or our Day to breake
> With Citizens? let Clownes, and Tradesmen breed
>> Their Sonnes to studie Arts, the Lawes, the Creed. (69–74)[43]

A few lines later the anti-Nennian quality of this stance becomes explicit:

> Let poore Nobilitie be vertuous: Wee,
>> Descended in a rope of Titles, be
> From *Guy,* or *Bevis, Arthur,* or from whom
>> The Herald will. Our blood is now become
> Past any need of vertue. (79–83)

But Jonson has hedged the critique: this shallow nobleman is not setting himself above just commoners; he is condescending to raised men "That in the Cradle of their Gentrie are" (84). With a svelte Horatian irony, Jonson's attack on false nobility becomes a defense of the admirable nobility who "serve the State by Councels, and by Armes" (85). Like Daniel, Jonson values his aristocratic connections, and for him the Nennian critique of nobility offers a position by which he can praise his social betters.

In *Poetaster,* act 5, scene 2, Caesar, insisting that the extremely deferential Virgil read the *Aeneid* which he is apologizing for, argues: "Vertue, without presumption, place may take / Above best Kings, whom onely she should make" (26–27).[44] This has its quotient of enigma, but it does seem to echo *Nennio* and to say that virtue is superior to nobility (or even royalty), though it also seems to say that good kings are virtuous. Virgil then defers one step further:

> It will be thought a thing ridiculous
> To present eyes, and to all future times
> A grosse untruth; that any *poet* (void
> Of birth, or wealth, or temporall dignity)
> Should with *decorum,* transcend CAESARS chaire.
> "Poore vertue rais'd, high birth and wealth set under,
> Crosseth heav'ns courses, and makes worldlings wonder." (28–34)

The equation of poetry and virtue is implicit in this denial, and yet the argument is also made for "decorum." We may remember Nennio's appeal to "custom," and the ambiguous status of that practical argument. Certainly, Virgil's claim here is not to justice but to civil order: if a poor virtuous poet were ever set above "high birth and wealth" the grotesqueness of the "crossing" would disrupt "worldlings." But Caesar, a man of virtue in this play, puts this ideal of justice ahead of "the course of heaven" and "all worldly custome." At this point Horace declares: "Custome, in course of honour, ever erres: / And they are best, whom fortune least preferres" (5.2.37–38). In one reading this is exactly Fabricio's line. But the denunciation of "custom" has a privileged ring to it; it is noteworthy that the line, which might be read to say with Chapman (see chapter 4, below) that obscurity is a sign of virtue, does not offend Caesar, the least obscure man in the realm. "Horace hath . . . spoke our thoughts," says Caesar. It is this royal sanction to the argument that suggests that here it has no particular social edge beyond its implicit contempt for the unvirtuous. Even such a provocative moment as this can plausibly be read as a praise of the conventional (virtuous) nobility.[45]

The term *virtue,* though Jonson is certainly capable of using it in the stoic sense of "worth," is given a narrow moral signification by Caesar. In 4.6 it is the blasphemy of Ovid and Julia playing gods that initially offends, and by Caesar's logic that blasphemy leads to an emptying of the idea of virtue, to licentiousness (53), and finally to the charge of "worship[ing] . . . that idoll, vice, / As if there were no vertue" (67–68). The minor offenders, such as Crispinus (Marston) and Demetrius (Dekker) are finally "purged" and pardoned, but Ovid and Julia are not, despite Maecenas's and Horace's brief appeals on their behalf. This moralistic base seems to replace the possible social critique that lies at the heart of the

Nennian language. And it is fitting that in the play Caesar is the best judge of poetry, and if in his words, "Sweet *poesies* sacred garlands crowne your gentrie" (5.1.17), the meaning is that poetry and conventional rank go hand in hand, to the benefit of learning and the nation.

In the light of the Nennian ideals we have been meditating on, *Bussy D'Ambois* and its later half-brother, *The Revenge of Bussy D'Ambois,* show up as complex expressions of the social dilemma that inspires Chapman. Bussy D'Ambois is an Achillean figure, and throughout the play issues of the source of nobility and its relation to virtue are debated. Bussy's virtue is something more than a moral posture; it is a critique of rank and of the prerogatives of conventional social position. It is fitting that Dryden some seventy-five years later should find *Bussy D'Ambois* a "hideous mingle of false poetry and true nonsense,"[46] for Dryden's aesthetic amounts to a triumphant repudiation of Chapman's dream of an obscure art that dignifies the "true nobility" of a small group of learned and virtuous readers.

Bussy D'Ambois is deeply concerned with the state of the virtuous man in the world, but it understands that virtue in Achillean terms, whereby virtue consists of the defense of a merit embattled against other criteria of rank and wealth. The play is wise about the world and it knows that virtue is not sufficient in itself. But it also envisions a world in which the virtue of obscure men becomes the essential guide for the great. Bussy poses the essential social image of virtue in his opening speech:

> And as great Seamen using all their powers
> And skills in *Neptunes* deepe invisible pathes,
> In tall ships richly built and ribd with brasse,
> To put a Girdle round about the world,
> When they have done it (comming neere their Haven)
> Are glad to give a warning peece, and call
> A poore staid fisher-man, that never past
> His Countries sight, to waft and guide them in:
> So when we wander furthest through the waves
> Of Glassie Glory and the Gulfes of State,
> Topt with all Titles, spreading all our reaches,
> As if each private Arme would sphere the world,
> We must to Vertue for her guide resort,
> Or we shall shipwracke in our safest Port.[47]

The important social point here is that the "great Seamen" need the "poore staid fisher-man," that is, that the powerful cannot do without the virtuous but obscure person. In his introduction to the play, Nicholas Brooke claims that Bussy is here posing "humble virtue" against "corrupt ambition" (xxviii). While such an opposition fits neatly into the dominant mode of thought—being already dominant it sees no need for ambition and easily preaches a selfless virtue—it ignores the ambition implicit when a poor man advocates virtue. Looked at from the perspective of a dominated man and in the context of the elaborate voyaging simile it caps, the couplet poses a somewhat different problem. Here a moral commonplace, which can be read complacently by those in power, has a covert signification that the virtuous non-noble will hear as distinguishing him above the great.

If we now go back to the opening lines of the play, we can see they have implications that most modern critics have tried to soften:

> Fortune, not Reason, rules the state of things,
> Reward goes backwards, Honour on his head;
> Who is not poore, is monstrous; only Need
> Gives forme and worth to every humane seed. (1.1.1–4)

In the inverted world of "the state of things," the wealthy are monstrous. As if in answer to Lear's "O reason not the need," Bussy says that it is the "Need," not the superfluities of wealth, that gives "form and worth." This is exactly the sense that the "great men," "our tympanous statists," fail to see when they think "they bear all the kingdom's worth before them"; in fact they are "nought but mortar, flint and lead." The premises that the play develops are radically social, and the ideal of the "virtuous man" is not a mystery of transcendent righteousness but an engaged integrity that exists, perhaps tragically, in constant tension with the world of rank and power that the duke of Guise represents.

In the taunting match with Guise that follows Bussy's boast to cleanse the court, the issue of nobility is made explicit. Monsieur tries to calm Bussy when Guise threatens him. Bussy responds,

> *Bussy.*   Let him peace first
>   That made the first war.
> *Monsieur.*   He's the better man.
>   *Bussy.*   And therefore may do worst?
> *Monsieur.*   He has more titles.
>   *Bussy.*   So Hydra had more heads.
> *Monsieur.*   He's greater knowne.

> *Bussy.* His greatness is the people's, mine's mine owne.
> *Monsieur.* Hee's noblie born.
> *Bussy.*   He is not, I am noble.
>   And noblesse in his blood hath no gradation,
>   But in his merit.
> *Guise.*   Th'art not nobly borne,
>   But bastard to the Cardinal of Ambois.
> *Bussy.* Thou liest proud Guiserd. (3.2.71–80)

I would want to emphasize the ambiguities of this exchange. Bussy's mockery of title and his distinction between a greatness coming from "the people" and an intrinsic one ("mine's mine own") are left standing. And the issue of Bussy's own nobility is completely ambiguous: he claims to be noble, but it is never made clear what is the basis for this claim.[48] The charge that Guise lies may mean that Bussy is not the son of the cardinal of Ambois, but it could just as well mean that he derives his "nobility" from his "virtue" rather than his "blood."[49]

The complement of this Nennian exchange occurs in *The Revenge of Bussy D'Ambois* when Clermont, after Monsieur has taunted him with his poverty and questionable gentry, points to the emptiness of Monsieur's claim to greatness:

> *Clermont.* You are a Kings sonne borne.
> *Monsieur.*   Right!
> *Clermont.*   And a Kings brother—
> *Monsieur.* True.
> *Clermont.* And might not any foole have been so too,
>   As well as you?
> *Monsieur.*   A poxe upon you!
> *Clermont.* You did no Princely deedes
>   Ere you're borne (I take it) to deserve it;
>   Nor did you any since that I have heard;
>   Nor will doe ever any, as all thinke.
> *Monsieur.* The Devil take him! Ile no more of him. (1.1.280–90)

Sarpedon's argument to Glaucus, which Chapman may have been translating at just this time, lurks behind this exchange. The play is filled with Chapman's outrage at great men, "servile nobles" (2.1.265) who are not truly noble but "sepulchres of noblesse" (2.1.154).[50]

In *Bussy D'Ambois* this critique of "blood" is more subtle. Monsieur parodies Nennian *virtue* when he invokes his fraternal relation with Henry:

> If every Nature held herselfe her owne,
> When the great Trial of a King and subject
> Met in one blood, both from one bellie springing:
> Now prove her *virtue* and her greatnesse One,
> Or make the t'one the greater with t'other
> (As true Kings should), and for your brothers love
> (Which is a speciall species of true *virtue*),
> Doe that you could not do, not being a King. (2.1.141–48, emphasis added)[51]

The "virtue" here has nothing to do with justice or right, only with "blood," the brotherly tie, and Henry in response to this appeal to a false idea of nobility acutely understands the claim being made—"Brother I know your suit"—and immediately cuts through to the deeper issue: "these wilful murders / Are ever past our pardon" (149–50). We hear behind this the debates in *Nennio* about the power of the king to confer nobility, and Henry's response here conforms to Fabricio's argument that blood and power are not the sources of virtue nor, therefore, of nobility.

Bussy is an "aspiring mind" who has a strong awareness of the social conditions that resist his success. He begins by denouncing the world that so obscures virtue, but as soon as he accepts Monsieur's patronage and begins to rise, this stance becomes complex. Monsieur is alert to how social position shapes attitude and how the critique of success and power may arise from disappointment. Bussy's resolve to "rise in Court with virtue" and thereby "bring up a new fashion" (1.1.120–30) entails a thinking through of the very idea of "virtue." He is a realist, aware that obscure virtue has no material advantage at all:

> Many will say, that cannot rise at all,
> Mans first houres rise, is first steppe to his fall.
> I'le venture that; men that fall low must die,
> As well as men cast headlong from the skie. (1.1.136–39)

If Bussy is unimpressed with the glories of height, he also with powerful irony rejects the moralism that takes pride simply in not succumbing to worldly ambition: the lowly will die just as surely as those Icarean figures "cast headlong from the sky."

From the other end of the social scale, the nobility has reason to feel threatened when the king favors a commoner, when, like Gismond in *Nennio,* he dignifies an unblooded man for his "virtue." In a later scene, after the king pardons Bussy for the duel, Guise angrily demands:

> D'Ambois is pardond: wher's a king? Where law?
> See how it runnes, much like a turbulent sea;
> Heere high, and glorious, as it did contend
> To wash the heavens, and make the stars more pure:
> And heere so low, it leaves the mud of hell
> To every common view. (2.2.24–29)

Guise, while he can admit the possibility of the justice of such an act (making "the stars more pure"), also sees it creating an arbitrary order that jeopardizes all "law," therefore the idea of kingship itself.[52] Essentially, Guise makes the same argument that Virgil made in *Poetaster:* "Poore vertue rais'd, high birth and wealth set under, / Crosseth heav'ns courses, and makes worldlings wonder" (5.2.33–34). And as if to confirm this latter reading, Henry again interrupts as a chorus in a famous speech praising Bussy as "man in his native noblesse" who "knows he comprehends / Worth with the greatest":

> Cosen Guise, I wonder
> Your equall disposition brookes so ill
> A man so good, that only would uphold
> Man in his native noblesse, from whose fall
> All our dissentions rise; that in himselfe
> (Without the outward patches of our frailtie,
> Riches and honour) knowes he comprehends
> Worth with the greatest: Kings had never borne
> Such boundlesse eminence over other men,
> Had all maintain'd the spirit and state of D'Ambois. (3.2.88–97)

These extraordinary lines, treating "riches" and "honour" as "the outward patches of our frailty" and finally acknowledging the equality of the king and the virtuous soldier, are a condensation of *Nennio*.[53] But, of course, this is all in the subjunctive: since "the spirit and state of D'Ambois" is exceptional, "Man in his native noblesse" may not now be a reasonable standard. And Chapman achieves further deniability by voicing such ambiguous sentiments through the mouth of the king: he dignifies monarchic authority even as he expresses an idea that would challenge such authority. Jonathan Goldberg sees this confusing doubleness as identifying *Bussy D'Ambois* as engaged in a Jacobean defense of monarchy,[54] but there are more complex issues of rank and class in play. *Virtue* is not only a mystifying quality that the aristocracy invokes to articulate its own worth, it is a key to a critique of the existing nobilities of wealth and inheritance in favor of a "true nobility."

Once we grasp the significance to Chapman and those around him of this phrase and the association they understand between it and a special sense of "virtue," we are in a position to appreciate the larger way social position shapes and hides meaning and how a failure to recognize the social angle can profoundly distort what is being said. The terms "true nobility" and "virtue" are more than simply elements of an obscure allegorical code; they serve to orient a perspective that leaves no social relation entirely untouched. The resentment we began to uncover in Marlowe's *Hero and Leander* and watched develop in Chapman's continuation and other early works aligns with an attitude that, despite the economic realities that continue inescapably to enforce the poor poet's humiliating social status, takes pleasure in imagining gestures of usurpation, making haughty claims of cultural superiority, and finally finding a way of speaking that both prevents retribution and displays repeatedly and at all levels the poor poet's obscure dignity. Once we understand the implications of this code we can begin to see how the very act of writing poetry at this moment and in this fashion becomes a claim for a social respect.

It is hardly surprising to find Marlowe sympathetic with such a program; after all, he was a daring and violent man, and all kinds of dangerous consequences follow from "overreaching." But it is unusual to think of Chapman as a critic of the "blooded" nobility. To a large extent it is Chapman's intention that we should have misinterpreted him for so long. As he describes himself after the sonnet commending *Nennio*, he speaks "*ex tenebris*," from the shadows, so that only what he calls in his letter to Roydon before *Ovids Banquet of Sence* "these serching spirits, whom learning hath made noble" (49) will understand him. His poetry is obscure, not because of an arbitrary stylistic whim, but because obscurity allows him freedom to speak social truths that can be perceived only by sympathetic, enlightened spirits who can pick out what matters to them. Once we begin to appreciate this social motive for his obscurity, the early work takes on a new significance as the most forceful and original English expression of a new idea of poetry, one that out of the motivation of class resentment is able to develop aesthetic ideals that become the basis for most modern aesthetics.

4

Virtues Obscured:
Social Perspective and Meaning

In rebutting the enemies of poetry who call it the father of lies, Sidney does more than just assert its moral pedagogic value; he translates the discussion to a different plane which defines poetry as a special discourse which is to be valued precisely because it "nothing affirms."[1] This privileged moral play, standing above the immediate debates of the age and material economic situations, speaking in universals, lays the ground for what Bourdieu identifies as the essential misrecognition of economic realities that lies at the heart of modern taste culture.[2] Sidney, therefore, seems modern, and just because many of his postures seem familiar to us, we may tend to ignore the extent to which Sidney's *Apology* is not disinterested but is the expression of a social strategy. Sidney speaks from and in defense of a distinct social position and voices his aristocratic authority through a myriad of subtle touches, from the casual references to aristocratic privilege ("When . . . we were at the Emperor's court") and the humor at the expense of the enthusiasms of nonaristocrats such as Pugliano, to its pervasive ironic detachment.[3]

Toward the end of the *Apology* a telling passage occurs in which Sidney argues against "art" in oratory on the grounds that "who doth generally use [it] any man may see doth dance to his own music, and so be noted by the audience more careful to speak *curiously* than to speak truly" (84, emphasis added). In the paragraph that follows he defends courtly *sprezzatura:* "Undoubtedly (at least to my opinion undoubtedly) I have found in divers smally learned courtiers a more sound style than in some professors of learning; of which I can guess no other cause but that the courtier, following that which by practice he findeth fittest to nature, therein (though he know it not) doth according to art, though not by art: where the other, using art to show art, and not to hide art (as in these cases he should do), flieth from nature, and indeed abuseth art" (84). In his next words Sidney goes on to link poetry and oratory in "this wordish consideration." The values advocated here are common enough, especially the idea of using art to hide art, but they are not universal or even self-evident.[4] The ideal of the hidden art of the "smally learned courtier," with the whole apparatus of social ease and grace associated with it, may well be resisted by a "professor of learning" coming out of a different economic situation.[5]

In his letter to Roydon accompanying *Ovids Banquet of Sence,* which was published in the same year as the *Apology,* Chapman explicitly inverts Sidney's argument: the valued art, which will be unappreciated by courtiers, is that which strenuously displays itself. As Lodge too was insisting at just about this time, poetry requires labor, both to produce and to appreciate. It is too important to be allowed to all or to be mistaken for nature. It is exactly in its artificially heightened difficulty that poetry needs to be distinguished from the oratory to which Sidney links it. Chapman scoffs, "But that Poesie should be as perviall as Oratorie, and plainnes her speciall ornament, were the plaine way to barbarisme: and to make the Asse runne proude of his eares; to take away strength from Lyons, and give Cammels hornes." He then goes on to define the quality that distinguishes "absolute poems": "That, *Enargia,* or cleerenes of representation, requird in absolute Poems is not the perspicuous delivery of a lowe invention; but high, and harty invention exprest in most significant, and unaffected phrase; it serves not a skilfull Painters turne, to draw the figure of a face onely to make knowne who it represents; but hee must lymn, give luster, shaddow, and heightening; which though ignorants will esteeme spic'd, and too curious, yet such as have the judiciall perspective, will see it hath, motion, spirit and life" (*Poems,* 49). As is abundantly clear elsewhere in this letter to Roydon and in the earlier one before *The Shadow of Night,* Chapman's hostility is directed against the leisured readers of poetry, those who read "to curtail a tedious hour." The "ignorants" who treat as "spiced and too curious" an art that shows art, the art Sidney has criticized as speaking "curiously," are the educated dilettantes, Sidney's "smally learned courtiers," who would diminish poetry to a gentleman's ornament, a fashion. This central passage for our understanding of Chapman counters Sidney's courtier aesthetic by inverting conventional rhetorical tropes and turning *enargia* from a technique of persuasion,[6] as it is in the courtly tradition, into a technique of exclusion.[7]

Chapman's use of the rhetorical term *enargia* is confusing, intentionally so. Traditionally, *enargia* is one of the rhetorician's most powerful tools of persuasion. For Quintilian *enargia* is "vivid illustration": "Consequently we must place among ornaments that *enargia* which I mentioned in the rules which I laid down for the statement of facts, because *vivid illustration,* or as some prefer to call it, *representation* [*enargia*], is something *more than mere clearness* [*plus est . . . quam perspicuitas*], since the latter merely lets itself be seen, whereas the former thrusts itself upon our notice" (emphasis added).[8] Chapman seems to have had this very passage in mind, but he makes telling modifications in it. He replaces the comparative (*plus est . . . quam perspicuitas*) with a negative ("enargia . . . is not the perspicuous delivery") and transfers the focus from the problem of *perspicuitas* ("perspicuous delivery") to "significance" and the distinction between high and low invention.

The importance of this subtle change will become evident if we elaborate on what *enargia* means for the orator. Quintilian asserts that the purpose of *enargia* is to "thrust" a scene on the notice of an otherwise indifferent audience, to make the audience pay attention and respond favorably. Linking *enargia* with the process of making the facts "attractive" he includes it under the heading of "lucidity" (*perspicuitas*) and calls it *evidentia* (2.85). In the comparison to the "skilfull painter" Chapman follows Quintilian in seeing mere representation as insufficient, but he departs from the rhetorical purpose in arguing that the point of embellishment is not to move the otherwise inattentive audience but to speak to "such as have the judiciall perspective." This *enargia* is not a tool of persuasion; rather, its complex display of art requires a special sensibility for appreciation. Where Quintilian teaches a style by which a good and wise orator can attract an audience and lead it to virtue, wisdom, and right actions, Chapman aspires to a style that distinguishes between audiences.

While occasionally allowing that poetry may be more obscure than oratory, Quintilian maintains that for a writer or speaker attempting to educate an audience obscurity is a drawback. "*Cacozelia,* or perverse affection [*mala adfectatio*] is a fault in every kind of style," he declares just before the passage on *enargia,* and he even accuses obscurity of being "childish" (*puerili*) (3.241, 243). Chapman again echoes Quintilian, "Obscurity in *affection* of words, & indigested concets, is pedanticall and *childish*"; but then he turns and makes a point of asserting that there is a kind of obscurity that is a virtue: "*but* where it shroudeth it selfe in the hart of his subject, utterd with fitnes of figure, and expressive Epethites; with that darknes will I still labour to be shaddowed" (*Poems,* 49; emphasis added). We can hear in that *but* a rejection of Quintilian's ideal of oratorical clarity and with it the persuasive purpose of poetry.

Presuming on his "understander's" attention and devoting his energies to "shadowing" his subject, Chapman distinguishes a special audience, a "cultural nobility," whose claim to eminence is precisely its ability to appreciate this special art. Quintilian's orator (and Sidney's courtier poet is similar "in this wordish consideration") must first of all prevent the audience's attention from wandering. "Our language," Quintilian declares, "will be approved by the learned and clear to the uneducated. . . . For we must never forget that the attention of the judge is not always so keen that he will dispel obscurities without assistance, and bring *the light of his intelligence* [*intelligentiae suae lumen*] to bear on the dark places of our speech" (3.209–11; emphasis added).[9] If the orator must convince a judge who fails to use the light of his intelligence, Chapman, by contrast, is proud that the very audience that Quintilian despairs of finding, "those that before-hand have a *radiant and light-bearing intellect*," will be able to understand what his poem says (*Poems,* 50; emphasis added).

We need to be careful at this point and distinguish Chapman's ideal of obscurity from others that pointedly serve the Sidneyean project. Court-oriented poets can also use a language of obscurity and veiling but without Chapman's resentful sense of embattled intellectual superiority. For instance, when Sir John Harington, Queen Elizabeth's godson, clearly writing from a dominant social position, outlines the traditional four levels of allegory, he never takes Chapman's step of insisting that obscure meaning makes the poetry exclusive. For the aristocratic Harington, allegory is generously democratic: after briefly sketching the traditional reasons for using "the vaile of fables and verse," he explains in language very unlike Chapman's that "the weaker capacities will feede themselves with the pleasantnes of the histories and sweetnes of the verse."[10] To the objection that poetry pleases fools, Harington wittily responds by observing that if the poetry improves the fools there is nothing wrong with pleasing them. While Chapman aggressively excludes from comprehension all but the heroic intellects who have endured "th'extremes incident to that *Herculean* labour" of overcoming "ignorance" and achieving "judgement" (*Poems,* 19), Harington, quoting Horace and echoing Sidney (*Apology,* 38), envisions a poetry that will "present unto us a pretie tale, able to keep a childe from play, and an old man from the chimnie corner" ("Preface," 207–8).

Spenser presents a more complicated case. He also falls easily into language which sounds much like Chapman's, but unlike Chapman he worries that his reader may not understand him and writes a prefatory letter so that Ralegh "may as in a handful gripe all the discourse which otherwise may happily seem tedious and confused."[11] Though he calls his "continued Allegory" a "darke conceit" and describes his "good discipline" as "clowdily enwrapped in Allegorical devises," he does not treat the darkness or the cloudiness as virtues in themselves. He quickly puts forth the conventional moral purpose of instructing by delighting, to the general end of fashioning "a gentleman or noble person in vertuous and gentle discipline." We need to be careful not to oversimplify Spenser's strategy; there is the possibility of a Nennian ambiguity here—does the virtuous discipline fashion the nobility or does it embellish a preexisting nobility? The letter to Ralegh does not explain the poem; but clearly, though he invokes the language of obscurity, Spenser differs from Chapman in the way he establishes his place as a poet in the world. The laureate stance entails a sense of national and civic responsibility that more or less precludes expressions of social hostility. The sixth book of *The Faerie Queene, Mother Hubberd's Tale,* and *Colin Clouts Come Home Again,* all show evidence of Spenser's disaffection with the courtly mode, but he always mutes his criticism. In the final analysis, he is too indebted to the queen and the courtly system to allow him to take Chapman's outrageous position.

Behind Chapman's rebuttal of Sidney's assertion of courtly superiority we hear the traces of the differences in their social power. The opinions of the powerful can be voiced with casual impunity, while those of the dominated must be spoken with diplomatic ambiguity but also with vigor if they are to be heard at all. Hegemonic power, which can never entirely control meaning and would have to silence all discussion were it to try to forbid all offensive implications, tolerates some possibilities so long as the larger issues of decorum and deference are maintained. From the other end of the social scale, the dominated, though they can never quite be sure they will escape censorial discipline, can speak in a way that avoids directly and unambiguously insulting their superiors. There is a zone, which changes at different times, within which the authorities will tolerate possible criticisms; writers and censors rely on a precarious understanding of what is permitted. Yet, periodically, as the boundaries of decorum begin to be pushed into dangerous areas or when powerful people find reason for feeling insulted, the authorities reopen the issue, usually by trying to assert a new discipline.[12] Much later, in 1614, Chapman would find himself on the wrong side of such a boundary when he roused the supporters of the earl of Essex by allegorizing him as the "barren rock" from which Somerset, playing Perseus, rescued Lady Frances, his Andromeda.[13] Thinking back to the logical difficulty of Phillip Stubbes's diatribe, which rallies the humble faithful while excusing the wealthy, we may recall Chapman's painting which "ignorants will esteeme spic'd, and too curious," but those with "the judiciall perspective" will appreciate.

We glimpse here a version of one of Chapman's favorite images, the perspective picture that under a murky, innocuous, and not very interesting meaning renders another more serious meaning. Though the idea of an image embodying different, even opposite, meanings is not uncommon in the period ("a natural perspective, that is and is not" says Orsino looking on Caesario and Sebastian together),[14] Chapman more than any other poet of the time is deeply attracted to it and repeats it in a variety of contexts.[15] At times, as in *Chabot,* one image is true and the others false:

> As of a picture wrought to optic reason,
> That to all pasers-by seems, as they move,
> Now woman, now a monster, now a devil,
> And till you stand and in a right line view it,
> You cannot well judge what the main form is.[16]

Here the "main form" must be distinguished from the false forms by what the poet later in this passage calls "the right laid line / Of truth" (78–79). It takes the "judiciall perspective" to understand aright. More confusing is the false image that is identical with the true. We see such identity/difference at the end of Chapman's translation of Virgil's epigram "A sleight man" whose

> imperfections yet are hid in sleight,
> Of the felt darknesse, breath'd out by deceipt,
> The truly learn'd, *is likewise hid,* and failes
> To pierce eyes vulgar, but with other vailes.
> And they are the divine beames, truth cast round
> About his beauties, that do quite confound
> Sensuall beholders. (59–65; emphasis added)[17]

The sleight man and the learned man are similarly hidden, one by cunning, the other by brilliance. Yet, as is typical of Chapman, the absolutely central distinction between the basest and the most valued is confused and is impenetrable to those "Sensual beholders" without inspiration. For Chapman poetry itself partakes of such doubleness at its very core: "This Hill of the Muses (which all men must clime in the regular way, to Truth) is said of ould, to be forcked. And the two points of it, parting at the Top; are *Insania,* and *divinus furor. Insania,* is that which every Ranck-brainde writer; and judge of Poeticall writing, is rapt withal; when hee presumes either to write or censure the height of Poesie; and that transports him with humor, vaine-glory and pride, most prophane and sacrilegious: when *divinus furor,* makes gentle, and noble, the never so truly-inspired writer."[18] This passage roughly translates Ficino's *epitome* of *Ion,* a favorite passage of Chapman's, which he quotes a number of times, apparently from memory.[19] In later chapters we will have occasion to emphasize the difference between divine furor and *insania;* now we need to pay attention to their near identity. It is at the very last stage of the climb up the hill of the muses that the path forks, "parting at the Top."

This identity/difference represents a deep habit of Chapman's thought; the true and valued is veiled by appearing as its opposite and will be overlooked and misjudged by the ignorant. It is telling that Chapman does not give us a way of identifying furor beyond the mystifying "truly-inspired." Divine furor is the only genuine source of poetry, but it is shadowed by an *insania* entirely without spiritual value but at times indistinguishable from divine furor. One state can always be read as another, divine furor as *insania,* or vice versa. Like charismatic aesthetics, such obscurity becomes a tool for distinguishing between social groups by appealing to deep structures of understanding that those who are excluded do not comprehend or may not even know to exist.

These multiple meanings rendered by the perspective picture are not only cognitive; they entail evaluation. The viewers who do not read the picture correctly will also misunderstand its value. Such works are, as Chapman says in "Eugenia,"

> like the pictures that are made,
> To th'optike reason; one way like a shade,
> Another monster like, and every way
> To passers by, and such as made no stay,
> To view her in a right line, face to face,
> She seem'd a serious trifle. (173–78)[20]

Religion, which is being described here, is often misconceived. Just so, Chapman's poetry itself depicts a truth that to the casual and hasty reader, "such as made no stay," seems a monster or a "serious trifle."[21] This last phrase may remind us of the dedication of *Hero and Leander* to Lady Walsingham and Chapman's game of apologizing for spending his "serious time" on "so trifeling a subject." Being taken seriously is a great problem, and one must allow that some will read as a trifle that which is written with labor and serious care, and at the same time one is content that the work be taken as a trifle by those who "made no stay" to read with a similar care.

The image of the perspective picture poses meaning as something different from the conventions of "veiling" by which meanings are "hidden." It is not a code that determines meaning, but "perspective," an attitude toward the meaning and the issue, a willingness to linger versus a haste that "makes no stay." Such an idea of meaning speaks to and from a social position; it does not take special training or esoteric knowledge to see the social implications of what is being said; it just takes social sympathy, and from that sympathy arises the attention that obscure verse demands. Incomprehension comes from a lack of interest, a social assurance that means one has no need to make the effort to understand difficult verse, combined perhaps with a suspicion that one would not find the meaning, once discovered, very interesting anyway. Such incomprehension is analogous to that which Bourdieu traces between the different social positions in modern society: the inhabitant of any position in social space finds certain aesthetic concerns important and for good reasons disregards or condescends to the art coming from a different social space. If the messages are implicitly political, they are hardly recognized as such; if they dare articulate something explicitly political, the message itself will be attacked separate from the form.

Though the discourse of perspective at some point must entail issues of censorship and secrecy, its importance for us is its conception of discourse as a complex of meaning that different perspectives read differently. I would thus agree with Richard Burt's criticism of a binary model of censorship which would treat the situation as simply an opposition between those who oppose censorship and those who censor.[22] Burt follows this complexity into the diplomacies of self-censorship and the countercensorship that Jonson's authority entails. I am interested in a different, more purely social, less individually psychological, model of how a hierarchic social structure generates a discourse within a certain fraction which out of necessity speaks *obscurely*—finds a voice that is hard to hear or difficult to interpret—as a way of establishing that fraction's social importance. Jonson is a complex presence in this social discourse; as I remark at numerous points, though he shares aspects of Chapman's project, he finally aligns himself with the blooded nobility in a way Chapman never does. I am not suggesting any political issue here; it may after all devolve down to Jonson as a better conversationalist and therefore able to hobnob more comfortably with nobility. Whatever the reason, Jonson consorts with the socially dominant, publishes verse letters he apparently writes to them, and, as the culminating gesture, praises the patronizing nobility in "To Penshurst." Chapman, though like most poets he makes the necessary gestures of dedication, writes his letters to such socially undistinguished men as Roydon and Harriot, and ends translating Juvenal's Fifth Satire on the humiliations of clientage.

The suggestive but deeply vague language of the *enargia* passage advocating an obscurity that speaks to "the heart of the matter," so seemingly resonant of symbolist implications, leaves obscure what exactly is, as Hamlet and Polonius would worry, the *matter.* What is the subject that benefits from such shadowing? Here, by seeming to invoke an ancient tradition of obscurity—the tradition that poets veiled truths to keep them from the vulgar[23]—Chapman in fact deflects attention from his more immediate subject: the public disregard for serious art and his own and his colleagues' social obscurity. For Chapman "obscurity" becomes a profoundly rich, self-reflective pun, denoting the style that identifies true art, the social place in which such art occurs, and the need to conceal the very fact that this is the issue. By his celebration of obscurity he foreshadows the paradoxical logic of modern taste culture whereby the disregard for profit validates cultural capital. Yet, despite these adumbrations of modernity, Chapman differs fundamentally from modern poets of difficulty in that he does not assume what Bourdieu calls the "distance from necessity" often associated with modern dominant taste. He generates something like "the sacred character, separate and separating, of high culture,"[24] not as a way of participating in an established taste culture but as a way of raising (cautiously, to be sure) issues of the economic hardship and injustice suffered by an intellectual elite. Within the transcendental mysteries of the "absolute poem" lies the expression of a social anger provoked by poverty. His obscurity is not, finally, "aesthetic" in any modern sense of the term; it is a way of voicing a social critique.

While the interlinked issues of obscurity, virtue, and nobility recur throughout his work, it is in his first published poem that Chapman makes the social implications of his project explicit. This four-hundred-line poem, "Hymnus in Noctem," and its matching "Hymnus in Cynthiam" compose one of the most difficult books of this period.[25] The book's mysterious title, *The Shadow of Night,* itself presents the kind of perspective picture we have just been looking at: is the shadow a deeper and thereby truer night? or is it a false night? Obscurity— expressed in the poem by the image of night and by extraordinarily ambiguous syntax—allows the poet to denounce the world while always leaving the exact object of his attack unclear. It is only by holding on to "the right laid line of truth" of Chapman's own social perspective, his impoverished learning, that we can begin to make coherent this depiction of chaos. At the same time, even our most assured reading of a passage will always be deniable—as it must be if the poet wishes to stay out of the Tower and to gain patronage. It is intrinsic to this form of obscurity that no one can ever prove a reading correct. And yet an understanding is "shadowed," and interested readers, like Vincentio, the lover in *The Gentleman Usher,* can "pick out" what they will. The angle of vision of the "light-bearing intellect" works the way "taste" does in modern culture, structuring the very terms of understanding.[26]

In a typical passage Chapman adumbrates the link between a difficult style and the social situation his poem addresses. After citing the enstellation of the "senseless Argive ship" as an instance of the reward for service, he continues:

> A thousand such examples could I cite,
> To damne stone-pesants, that like Typhons fight
> Against their Maker, and contend to be
> Of kings, the abject slaves of drudgerie:
> Proud of that thraldome: love the kindest lest,
> And hate, not to be hated of the best. ("Hymnus in Noctem," 117–22)

The passage seems at one level contemptuous of ambitious "stone-pesants" who would upset the social hierarchy, but it turns out that they are not social rebels at all but the "slaves" of kings and "Proud of that thraldome." These are not literal peasants; they are powerful timeservers, ambitious courtiers who fail to reward affection ("love the kindest lest [i.e., least]") and discriminate not according to actual value but as a social strategy ("hate, not to be hated of the best"). The dangerous, even traitorous charge that, to put it crudely, the thralls of the king are rebels against God ("their Maker") is hidden by the deeply enigmatic grammar, which might just as well be read as treating "kings" and "their Maker" as identical. The strange, unidiomatic locution, "contend *to be / Of,*" could almost mean "contend against," but it turns out to suggest something else, a rivalry among the courtiers for "thraldome." The ideal of duty represented by the Argive ship at the passage's beginning shifts before our eyes into a contemptuous sense of the politics of the court.

Exactly such outrageously opposite meanings are rendered by the poem's blatant inversion of the iconography of conventional morality. After invoking Night as the patron of inspired trance, the poem praises the night of the primal chaos that preceded the present outrageous state of things. In the primal night:

> Nothing, as now, remainde so out of kinde,
> All things in grosse, were finer than refinde,
> Substance was sound within, and had no being,
> Now forme gives being; all our essence seeming,
> Chaos had soule without a bodie then,
> Now bodies live without the soules of men,
> Lumps being digested; monsters in our pride. (43–49)

Since in the present monstrous world form is deformity, obscurity and chaos are the only possible moral figures.

But, in a way that echoes the epigram on "the sleight man" and the identity of divine furor and *insania,* Chapman complicates this already shocking intellectual structure by further splitting his symbols and describing a symmetrically antithetical night, "A stepdame Night of minde," who patronizes confusion (63–74). In "Hymnus in Noctem" the darkness of blindness of the mind is public and scandalously open, while true night is a "covert" in which treasures remain unknown. Under the false shadow of "stepdame Night,"

> All are transformed to Calydonian bores
> That kill our bleeding vines, displow our fields,
> Rend groves in peeces; all things nature yeelds

> Supplanting: tumbling up in hills of dearth,
> The fruitfull disposition of the earth,
> Ruine creates men: all to slaughter bent,
> Like envie, fed with others famishment. (84–90)

In these extraordinary lines an energetic ruin perverts all generative impulses. There is no direct way to do good under these conditions, and there is no way to write instructive poetry.

In "Hymnus in Noctem" Chapman creates a perspective picture to depict our interpretive problem:

> And as when Chloris paints th'ennamild meads,
> A flocke of shepherds to the bagpipe treads
> Rude rurall dances with their countrey loves:
> Some a farre off observing their removes,
> Turnes, and returnes, quicke footing, sodaine stands,
> Reelings aside, od actions with their hands;
> Now backe, now forwards, now lockt arme in arme,
> Now hearing musicke, thinke it is a charme,
> That like loose froes at Bacchanalean feasts,
> Makes them seeme franticke in their barraine jestes;
> And being clusterd in a shapelesse croude,
> With much less admiration are allowd. (181–92)

The observer's perspective determines how the shepherds' dance is read. To "Some a farre off" it appears as a "franticke," "shapelesse croude," and they grant the intricate pattern ("Turnes, and returnes, quicke footing, sodaine stands, / Reelings aside") "much less admiration" than would someone closer.[27] In the next lines the simile completes itself and the problem of reading the dance becomes the problem of understanding the virtuous but obscure poet:

> So our first excellence, so much abusd,
> And we (without the harmonie was usd,
> When Saturnes golden scepter stroke the strings
> Of Civill governement) make all our doings
> Savour of rudenesse, and obscuritie,
> And in our formes shew more deformitie,
> Then if we still were wrapt, and smoothered
> In that confusion, out of which we fled. (193–200)

This may say that we partake of the degeneracy of the age, but it may just as well say that the "rudenesse," "obscuritie," and "deformitie" that "our formes shew" are the misconstructions of unsympathetic, "farre off" observers. Or such deformity and obscurity, recalling the virtues of the primal chaos, may in fact be the shapes of "true nobility." There is no clear reading of this simile. But that difficulty is appropriate to the poem's mode, and in the confusion we can discover the poem's central theme: that obscurity is both a deformity and the only moral posture.

The verse does not pose this doubleness (logically it may well be a contradiction) as a neat paradox but as a deeply entangled ambiguity. *Obscurity* identifies both a place of virtue (in a corrupt world only the obscure can be virtuous) and a consequence of social injustice (the world, failing to reward virtue, leaves virtuous men obscure).

> Meane while, accept, as followers of thy traine,
> (Our better parts aspiring to thy raigne)
> Vertues obscur'd, and banished the day,
> With all the glories of this spongie sway,
> Prisond in flesh, and that poore flesh in bands
> Of stone, and steele, chiefe flowrs of vertues Garlands. (241–46)

"Vertues obscur'd, and banished the day" may be a self-pitying observation about unrecognized merit, but given the poem's rejection of "day" and praise of obscurity, it also defines true nobility. The idea that the flesh is inimical to virtue is familiar from Platonic tradition, but the very imprisonment that the flesh performs on virtue is then performed on the flesh so that the act of obscuring becomes, paradoxically, an act of display as the "bands / Of stone, and steele" turn into "vertues Garlands." The passage is both an objection to the unjust world which obscures virtue, and a praise of a hermetic virtue that transcends the "glories" of the day. The obscure man is both a victim of injustice and a figure of integrity.

The poem is filled with such perspective tricks that describe in a single formulation the dignified humiliation of virtue and the arrogance of power:

> But wo is wretched me, without a name:
> Vertue feeds scorne, and noblest honor, shame:
> Pride bathes in teares of poore submission,
> And makes his soule, the purple he puts on. (320–23)

From one perspective the lines say that virtuous men without title, "without a name," are scorned and shamed. Such men abase their pride in tears of submission and make their souls their only accoutrements. But from another perspective the lines say that in this world the putatively virtuous are scornful and the putatively noble shame themselves. The proud man, in this second reading, revels in the pitiful submission of others and makes his social position ("the purple he puts on") his whole and only virtue ("soule").[28] And the critical social thrust of the whole conception is rendered especially ambiguous by the term "virtue," which, as we have seen, allows Chapman to pose a social critique under the guise of a moral ideal.

The explicit statement of the social idea at the core of "Hymnus in Noctem" is to be found carefully hidden and surrounded by a context that allows it to be denied repeatedly:

> From the silke vapors of her Iveryport,
> Sweet Protean dreames she sends of every sort:
> Some taking formes of Princes, to perswade
> Of men deject, we are their equals made,
> Some clad in habit of deceased friends,
> For whom we mournd, and now have wisht amends,
> And some (deare favour) Lady-like attyrd,
> With pride of Beauties full Meridian fir'd:
> Who pitie our contempts, revive our harts:
> For wisest Ladies love the inward parts.
>   If these be dreames, even so are all things else,
>   That walke this round by heavenly sentinels. (340–51)

This passage actually speaks the happy dream that "we," "men deject," are encouraged by princes to understand our equality with them. King Henry's famous speech in *Bussy D'Ambois* praising Bussy as "man in his native noblesse" enacts precisely this dream of a prince acknowledging equality.[29] But the radical social assertion is spoken in such a way and in such a context that one can never quite say it has been asserted. Grammatically "their" might refer to "men deject," and the lines might say we dream of princes persuading us that we are the equals of dejected men. And perhaps, like all dreams issuing from the ivory port, the wish-fulfilling idea of equality with princes is a delusion, as are the other dreams, that the beloved dead are not dead, or that a woman pities our "contempts" (i.e., our obscurity) and loves us for our "inward parts." And yet the next section begins declaring that these are no more "dreames" than night's other productions. A few lines later even this line of assertion is conditionally disclaimed: "If these seeme likewise vaine, or nothing are / Vaine things, or nothing come to vertues share: / For nothing more then dreames, with us shee findes" (356–58). Perhaps even true dreams are vain. The play on "nothing" allows this last passage to say both that virtue is unrewarded in this world and that the "nothing more than dreames" is the essence of value. For those willing to read it so, Chapman in affirming nothing has affirmed something quite extraordinary, for in that space of "nothing" lies the realm of culture, the mysterious treasure that is economically without value and yet is the true reward of "virtue" and superior to "all things else."

Chapman anticipates partners in this obscure discourse of virtue and resentment. Toward the end of "Hymnus in Noctem" he rallies a cohort of "nimble and aspiring wits" "possest with indepressed spirits":

> Come consecrate with me, to sacred Night
> Your whole endevours, and detest the light.
> Sweete Peaces richest crowne is made of starres,
> Most certaine guides of honord Marinars,
> No pen can any thing eternall wright,
> That is not steept in humor of the Night. (372–77)[30]

Different from, even hostile to, the educational mode pursued by Harington, and Sidney, the pen that is "steept in humor of the Night" will depict with a dark art not just moral virtues and failings but the injustice of the social structure itself.

The paradoxical stance of the obscure poet who begrudges his social insignificance and at the same time takes pride in his alienation from the society that disregards him is most elegantly elaborated in the extraordinary sequence of ten difficult, linked sonnets, "A Coronet for His Mistresse, Philosophie."[31] In this poem the contradiction is structured in the form itself. The poem, which has received little detailed attention, though it is occasionally invoked (wrongly, again, as will be apparent) as evidence of Chapman's moralism, appears a year after "Hymnus in Noctem" in a small book, *Ovids Banquet of Sence,* which also includes, along with the major title poem, two strange erotic narratives, "The Amorous Zodiac" and "The Amorous Contention of Phillis and Flora." Though these last two poems are generally thought to have been written by someone other than Chapman, they nevertheless suggest a lighter and more erotically playful tonality than the modern moral reading of the "Banquet" and the "Coronet" would tolerate. I note the companion poems to suggest that the agenda of the book may not be as ascetically dour as much recent criticism has assumed.

At the beginning of the chapter on nobility we had occasion to consider the social position manifested by the lines in the "Coronet" denouncing "titles of primacy, / Courtship of antick jestures, braineles jests, / Bloud without soule of false nobilitie." We saw this important social awareness reappearing in the ninth sonnet when the poet declares that, though Philosophie will make up for his neglect, "Honor, and Error, which the world bewitches, / Shall still crowne fooles, and tread upon desert" (9.11–12). Marlowian resentment speaks clearly here. The poet compensates for "the wrongs [his] fortunes show," the rule of "fooles," and the treading down of "desert" by trusting a Philosophy who both "aswages" his pain and represents, herself, "riches," a form of cultural capital. The poet is clearly aware of the social injustice of his obscurity, but he also poses a value for Philosophy that puts her and the poem to her above the popular poems "that Fames loose feathers beautifie."

The opening lines of sonnet 4 develop the paradoxes of obscurity we have observed in "Hymnus in Noctem:"

> So her close beauties further blaze her fame;
>   When from the world, into herselfe reflected
>   Shee lets her (shameles) glorie in her shame
>   Content for heav'en to be of earth rejected,
> Shee thus deprest, knocks at *Olympus* gate. (1–5)

The heavenly values that compensate for earthly rejection mutate into the more abstract, moral categories of the sacred and profane in the second part of the sonnet:

> And in th'untainted Temple of her hart
>   Doth the divorceles nuptials celebrate
> Twixt God and her; where loves prophaned dart
> Feedes the chast flames of *Hymens* firmament,
>   Wherein she sacrificeth, for her part;
>   The Robes, lookes, deedes, desires and whole descent
>   Of female natures, built in shops of art
> Vertue is both the merit and reward
> Of her remov'd, and soule-infusde regard. (6–14)

The lines argue that the energies of the profane, material world sustain ("feed") Philosophy's "remov'd, and soule-infusde regard." The fires fed by "loves prophaned dart" become the "chast flames of *Hymens* firmament," and all the apparatus of the conventional human mistress, all her "art," Philosophy "sacrifices," that is, she consumes it but in doing so she grants it value.[32] Virtue as "both the merit and reward" of Philosophy captures the tight circularity of this "removed" yet intensely engaged enterprise.

Philosophy is not a principle of ascetic moral judgment, as is sometimes suggested; she is an extraordinarily complex insight that encompasses opposites. The vices, like "loves prophaned dart," are digested and rendered as virtues. In sonnets 6 and 7 philosophical love is seen as a salvation from a world of "protean rages," but then that love turns out to be more protean than the world itself: "Nor any folly that the world infests / Can alter her who with her constant guises / To living vertues turns the deadly vices" (6.12–14). The next sonnet figures for us the "constant guises" which are expressed in a series of paradoxes about the virtues of vices. The ingenuity of sonnet 7 should not blind us to the radical violation of moralistic rigor Chapman is envisioning. Philosophy, while preserving "constant" balance and singleness, partakes of all extremes and deficiencies.[33] The alternative to a pied world of "Protean rages" is not a puritan black or a moralist gray but an extravagant insight that transcends the contradictions and follies of appearance while engaging in them.

Circularity, that is, contradiction, structures this poem. Vice becomes virtue; virtue, vice. Rejection becomes salvation. Contemplation becomes passion. The corona form—the last line of each sonnet becoming the first line of the next— allows each sonnet to spin the idea of the last in a new way. And the whole circular form, which entails that the first and last lines are identical, constructs a contradiction that is, thanks to the transcendent generosity of Philosophy, not a contradiction at all. In sonnet 1 the "Muses that sing loves sensuall Emperie" are certainly being rebuked, urged to "Abjure those joys, abhore their memorie" and to turn aside from sensuality. "Let my love," that is Philosophy, "the honord subject be / Of love, and honors complete historie." Yet, after tracing Philosophy through her complex engagements with material reality, the circle completes itself, and we return to these same "muses" with an attitude very different from that with which we began: "And let my love, adorne with modest eyes, / Muses that sing loves sensuall Emperyes" (10.13–14). "Loves sensuall Emperies" are not rejected at all. To do so would be to reject an essential motivation of the universe and to destroy the circular harmony that preserves it. But to accept "sensuall Emperies" is not to succumb to mere sensuality; the harmony that arises from love depends on Philosophy to enable the movement from sense to mind, and this process seems clearly the one Chapman is referring to when he asks that his love "adorn with modest eyes" the sensual muses. The failure of the lovers described in the first sonnet is not that they have used the senses or even that they have allowed the senses empire, but that they have been content with that; they have not engaged in the circular process that involves sensuality as it transcends it.

Sonnet 8 stands out by making complex reference to the nature of obscurity:

Nor riches, to the vertues of my love,
>   Nor Empire to her mighty government:
>   Which fayre analisde in her beauties grove,
>   Showes Lawes for care, and Canons for content:
And as a purple tincture gyven to Glasse
>   By cleere transmission of the Sunne doth taint
>   Opposed subjects: so my Mistresse face
>   Doth reverence in her viewers browes depaint,
And like the Pansye, with a little vaile
>   She gives her inward worke the greater grace;
>   Which my lines imitate, though much they faile
>   Her gyfts so hie, and tymes conceits so base:
Her vertues then above my verse must raise her,
For words want Art, and Art wants words to praise her.[34]

The simile of Philosophy as tinted glass expresses the basic paradox of obscurity. Philosophy is both darkening and enlightening, and in this it imitates love itself. In the simile the glass is between the sun, the equivalent of truth itself, and the viewer. The transmission is clear, but it colors the viewer. By looking through this purple glass, Chapman's special reader will recognize that which he or she knows, which is a complex understanding of the ideal that is by now familiar to us, a learning that is unrecognized but nevertheless superior to the behaviors and positions that the world honors. Such understanding is not available to aristocratic love poets or to puritans inspired by pious asceticism. Heroic learning and discipline are required to achieve such "true nobility." And though on one level such "nobility" may be merited by learning, it is also, like "taste" in modern aesthetics, a mysterious given. It is to this idea, most notoriously represented by the Platonic doctrine of *furor poeticus,* we must next turn. The doctrine is frequently invoked by religious and amorous courtly poets, but for Chapman and the poor poets we are studying, it has a special significance: it is the coded sign of poetic culture itself, with all the implications of resentment and social critique we have been tracing.

5

"Nobler Than Nobility": The Social Meaning of Poetic and Amorous Rapture

> But my love is the cordiall of soules
> Teaching by passion what perfection is.
> —"Coronet" 2.9–10

For Spenser, the public poet who can never forget the court even if he may resist it, the idea of poetic furor can have provocative and ambiguous social implications, as in the following passage from *Colin Clouts Come Home Again* praising the queen:

> Her great excellence
> Lifts me above the measure of my might:
> That being fild with furious insolence
> I feele my selfe like one yrapt in spright.[1]

Insolence is a socially difficult word; while the modern sense of "impudence" does not become common until the end of the seventeenth century, the pride the term denotes is nevertheless presumptuous in all people but those of the very highest rank. The editors of the *OED* solve the difficulty of Spenser's "furious insolence" by discovering a positive meaning of insolence, "exultation," for which the passage cited above is the only quoted instance (*Insolence,* def. 2).[2] They derive this meaning from another unique example, Puttenham's describing Ralegh's style as "loftie, insolent, and passionate." There the *OED* editors, prefacing their conjecture with a question mark, pose the meaning "Swelling, exulting: in a good sense" (*Insolent,* def. 4). But the more conventional meaning of *insolence* makes sense in Spenser's lines. If the "excellence" of the queen inspires poetic "might," that inspiration threatens a social breach, not just because of the power the poet has over the representation of the queen,[3] but because of the independent worth of the "insolent" figure of the "furious" poet. By inventing a special meaning, the dictionary editors efface the signs of a disruptive social ambition implicit in the claim to inspiration.

One does not normally think of Spenser as insolent, and we need to reconsider the social meaning of Platonic rapture to understand why such an earnest poet should invoke it. For the poets that most interest us here, the idea of poetic furor resumes some of its primitive vatic emphasis and identifies a mysterious seriousness and power in poetry that is out of reach of courtly poetasters. But in the cases of Spenser and Chapman the social gesture of defending poetic rapture is complicated by what seems a philosophical contradiction; even as they invoke ecstatic rapture they also express a distrust of irrationality and a sympathy with the stoic idea of tranquillity. I want to consider the social strategies of such apparent contradictions. Spenser, though drawn to the social declaration implicit in the idea of Platonic inspiration, will always temper the radical suggestions of rapture. But Chapman, by insisting on forcing just such a contradiction to the center of his discourse, expounds a "philosophy" that cannot be "placed" in any tradition and thereby defines a cultural place for himself that is outside and above the available categories, social and intellectual.

A tension has always existed in Neoplatonism between a tradition that denies the body and maintains reason and decorum and one that treats the Platonic concept of inspiration (*furor poeticus*) as a mode of understanding that links the mind with energies and insights beyond the reach of unaided reason.[4] Furor identifies an aspect of Neoplatonism that, though intrinsic to its conception of the intellectual role of beauty, is diluted and evaded by the fashionable Neoplatonism promoted in the Italian courts. While the ecstatic tradition has its important representatives in the Renaissance—one thinks particularly of Leone Ebreo and Giordano Bruno—the more cautious and "spiritual" tradition has tended to dominate the English interpretation.

The great expression of the ascetic, spiritual tradition is Cardinal Bembo's speech at the end of Castiglione's *The Courtier.* In a formulation that will shape much of later Platonism, Bembo insists that love be restrained "with the bridle of reason" and that "reasonable love is more happy than sensuall."[5] The following passage is typical of his conception of love as a matter of rational and civil decorum:

> Therefore when an amiable countenance of a beautifull woman commeth in his sight, that is accompanied with noble conditions and honest behaviours, so that as one practised in love, hee woteth well that his hew hath an agreement with hers, as soone as hee is aware that his eyes snatch that image and carrie it to the hart, and that the soule beginneth to behold it with pleasure, and feeleth within her selfe the influence that stirreth her, and by litle and litle setteth her in heate, and that those lively spirits, that twinckle out through the eyes, put continuall fresh nourishment to the fire: he ought in this beginning to seeke a speedy remedie and to raise up rea-

son, and with her to sense the fortresse of his hart, and to shut in such wise the pas-
sages against sense and appetites, that they may enter neither with force nor subtil
practise. (312–13)

Amorous arousal, so teasingly depicted in the first half of the passage, must be
controlled by reason, appropriately conveyed in the image of the fortress and the
blocking up of "the passages against sense and appetites." Only at the very end
of the ascent to love, when the soul has achieved "universall understanding," has
"couple[d] her selfe with the nature of Angels," and has "cleane forsake[n] sense,"
will she have "no more neede of the discourse of reason" (312). To be sure, at the
end of his speech Bembo himself is seized by what he calls "the holy fury of love,"
but in a gesture of extraordinarily tactful irony, Lady Emilia, taking "him by the
plaite of his garment, and plucking him a little said. Take heed (maister Peter)
that those thoughts make not your soule also to forsake the body" (615). The "holy
fury" is so purely spiritual that it becomes a courtly joke.

Because traditional Neoplatonism emphasized an immaterial and intellectual
conception of love, Ficino, who comes to Plato much influenced by Plotinian
commentary, understandably might have reason to distrust the erotic abandon
described at moments in the *Phaedrus* and the *Symposium*.[6] Nevertheless, at cru-
cial points Ficino can envision love as a rapture, a madness, a furor in which the
lover, overcome by the divine afflatus, relinquishes rational self-control. He opens
his *epitome* of *Ion* by reminding his readers of the *Phaedrus*'s emphasis on ecstat-
ic irrationality and its similarity to dementia: "Our Plato, greatest Laurentius, in
Phaedrus has defined furor as the alienation of the mind. However, he has recount-
ed two kinds of alienation, one from human sickness, the other deriving from
God. The former he calls insanity; the latter he calls divine furor. By insanity a
man is cast down beneath the form of man and is returned in a certain measure
from man to brute. By divine furor he is lifted above the nature of man and he
passes into God."[7] The pairing of *furor* and *insania*, while it can be interpreted
as an opposition, can also very reasonably be viewed as a point of near identity
at the start. Both are "alienations of the mind." The rhapsodic version of furor,
shadowed by its parody, *insania*, defies Bembo's cautious and rational love. Fici-
no takes seriously Socrates' denunciation of the "fool" who tempers love with
"mortal prudence" in order to adopt "mortal and parsimonious rules of conduct"
and the "narrowness which the common folk praise as virtue" (*Phaedrus*, 256e–
257a).[8] Elsewhere in the commentary on the *Phaedrus* Ficino can even suggest
that an intemperate love has intellectual value:

Love is threefold: intemperate, temperate, and divine. The first hurls the soul down
towards corporeal beauty; the second turns it back towards animate beauty, that is,

to morality and wisdom; the third recalls it to intelligible and ideal beauty. Socrates and Lysias have openly censured the first; Socrates has secretly praised the second; and now at last Socrates is about to praise the third. Anyone who absolutely disapproves of love necessarily errs; and anyone who condemns intemperate love on the grounds that it is a frenzy, that is, an alienation of the intelligence, also errs.[9]

The ambiguity of this passage, which first seems to condemn intemperate love but then unexpectedly defends it at the end, allows Ficino to support rational morality while simultaneously refusing to curb the rhapsody. It is important to understand why for Ficino the intemperate frenzy is in itself unobjectionable; if it is to be censured, that is not because it is an irrational "alienation of the intelligence" but because it fails to move beyond the corporeal. While the terms remain vague, Ficinian furor would enlighten rhapsodes by carrying them intemperately beyond reason and reason's constraints.[10]

In Renaissance England this concept was greeted by court-directed poets with skepticism. A courtier like Sidney, who despite personal political and courtly disappointments remains content with the social structure and finds little need to attempt to speak to a "true nobility" outside the accepted court, disclaims the doctrines of inspiration and treats them with amused and condescending irony. Though at the end of the *Apology for Poetry* he asks us to believe that poets "are so beloved of the gods that whatsoever they write proceeds of a divine fury," clearly the claim is self-mockingly extravagant, and elsewhere in the *Apology* he is skeptical of the idea of Platonic inspiration.[11] His style registers his skepticism: "that same exquisite observing of number and measure in the words, and that high-flying liberty of conceit proper to the poet, did *seem* to have some divine force in it" (106, emphasis added). Such moments are part of a complex ironic rhetoric by which Sidney, in a gesture which radiates aristocratic assurance, plays with serious ideas.[12] As O. B. Hardison emphasizes, the last section of the essay holds up the standards of neoclassic poetry: "Art, Imitation, and Exercise" (*Apology*, 72) not divine inspiration or "learning" make the poet.[13] In general, Sidney supports an ideal of civic and moral pedagogy as the purpose of poetry. Though Astrophel may have a perspective different from that of the author of the *Apology*, he shares the theorist's mocking skepticism about the claim to inspiration:

> I never drank of Aganippe well,
> Nor ever did in shade of Tempe sit,
> And Muses scorn with vulgar brains to dwell,
> Poor layman I, for sacred rites unfit.
> Some do I hear of poets' fury tell,
> But, God wot, wot not what they mean by it.[14]

The aristocrat, with a casual acknowledgment of ignorance that only the socially secure can make, denies that he partakes of inspiration.[15] In a similar gesture Shakespeare has the king in *Love's Labour's Lost* mock Berowne's claim that Rosalind is superior to the princess by asking, "What zeale, what furie hath inspired thee now?" (4.3.246). And, of course, Shakespeare accuses the rival poet of being "gulled" by inspiration.[16] These are social gestures. By trivializing the idea of poetic furor Sidney and Shakespeare are belittling the strategy by which Chapman emphatically and Spenser more cautiously distinguish themselves from courtly poetry and its conventions.[17]

By invoking the archaic doctrine of poetic furor nonaristocratic poets are not proposing a psychology but are creating a mysterious mark that will identify a "true" poetry directed to the by now familiar "true nobility," a learned but unprivileged audience. Unlike Sidney and Shakespeare, Chapman unequivocally assumes the stance of a believer in Ficino's version of Platonic inspiration. He seems to have memorized the passage contrasting divine furor and *insania,* for he recalls it in his prefatory dedications to Somerset of his translation of the *Odyssey,*[18] quotes from it for a gloss to his epistle to Somerset accompanying the *Hymns of Homer,*[19] and elaborates on it in his defense of *The Masque of the Middle Temple and Lincoln's Inn:* "This Hill of the Muses (which all men must clime in the regular way, to Truth) is said of ould, to be forcked. And the two points of it, parting at the Top; are *Insania,* and *divinus furor. Insania,* is that which every Ranck-brainde writer; and judge of Poeticall writing, is rapt withal; when hee presumes either to write or censure the height of Poesie; and that transports him with humor, vaine-glory and pride, most prophane and sacrilegious: when *divinus furor,* makes gentle, and noble, the never so truly-inspired writer."[20] We have looked at this passage before, as one of a number of instances in which Chapman renders difference and identity problematic.[21] Even more than Ficino, Chapman sees *insania* as nearly identical to furor: it is only at the "top" that the two states become antithetical. Chapman avoids sanctioning immoral behavior; nevertheless he advocates an idea of inspired madness that Bembo's rational Platonism would find deeply suspect. By the habit of mind for which the perspective picture is the paradigm, he creates a doctrine that is both intensely moral—it denounces *insania*—but also entirely open to a mysteriously rapturous and intuitive knowledge that identifies the true poet and the serious reader.

Despite his clear debt to Ficino's concept of inspiration, Chapman uses it for quite different purposes. The doctrine that Socrates develops in *Ion* and which Ficino follows loosely in his *epitome* requires only that the poet, Homer in Plato's example, be inspired by a muse. His inspiration will then communicate itself to Ion, who, significantly, does not understand the poetry rationally; Ion will then communicate the inspiration to his audience. Neither Ion nor the audience need to be readied for insight; given the initial furor of the poet, the rhapsode and the audience are drawn in irresistibly. Socrates' famous image is that of a lodestone which magnetizes the pieces of iron suspended from it.[22] In his *epitome* of *Ion* Ficino describes the soul moving between the One Itself and the multiplicity of matter in four steps which correspond to four levels of furor.[23] As the first term of the progression, the poetic furor is at times a soothing preparatory moment before the more powerful raptures, and at other times it is itself a rapture using words to reach an understanding beyond words. The different meanings can be casually listed in a single passage: the poetic furor "arouses by musical tones those who languish, . . . soothes through pleasing harmony those who are disturbed, and finally, through diverse consonance drives out dissonant discord and orders the various parts of the soul."[24] The "arousing," "soothing," and "ordering" of the soul is a mysterious process that is quite distant from Bembo's conception of the "bridle of reason." Elsewhere, in a letter entitled "De divino furore," Ficino calls those who "imitate the celestial music by harmony" "superficial and vulgar musicians." He prefers poets, who render the "inner reason" of that harmony. Music "does no more than sooth," while inspired verse "expresses with fire the most profound and, as the poet would say, prophetic meanings, in the numbers of voice and movement. Thus not only does it delight the ear, but brings to the mind the finest nourishment most like the food of the gods." Such "supreme words" are difficult to comprehend, for the poets themselves "when the rapture has left them . . . scarcely understand what they have uttered."[25] Ficino (and Plato) are accounting for the mystery of rhetoric itself.[26]

Chapman, however, ignores this rhetorical aspect of furor.[27] For him furor does not pass from poet to audience but is a sign of their common fitness for understanding. Not only "every Ranck-brainde writer" but also almost every "judge of Poeticall writing" succumbs to *insania* instead of divine furor. Chapman insists that his audience be fit; in his earliest critical prefaces, the two letters to Matthew Roydon, he attacks not simply uninspired poets but uninspired readers. "Now what a supererogation in wit this is, to thinke skil so mightilie pierst with their loves that she should prostitutely shew them her secrets, when she will scarcely be lookt upon by others but with invocation, fasting, watching; yea not without having drops of their soules like an heavenly familiar."[28] In bypassing the central communicative dynamic of Ficino's and Plato's idea of furor, Chapman contrives to make furor one of the marks identifying the intellectual elite.

There is a deep circularity implicit in Chapman's idea of furor, for it takes work (virtues of the mind, such as "invocation, fasting, watching") to attain such a state, and the state once attained confers a type of "true nobility." For the enthusiast of *Nennio's* critique of nobility of blood, the assertion that *"divinus furor,* makes gentle, and noble, the never so truly-inspired writer" is not idle flattery. Gentleness and nobility, often, as in Spenser, the prerequisite for recognition, here follow from furious inspiration. In effect Chapman is posing an alternative basis of social rank, an aristocracy of the inspired in place of the aristocracy of birth. Throughout Chapman's early prefaces one hears allusions to the special qualities required of the audience of his dark work, and Homer's "more than Artificiall and no lesse than Divine Rapture" speaks to "no mere reader" but an "Understander."[29] Even among the aristocracy, "the admirable luster of their true Nobility" belongs only to those who embrace the cause of divine learning (Chapman, *Poems,* 19).

The important point of difference between Chapman and Sidney represented by their different approaches to *furor poeticus* has been confused because Matthew Roydon, to whom Chapman addresses the letters in which he first announces his rhapsodic poetic principles, was best known at the time as the author of an elegy for Sidney. It is therefore commonly assumed that Roydon and Sidney share the same poetic ideals. But Roydon's elegy for Sidney subtly enlists Sidney and his reputation in the cause of the Platonic inspiration which Sidney explicitly renounces. Roydon's poem does not, however, flaunt its manipulation of Sidney's position. It is careful to cloak its creation of a learned and rhapsodic Sidney in the language of courtly Platonic commonplaces. The poem is both a rereading of Sidney and a diplomatic tour de force which in its very ambiguities marks a point of struggle over the importance and social uses of poetry.

Roydon's elegy stands apart from the many other elegies for Sidney by neither praising him as a courtier poet nor mentioning his birth or family connections.[30] It places Sidney in Arcadia, but it defines him by reference to the amorous situation of *Astrophel and Stella,*[31] and it makes love a source of Sidney's insight. It is striking that the elegy does not admire Sidney for rendering the conflicts and paradoxes of love, or for his critique of Petrarchism. In the face of the evidence to the contrary in *Astrophel and Stella,* the elegy asserts that Sidney, inspired by Stella's beauty, attains a high vision denied to "any other": "He that hath love and judgement too, / Sees more than any other doo" (143–44). Sidney is pictured as a learned, inspired Platonist:

> Then being fild with learned dew
> The Muses willed him to love,
> That instrument can aptly shew

> How finely our conceits will move
> > As *Bacchus* opes dissembled harts,
> > So love sets out our better parts. (121–26)

A casual reading of this praise of love might see it as conforming to Bembo's rational and decorous Neoplatonism, but the final couplet of the stanza, which equates love with drunkenness,[32] clearly puts Sidney in the company of inspired poets. Learning is not the restraint that harnesses love; it is the preparation that makes rapturous love possible. Sidney here, quite contrary to his own assertions, is depicted as a furious initiate.

It is a telling sign of how radically Platonic Roydon's poem is that it seems aware of the illicit nature of Astrophel's affair with Stella. Without ever quite praising adultery, it explicitly sanctions it:

> > Above all others this is hee
> > Which ferst approved in his song
> > That love and honor might agree,
> > And that pure love will do no wrong,
> > > Sweet saints it is no sinne nor blame,
> > > To love a man of vertuous name. (151–56)

It would be inappropriate for Roydon to raise the issues of honor, sin, and blame if he thought (as Spenser seems to have believed) that Stella was Frances Walsingham, Sidney's wife.[33] Spenser's elegy depicts Stella dying with Astrophel (lines 175–80), while in fact Sidney's widow married Robert Devereux, the earl of Essex and the brother of the real Stella (Penelope Rich). Spenser, apparently unconscious of the implications of the word "rich," casually uses it to describe Astrophel's wit (line 62). Roydon, however, pointedly associates the word "rich" with Stella: "*Stella,* a Nymph within this wood, / most rare and rich of heavenly blis, / The highest in his fancie stood" (127–29). Roydon never implies that Astrophel and Stella were married. The fourth line in the foregoing stanza ambiguously allows for a moral and a rhapsodic reading: it says both that "pure love" will abstain from "wrong" and that whatever "pure love" does is right. The "purity" of this love is not a function of marriage, and Sidney's "vertuous name" betokens neither Protestant piety nor aristocratic lineage but a mysterious power that accrues to the inspired poet.

The elegy's final praise of Sidney as a poet, before it moves to praise him as a soldier, might be read as a description of a successful courtier complimenting his mistress, but again the simple lines suggest something more:

> Did never love so sweetly breath
> In any mortall brest before,
> Did never Muse inspire beneath,
> A Poets braine with finer store:
>> He wrote of love with high conceit,
>> And beautie reard above her height. (157–62)

The link between love's breathing and the muse's inspiring the store of the poet's brain suggests more than poetic tact. The final line clearly sees the movement as transcendent. This is a love poet who, in good Platonic fashion, renders the universal by describing the particular beauty. Rather than succumbing to lust, he rises to high insight and by art elevates the beloved's beauty beyond itself.

Unlike Chapman's poems published a few years later, Roydon's poem does not belabor its Platonism, and a casual reader might easily understand it as simply a courtly compliment. But the court and all its graces are absent, and the lines hint with considerable subtlety at a radically Platonic vision. Roydon signals this double reading in a strangely elaborate stanza near the beginning of the poem:

> In midst and center of this plot,
> I saw one groveling on the grasse:
> A man or stone, I knew not what.
> No stone, of man the figure was,
>> And yet I could not count him one,
>> More than the image made of stone. (43–48)

The poem here is contradictory. The third line declares that the poet cannot tell if the figure is a man or a stone; the fourth declares it a man; the final couplet declares it a stone. In stanza 3 of Chapman's "Ovids Banquet of Sence" a similarly ambiguous image appears: a statue of Niobe

> So cunningly to optick reason wrought,
>> That a farre of, it shewd a womans face,
> Heavie, and weeping; but more neerely viewed,
> Nor weeping, heavy, nor a woman shewed. (6–9)

Chapman's image is more intricate than Roydon's in that, since Niobe herself was turned to stone, a stone Niobe might actually be Niobe; but the same puzzle to "optick reason" shapes both images. As critics of Chapman's poem have suggested, such an ambiguous image may be a sign that the poem to come is itself an optical illusion that can be read two ways.[34] Similarly, beneath Roydon's praise of the poet of love lies the more intricate description of the inspired poet.

Decades later Ben Jonson performs a similar co-opting of Sidney into the tradition of furor in his poem to Sidney's daughter, the countess of Rutland.[35] Few poets are less given to ecstatic poses than Jonson; nevertheless in this poem he attributes fame to "poets rapt with rage divine" (63). Toward the end of the poem he promises to sing Orpheus-like of the countesses of Bedford and Rutland:

> not with tickling rimes
> Or common places, filch'd, that take these times,
> But high, and noble matter, such as flies
> From braines entranc'd, and fill'd with extasies;
> Moodes, which the god-like *Sidney* oft did prove. (87–91)

The trick here is to couple an aristocratic poet with ecstatic verse and to then call it "high and noble." Here is the "true nobility," again.

Spenser's sensitivity to the social implications of the claim to poetic furor registers in his complicated attempts to accept and adjust the doctrines of inspiration. Throughout his career he invokes the poetic and amorous furors, but he always hesitates before admitting full rapture. As a pensioner of the queen he is dependent on the court, but as an outsider, both by birth and by location, he is in a position to see the limits and problems of the court. The language of inspiration is repeatedly tempered by the language of courtly values; all inspiration risks *insania* and threatens to disrupt social decorum; love beyond reason becomes disloyal lust. However, in the late pastoral poems he allows the furor some freedom and gestures toward the "insolent" idea of the seriousness of inspired poetry and its superiority to courtly decorum.

In Spenser's most explicitly Platonic poems, *The Fowre Hymnes,* a courtly Neoplatonism, which like Bembo's puts value on moral behavior and social grace, repeatedly interrupts and qualifies the inspiration. In the "Hymn in Honour of Love" the poet calls on the God of Love to inspire him with "gentle furie" (28) so that he can praise the inspirer. Love orders the universe, tempers oppositions (71–91), and inspires all things so that they "their being have and dayly are increast / Through secret sparks of his infused fyre" (96–97). "Infused fyre," acceptable as a cosmic principle, becomes problematic at the human, moral level. While all "within this goodly cope" (95) are "moved" by love "to multiply the likenesse of their kynd" (99–100), humans are excepted. Man "that breathes a more immortall mynd / Not for lusts sake, but for eternitie, / Seekes to enlarge his lasting progenie" (103–5). After amorous energy has been divided into "lust" and that mysterious urge which is "for eternitie," courtly moral behavior becomes the sign of inspiration:

> For love is Lord of truth and loialtie,
> Lifting himselfe out of the lowly dust,
> On golden plumes up to the purest skie,
> Above the reach of loathly sinfull lust. (176–79)

In this formulation the possibilities for insight are submerged in the concern for loyalty and the avoidance of lust.[36]

There is one moment in the *Hymnes* when furor promises something like abandon. "The Hymne in Honour of Beautie" begins with a moment of rapture in which the poet claims to have ceded control to love and desire: "Ah whither, Love, wilt thou now carrie mee? / What wontlesse fury dost thou now inspire / Into my feeble breast, too full of thee?" (1–3). However, this "wontlesse fury" soon gives way to careful distinctions between the "perfect Beautie which all men adore" (40) and the material bodies through which it shines, and a Protestant sense of *contemptus mundi* distorts the Platonic process. After saying beauty is not "an outward shew of things that onely seeme" (91), the poem discounts all material beauty because it "shall decay," "shall fade and fall away," and "Shall turn to dust" (93–98). Then, when the poem tries to make the conventional Platonic argument that beauty reveals itself in beautiful bodies ("For soule is forme, and doth the bodie make" [133]) it almost immediately tangles itself in contradictions. The poet knows better than to trust a morality of beauty and love. He may assert that "all that faire is, is by nature good" (139), but in the next stanza he must admit that some beautiful souls, "through unaptnesse of the substance fownd" (144), dwell in "deformed tabernacle[s]" (142). A further problem is that "goodly beautie . . . Is foule abusd" (149–50) and "Made but the bait of sinne, and sinners scorne" (152). The fault, the poet easily says, is not fair beauty's "But theirs that do abuse it unto ill" (156). "Disloyall lust" (170) is again abjured, and ladies are urged to pick their lovers with care that they have a sympathy with "your forms first sourse" (192). Love becomes unmaterial, "a celestiall harmonie" (197) leading to "true content" (200).

Spenser hedges his idea of rapture with moral limitations and puts it in the service of courtly wooing. He asks "beauties Queene" (267) to grant that his beloved will give him "one drop of grace" (277), "one drop of dew reliefe" (284), and the poem closes, not with any furious revelation, but with a prayer for an end to "my harts long pyning griefe" (285). As many critics have remarked, such poems hardly warrant the palinode of the hymns to "Heavenly Love" and "Heavenly Beauty." The "gentle fury" with which Spenser begins never breaks with a courtly decorum subtly but explicitly linked to the mystique of aristocratic ancestry, "For all that faire is, is by nature good; / That is a signe to know the gentle blood" (139–40).[37] Spenser in these hymns honors aristocratic lineage as a precondition for the gift of Platonic beauty.

In *The Shepheardes Calender* a more complicated idea of furor had appeared, though it is one which still displays some distrust of inspired rapture. In his epistle to Harvey, E.K. mocks claims to furor. It is impossible to tell if Spenser or Gabriel Harvey is dictating some of these attitudes. Elsewhere, as G. C. Moore Smith notes, Harvey makes bold claims to learning and appears to honor the Ficinian tradition of furor. "Alae Platonicae. Nemo magnus sine quodam furore. ficinus saepe in Epist." "Great" (*magnus*) here is a general term that applies to worldly accomplishment, and furor is almost synonymous with zeal. Thus, in a rubric to his notes on Quintilian, Harvey can talk of "the divine madness of great men such as Sforza, Luther, Parocelsus."[38] He seems to understand the tradition in what we might call civil terms and to see its signs not in great poetry but in significant social presence. Here in the *Calender* E.K. at first seems to assume an aristocratic skepticism about inspiration, distinguishing Spenser's verse from that produced by "ragged rymers" who "without learning boste, without judgement jangle, without reason rage and fome, as if some instinct of Poeticall sprite had newly ravished them above the meaneness of commen capacitie" (17). E.K. here treats furor as *insania*. But in the October Eclogue Cuddie can instruct Piers "howe the ryme should rage" (175, line 109), and in language that echoes his earlier mockery E.K. can comment, "He seemeth here to be ravished with a Poeticall furye. For (if one rightly mark) the numbers rise so ful, and the verse groweth so big, that it seemeth he hath forgot the meaneness of shepheards state and stile" (182, E.K.'s note to line 110). E.K. thus explains the emblem at the end of the eclogue: "Poetry is a divine instinct and unnatural rage passing the reach of common reason" (183). The word "rage," which appears repeatedly in all these quotations, evokes the irrational "alienation of soule" that characterizes furor and also the wildness of lust. It is hard to know just how to read Spenser at this point. The breach of decorum might have social implications: a shepherd here speaks above his station. But it may simply be a polite fiction that treats such a violation of protocol as a form of praise rather than an arrogation of the style of one's betters.

In *Colin Clouts Come Home Again* Spenser invokes the furor in a way reminiscent of the October Eclogue, but this time the context and the language suggest that the idea of inspiration, while at first a trope of praise, also bespeaks truths that cannot be spoken and conceals an element of social complaint. Colin, describing Cynthia's court, finds his language escalating from the homely pastoral images of honey and grapes through the "beames of the morning Sun" to a language that is new to the poem (608–15). Cuddie cautions Colin that "Such loftie flight base shepherd seemeth not, / From flocks and field, to Angels and to skie" (618–19). Colin answers with the lines quoted in the first paragraph of this chapter. The phrase "furious insolence" expresses the social danger that such inspiration presents. A shepherd praising a queen in heightened language is a form of social presumption. When furor arises a second time in *Colin Clouts Come Home Again,* Colin complains of the triviality of courtly Platonism—"all the walls and windows there are writ, / All full of love, and love, and love my deare" (776–77)—and he defends a more powerful idea of love whose "mightie mysteries they do prophane" (788). As he rhapsodizes on love's power (823–26), the change in style is again noted, and Colin has to explain that to "speak" of love's perfection or to define his nature "passeth reasons reach" (837). But the power of Love to stimulate "each one his like to love / and like himselfe desire for to beget" (863–64) forces Colin again into territory that Spenser finds morally difficult:

> But man that had the sparke of reasons might
> More than the rest to rule his passion
> Chose for his love the fairest in his sight,
> Like as himselfe was fairest by creation.
> For beautie is the bayt which with delight
> Doth man allure, for to enlarge his kynd. (867–72)

We can appreciate the difficulties the strange logic of this passage overcomes. The introduction of reason and the ruling of passion is gratuitous at this point, and might even be considered a contradiction of the thesis on love's power. What is remarkable here is that the verse then ignores reason's restraint and goes on to describe love's power, against which "nor God nor man can fynd / Defence" (875–76). The recurrent uneasiness about erotic energies never disappears, but it also remains ambiguous and allows for inspiration.

> Thus ought all lovers of their lord to deeme:
> And with chaste heart to honor him alway
> But who so else doth otherwise esteeme,
> Are outlawes, and his lore do disobay.
> For their desire is base, and doth not merit,
> The name of love, but of disloyall lust. (887–92)

This ambiguous passage may say that desire is lust, or it may say that the desire of those who honor love is not lust.

The moral dilemma Spenser poses masks a social one. While he cannot comfortably allow that desire beyond the control of reason might serve a philosophic purpose, he is becoming disillusioned with the very social code that holds up "disloyall lust" as a prime offense.[39] To identify all rapture with lust, to see in the alienation of mind only *insania,* is to lose the opening that Ficino's *divinus furor* offers for an insight beyond simply the reasonable behavior of courtly decorum. In this poem Colin's "insolence" becomes admirable precisely because his ability to partake of a rhapsodic furor sets him apart from and above the decorous Platonic courtiers. The implications of such an idea—that the lowly but inspired poet is superior to the titled courtier—are not made explicit in the poem, but they are implicit in the trope of furor, and Spenser's very caution as he broaches the idea suggests that he is not altogether deaf to them.

The problem of the status of the inspired poet in a situation in which courtiers are powerful is rendered emblematically on Mount Acidale when Calidore, the knight of courtesy, intrudes upon Colin, the visionary poet, and unintentionally disperses the dancing Graces (*Faerie Queene,* 6.10.27–28).[40] Spenser's Colin is a Platonic poet-lover who, inspired by the beauty of his beloved, renders his beloved more beautiful. Spenser here brings to a point the social dilemma that motivates *Colin Clouts Come Home Again.* The social differences between Calidore and Colin are explicit, and Calidore's apology for disturbing his social inferior denotes a social awareness that is special.[41] But more important for our current purposes is the puzzle posed by Calidore's relation to vision and truth:

> Much wondred *Calidore* at this straunge sight,
>> Whose like before his eye had never seene,
>> And standing long astonished in spright,
>> And rapt with pleasaunce, wist not what to weene;
>> Whether it were the traine of beauties Queene,
>> Or Nymphes, or Faeries, or enchaunted show,
>> With which his eyes mote have deluded beene.
>> Therefore resolving, what it was, to know,
> Out of the wood he rose, and toward them did go. (6.10.17)

Though the term *furor* is not used, the phrases "astonished in spright," and "rapt with pleasaunce" reassemble the terms of the phrase that describes the "furious" Colin in *Colin Clouts Come Home Again,* "like one yrapt in spright." For a moment Calidore has a glimpse of an ecstatic poetic truth.

As a responsible courtier, however, Calidore must question what he has glimpsed, and he comes forward to "know" whether "his eyes mote have deluded beene", whether this is poetic furor or *insania,*[42] and he turns to the poet in the hopes that "he the truth of all by him mote learne" (6.10.18). "The truth of all" may refer to the vanished scene, but it also suggests that there is a whole level of knowledge that Colin understands and Calidore does not. After Colin has explained the vision, Calidore asks pardon for having "rashly sought that, which I mote not see" (6.10.29). "Mote not see" could be interpreted to suggest not just that Calidore is unable to see the vision but that it would be wrong for him to see it. We are on the edge of the tradition of mysteries that only the prepared initiate, that is, Colin, the Platonic poet, can see, and Calidore himself declares himself a layman.

Spenser is too diplomatic to set up a stark opposition between poetic vision and courtly grace. The Graces, as figures of hierarchy and order, return us to the issues of courtesy at a higher plane:

> all the complements of curtesie:
> They teach us, how to each degree and kynde
> We should our selves demeane, to low, to hie;
> To friends, to foes, which skill men call Civility. (6.10.23)

At the same time the woman at the center of the dance suggests a more mysterious insight: while a "countrey lasse" she is nevertheless also a "goddesse," the epitome of all women. Yet even this hint of the idea of beauty itself shies from the mystical and concludes by reenlisting the beloved in the social world of "Firme Chastity" and "courtesie" (6.10.27) and by apologizing to Gloriana for so dignifying her handmaid. At the end the decorums of social rank are explicitly and carefully maintained.

The confusion in Spenser's allegiance to the idea of inspiration is a function of the complexity of his social position. He is thoroughly invested in the laureate idea, with its clear understanding that poetry has a civic function and finally may not have meaning apart from the court, even if it is at times somewhat critical of that court. His sympathy and identification with a rapturous Colin must be muted, for he also owes a debt to Calidore. The mysterious scene on Mount Acidale is an emblem of the incompatibility Spenser experiences as a nonaristocratic poet indentured to the court, and the obscurity of the allegory at this point is necessary lest his own "despight" become evident to his patron.

Years later in *Euthymiae Raptus* Chapman tells us that Homer appeared to him, assured him of the "inward" value of his understanding, and reminded him of his first visit:

> I am (sayd hee) that spirit *Elysian,*
> That (in thy native ayre: and on the hill
> Next *Hitchins* left hand) did thy bosome fill,
> With such a flood of soule; that thou wert faine
> (With acclamations of her Rapture then)
> To vent it, to the Echoes of the vale.[43]

The rapture here resembles religious zeal and its consequent disregard of the courtly world, but it is a zeal devoted to the project of poetry itself and to the absolute value of the rapturous poet. Colin, on a different hill, has a similar rapture, but it is interrupted, and at the center of his vision is not the master poet, Homer, but a beautiful representative of the queen. By resurrecting the archaic ideology of inspiration these poets find a way to assert, over morals, courtesy, rank, and political power, the value of "culture," which the poet alone possesses, and they thereby begin to create cultural capital and with it the modern aesthetic stance.

Chapman's language of the full bosom and the flooded soul recalls another tradition of inspiration that very much complicates our understanding by reserving fury for devotional enthusiasm and expressing it in conventional rhetorical forms. While this line of tradition shares a debt to Ficino, it represents a very different social gesture. In 1596 Barnabe Barnes, having abandoned the lascivious ambitions of *Parthenophil and Parthenophe* (1593), invokes spiritual inspiration for his religious verse:

> And if any man feele in himselfe (by the secret fire of immortall Entheusiasme) the learned motions of strange and divine passions of spirite, let him refine and illuminate his numerous Muses with the most sacred splendour of the holy Ghost, & then he shall (with divine Salust the true learned frenche Poet) finde that as humane furie maketh a man lesse then a man, and the very same with wilde unreasonable beastes: so divine rage and sacred instinct of a man maketh more than man, and leadeth him (from his base terrestriall estate) to walke above the starres with Angelles immortally.[44]

The parallel between "humane furie" and "divine rage" is familiar; it is a version of Ficino's *insania* and *divinus furor.* The language of "lesse then a man" and "more than man" clearly derives from Ficino, but Barnes's immediate source here is Du Bartas, "the true learned frenche Poet." In the thirtieth stanza of "Urania, Or, The Heavenly Muse," Du Bartas declares, in Sylvester's translation:

> For, as a humane Furie makes a man
> Lesse then a man: so *Divine-Fury* makes him
> More then himselfe; and sacred *Phrenzie* then
> Above the heav'ns' bright flaming arches takes-him.[45]

The frenzy that Du Bartas invokes is a religious inspiration, the voice, not of a muse or a minor deity, but of truth itself. Such inspiration is not in any enigmatic relation to "humane furie"; it is such fury's antithesis.

The righteous enthusiasm that Urania sanctions and that Barnes takes up is significantly different from Chapman's obscure furor in a number of ways. Du Bartas's inspired verse is undistinguished stylistically, and he sees inspiration as working in the traditional moral-rhetorical tradition:

> *He the Laurel Crown doth merit,*
> *Who wisely mingles profit with his Pleasure.* (71.3–4)

> So prudent Writers never doe divide
> Knowledge from Mirth, Mirth from Instruction's lore. (72.3–4)

And if divinely inspired verse is profitable, secular verse is dangerous, for it "must intice / Your heed-lesse *Readers,* your loose Race to follow: / And so for *Virtue,* make them fall to *Vice*" (38.2–4). Du Bartas's Urania is firmly in the moral-ped-agogic tradition and the poetry she inspires serves a proselytizing purpose. Du Bartas has none of George Herbert's sensitivity to the paradoxes of poetic ambi-tion in a devout poet, and he repeatedly declares that it is the hope to be famous, the "brave desire t'immortalize [his] name" (1.2), that drives him.[46]

Toward the end of "Urania" it appears that the subject matter rather than style is the issue: "Base argument, a base style ever yeelds" (57.1). Unlike Chapman, who in "consecrating" his energy to the humor of the Night advocates a difficult style as the essence of serious poetry, Du Bartas urges poets, "Then consecrate-me (rather) your Wits' miracles, / To sacred Stories" (61.1–2). The key to making lasting verse is to reiterate biblical stories rather than classical subjects. Never-theless, it is difficult to determine exactly what, beyond Protestant piety, Du Bartas is finally advocating, for if at the end he seems to denigrate classical narratives, earlier in the poem he has held up Homer and Ovid, alongside David, as instances of inspired poets:

> Thence is't, that many great *Philosophers,*
> Deep-learned *Clarks* (in *Prose* most eloquent)
> Labour in vain to make a gracefull *Verse,*
> Which many a Novice frames most excellent.

> Thence is't, that yerst, the poor *Meonian* Bard,
> Though Master, means, and his own eyes he misses,
> Of Old and New is for his Verse preferr'd,
> In's stout *Achilles,* and his wise *Ulysses.*

> Thence is't, that *Ovid* cannot speak in *Prose:*
> Thence is't, that *David* (Shepheard, turned *Poet*)
> So soon doth learn my *Songs:* and Youths compose
> After our *Art,* before (indeed) they know it. (23–25)

Emphatically, it is the *unlearned* quality of inspired verse that identifies it. If religious enthusiasm lies at the heart of Du Bartas's inspiration, it is a source that is open to all, not just to those who, in Chapman's words, "endure the Herculean labour of learning." In this respect Du Bartas's idea of inspiration is closer to Plato's than is Chapman's. We need to observe the important social consequences of this openness. The very arrogance of unlearned youth that Chapman so scorns in the letters to Roydon becomes for Du Bartas a sign of inspiration. For Du Bartas "many a Novice" can write inspired verse. This is a religious analogue to Sidneyean *sprezzatura;* the novice, like the "smally learned courtier," is spontaneously superior to "Deep-learned Clarks."

Socially, moralists such as Du Bartas and Sylvester are less radical than Chapman. They trust the rhetorical tradition of art to make the case for piety. If in "Urania" Du Bartas can, like Chapman, hate the humiliations of patronage, he disclaims epideictic poetry without considering a change in the social values:

> Anon, I meant with fawning Pen to praise
> Th'un-worthy Prince; and so, with gold & glorie,
> T' inrich my Fortunes, and my Fate to raise,
> Basely to make my *Muse* a Mercenarie. (6)

The ambiguity of this disclaimer is deep, especially in the English translation. This quatrain might mean that princes themselves are "un-worthy," but "Th'un-worthy Prince" might be a particular noble[47] or bad king, and the poet might be quite willing to praise a "worthy" prince. And if the French poet might speak of *his* monarch this way, the English translator, by dedicating the whole of the *Weeks* to "James Stuart: A Just Master," makes it clear that he intends no such critique.

Since for Du Bartas the inspired poem is identified by its pious theme, his invocation of divine furor reinforces his moralism. Barnes, too, sees his shift in 1596 from the love poetry of *Parthenophil and Parthenophe* (1593) as a conversion, as a movement between incompatible genres and moral stances.

> No more lewde laies of Lighter loves I sing,
> Nor teach my lustfull Muse abus'de to flie,
> With Sparrowes plumes and for compassion crie,
> To mortall beauties which no succour bring.
> But my Muse fethered with an Angels wing,
> Divinely mounts aloft unto the skie.
> Where her loves subjects with my hopes doe lie:
> For Cupids darts prefigurate hell's sting.
> His quenchlesse Torch foreshowes hell's quenchles fire,
> Kindling mens wits with lustfull laies of sinne:

> Thy wounds my Cure deare Saviour I desire
> To pearce my thoughts thy fierie Cherubinne,
> (By kindling my desires) true zeale t'infuse,
> Thy love my theame and holy Ghost my Muse. (sonnet 1)

Barnes sets up an opposition here that develops through the sequence: Cupid's torch is rejected in favor of the "fierie" Cherubim, the "lustful Muse abus'de" in favor of the Holy Ghost.

Chapman sets up a similar-looking opposition in the first sonnet of "A Coronet for His Mistresse, Philosophie," but there are subtle and profound differences between Chapman's intellectualism and Barnes's pious moralism:

> Muses that sing loves sensuall Emperie,
>   And Lovers kindling your enraged fires
>   At *Cupids* bonfires burning in the eye,
>   Blowne with the emptie breath of vaine desires,
> You that prefer the painted Cabinet
>   Before the welthy Jewels it doth store yee,
>   That all your joyes in dying figures set,
>   And staine the living substance of your glory,
> Abjure those joyes, abhor their memory,
>   And let my love the honord subject be
>   Of love, and honors complete historie;
>   Your eyes were never yet, let in to see
> The majestie and riches of the minde,
> But dwell in darknes; for your God is blinde. (sonnet 1)

Though "*Cupids* bonfires burning in the eye" shares the lustful quality of "Cupids darts" that Barnes disclaims, Chapman does not correct passion by pious rigor. In place of the "sensual Emperie" Chapman offers the "riches of the mind," something quite different, even antithetical to the ascetic religious spirituality that Du Bartas and Barnes advocate, something more akin to an anticipation of "cultural capital" than to "moralism."

One reason criticism has had difficulty seeing the difference between Chapman's idea of inspiration and Protestant religious enthusiasm is that Chapman further complicates the Platonic doctrine by combining it with a Stoic doctrine. In the title of his late-middle poem, *Euthymiae Raptus, euthymia* is an essentially Stoic concept that looks back to the original Stoics' idea of ἀπάθεια.[48] Plutarch describes ευθυμία as the aim of Stoic philosophy, which is finally achieved more by psychological than by philosophical understanding.[49] Seneca's "de tranquillitate animi" reveals the same moral and psychological concern when he gives his friend practical advice on how to achieve "this abiding stability of mind the Greeks call *euthymia*" and which Seneca translates as *tranquillitas*.[50] Thus, in the contexts with which Chapman would be familiar, *euthymia* makes specific reference to that quality of Stoic philosophy most antithetical to rapture. *Raptus,* on the contrary, while it suggests *abduction,* also recalls rapture, the "alienation of soul," that is part of the divine furor. Here is the center of Chapman's philosophical difficulty, for surely this is a union that should offend Platonists and Stoics alike. Yet, what looks like philosophical confusion makes sense as a social strategy. This paradoxical *euthymia* is a term of distinction in Bourdieu's sense. It separates Chapman's own brand of inspired stoicism, which is ecstatic about the very idea of tranquillity, from the conventional, Du Bartasian moralism. And at the other pole of the social struggle, it poses a state of intellectual virtue that is unattainable, even incomprehensible, to the amorous courtly poet. *Euthymia* must be ungraspable. It is the mysterious heart of culture itself, a state that only the truly noble man of Nennian virtue of the mind can understand. Like "obscurity," *euthymia* is both content and form, an ideal and the enigma that hides that ideal.

The questions that now arise are how can one embrace both Stoic prudence and Platonic rapture? and what does it mean socially to do so? First of all, we should remember that the union, while certainly difficult and disconcerting, has a reasonable genealogy: both Platonism and Stoicism derive ultimately from Socrates.[51] Stoic moral wisdom is compatible with the early stages of knowledge in Ficinian Platonism.[52] If Ficino places less emphasis on the consoling aspect of philosophy than do such Stoics as Plutarch and Seneca, nevertheless he allies himself with them in his emphasis on the importance of virtue.[53] Where Ficino parts with such Stoicism is over the value and possibility of intellectual virtue. The moral virtue that is the goal of the Stoic's philosophical struggle is, for the Platonist, only the necessary first stage for an ascent to higher understanding. Socrates is Ficino's model for such understanding.[54] Only by becoming an exemplary moral figure can Socrates become an exemplary intellectual figure.

In the difficult allegory of Cynthia's hunt at the center of Chapman's early "Hymnus in Cynthiam," this mysterious union is elaborated and its social significance suggested. In order "to take the pleasures of the day," Cynthia creates "A goodlie Nimph" named *Euthymia*. The goddess also creates hunters and hounds which give chase to Euthymia, who changes shapes as she flees and, as a panther, takes refuge in a thicket "all armd in thorne" which repels the dogs. The hunters, mounted on "Lyons, Bores, and Unicorns, / Dragons and wolves" repeatedly charge the thicket, and even gain entry, but finally, overcome by fear, they re-treat. Chapman uses the occasion to introduce a long simile comparing the fear found by the hunters to that felt by the troops under "the Italian Duke" caught in an ambush set up by the English under "Fame-thriving Vere." Euthymia, still a panther, flees to a "fruitful island," turns into an enormous boar, and then Cynthia suddenly stops the performance.

Euthymia's disguises as boar and panther and the fact that the hounds are named after those of Acteon have led critics to see the passage as a moral allego-ry about the destructiveness of bestial passion.[55] But the stoic origin of *euthymia* suggests that we should not be too quick to see it as unworthy, even if the hunt-ers are not themselves worthy. And on the Platonic side, we should remember Bruno's allegory of Acteon, which overturns the traditional moral reading and understands the allegory as the depiction of the seeker of truth who becomes one with the nature he observes.[56] By naming the nymph "Euthymia" Chapman hints at a basic paradox that underlies both hymns: that the most passionate act is quiet contemplation. In the "Coronet" Philosophy is "Drunk with extractions stild in fervencie / From contemplation and true continence" (7.7–8). The passionate hunt is not necessarily merely that of the passions for their earthly object; it is a hunt for the moment of balanced passion itself, contentment, in which, accord-ing to the Stoics, one is wise.

The image of the chase, with its un-Stoic language of desire and pain, becomes an image of the struggle of the learned poet himself. If Platonic desire urges him on, a Stoic awareness of the dangers of desire and of the "toyles" of the world is never absent. In this philosophically ambiguous space, where values can be read as their opposites, a powerful social ideal lurks, one which depends on obscurity but which dreams of a strong outspokenness. The poet tells us not to marvel that "a Nimphe so rich in grace / To hounds rude pursutes should be given in chase" (224–25); it is an instance of the way of the world:

> Wealth faunes on fooles; vertues are meate for vices,
> Wisedome conformes her selfe to all earths guises,
> Good gifts are often given to men past good,
> And Noblesse stoops sometimes beneath his blood. (228–31)

The pessimistic and satiric reading says that the rich are fools, that the wicked prey on the virtuous, that wisdom is forced to compromise, that evil men get all the breaks, and that the nobility fails to live up to its "blood." But the logic of the instance also says that though wealth is misplaced and virtue victimized, wisdom still is able to be found in the world's "guises" (Euthymia "could turne her selfe to everie shape" [226]), that it is not wrong that such wisdom be made available to "men past good," or that she should demean herself. A corrupt world still has treasures for the prepared initiate, at the very least an insight into its corruption.

The huntsmen arrive to find their hounds retired from the thicket "licking their sores." The hunters, however, spur their beasts forward into the thorns and, surprisingly, make a way (300–327). It is a very difficult passage to make sense of because the meaning keeps veering in unexpected directions. No sooner have the hounds entered the thicket than they are terrified by "her Stigian fumes of miseries." Yet the stygian fumes clear the hunters' horses heads, and for a moment they resemble "the fierie coursers of the sunne." But then further revelation of "cursed sights" leads to terror. At the center of this passage, at the moment of terror and insight, is language that echoes closely the concerns of "Hymnus in Noctem," "the vaporous subject of the eye / Out-pierst the intellect in facultie. / Baseness was Nobler then Nobilitie" (311–13). Here again is a line that can be read to say opposite things with equal plausibility. It may say that the base eye has supplanted the noble mind, and thus be an aristocratic complaint about the corruption of values. But the ambiguity of the terms allows for an antithetical reading, that a base nobility (i.e., a nobility of blood) has triumphed over "true nobility," the "virtues of the mind." Or it may say the radically Platonic idea that the man inspired by beauty, base as he may be, is nobler in the Nennian sense than the nobility. In this inverted state all acts of learning and morality become parodies of their true worth. The "inspiration" experienced within the thicket creates a vision which "Out-pierst the intellect in facultie," a line which could in other circumstances describe gnostic revelation, but here, because the souls are unprepared, the line may say that inspiration is blind and leads to a false pity which in turn leads to fear. The foggy and stygian surroundings resemble those encountered halfway through "Hymnus in Noctem," a world in which the poet finds solace from the world of day (cf. "Hymnus in Noctem," 268–77). Entering into this deathlike state of vision without the proper moral and intellectual preparations, however, leads not to insight but to confusion and terror.

This is by now familiar territory. Like the perspective picture, like the close conjunction of furor and *insania,* like obscurity itself, *euthymia* entails a double meaning which speaks in its hidden way to the issues of true nobility. By these various and seemingly contradictory enthusiasms Chapman repeatedly but always deniably develops his vision of a society in which learning and integrity earn regard and poetry and philosophy respect, and any deficiencies of birth or fortune are irrelevant. Having developed this ideology and come to an understanding of the manner of the strange style that it is forced to cloak itself in, we are finally in a position to engage "Ovids Banquet of Sence," Chapman's most ambitious and most outrageous poem.

6

Ovid and the Social Value of Literature

Chapman aspires to something far more complex than ascetic moralism. Neither a puritan nor an intimate of aristocrats, he advocates a philosophical eroticism, an energy whose goal is not the conquest of the resisting woman but a rectification of social injustice and a realignment of social rewards. Like Ovid, he plays at the edge of the aristocratic system. As I have been arguing through the whole course of this book, he defines himself by his "virtue," his integrity, and his dignified obscurity, with all the risks associated with that remarkable position. Against the background of the issues of resentment, the critique of nobility, the defense of obscurity, and the social meaning of poetic furor, in this chapter we turn to the place of Chapman's enigmatic poem, "Ovids Banquet of Sence." But first we should observe that to make Ovid the central character in a poem at the middle of the decade of the 1590s is to engage a number of poems that had just appeared. There is good reason to think that Chapman has Shakespeare and Barnes in particular in mind as he produces this major poem about eros and inspiration.

It is not clear exactly who are the "English Ravens" in their "nests of basest obscurity" Barnes insults in his letter before *Pierces Supererogation,* but it is plausible to think that Chapman found reason to take offense, for within a year he publicly defended obscurity and in "Hymnus in Noctem" allied himself with the ravens and owls whom Barnes scorns. He would find Barnes's bright art trivial: as he mockingly says at the end of the hymn, "I can not (do as others), make day seeme a lighter woman then she is, by painting her." In the dedicatory letter to Matthew Roydon prefixed to *The Shadow of Night,* while asserting his familiar idea of the special value of poetry, Chapman had already made an oblique reference to Harvey's book: "Now what a *supererogation* in wit this is, to thinke skil so mightilie *pierst* with their loves, that she should prostitutely shew them her secrets, when she will scarcely be lookt upon by others but with invocation, fasting, watching; yea not without having drops of their soules like an heavenly familiar" (19, emphasis added). Frances Yates years ago observed the forced conjunction of "supererogation" and "pierst."[1] If the reference is to Harvey's *Pierces Supererogation,* then there is reason to think that Barnes's notorious claim to poetic significance may have inspired Chapman's diatribe to Roydon and that the "Coronet for His Mistresse, Philosophy" is in part at least directed against this kind of trivial lascivious poetry.

Along with Barnes's *Parthenophil and Parthenophe* (1593) Chapman might also include such works as Shakespeare's *Venus and Adonis* (1593) and even Donne's *Elegies* which also find in Ovidian eroticism an opportunity for a poet to become "courtly" without being a member of the court.[2] Chapman and Marlowe before him, by contrast, find in the Ovidian fashion an opportunity to revise the very nature and value of poetry itself, to make poetry an alternative to the court. It is a project that can be understood only in the light of its opposition not to eroticism—it is not a puritan morality—but to a misuse of poetry, to a failure to take advantage of the extraordinary cultural power of verse.

The distinction I am making here is at first difficult to see just because both traditions identify themselves by their contempt for the vulgar. Shakespeare quotes Ovid to just this effect in his epigraph to *Venus and Adonis:*

> Vilia miretur vulgus: mihi flavus Apollo
> Pocula Castalia plena ministret aqua.

[Let the vulgar admire the vile: to me Golden-haired Apollo ministers cups full of the Castalian water.]

Less than two years later Chapman puts Persius as the epigraph to *Ovids Banquet of Sence:* "Quis leget haec? Nemo Hercule Nemo, / vel duo vel nemo" [Who reads this? No one, by Hercules, no one, or a couple or no one]. This may sound like a similar gesture, but it is not. Shakespeare's epigraph is a conventional trope distinguishing an aristocratic sensibility from that of the vulgar and popular.[3] The art that appeals to this taste pointedly avoids social comment; mythological erotic narrative becomes primarily an opportunity to display style.[4] Chapman's, on the other hand, identifies a learned coterie, a "two or none" of the "true nobility," alone and removed from the conventions of social hierarchy, who must earn their ability to read his uncourtly and strange verse. Chapman's is a learned project that will find in Ovid, not an idle sensuality, but a style of social alertness that can be used to reinstate the classical dignities of poetry.

The Ovidian component, the sense of rich inspiration entailed in the phrase

"Pocula Castalia plena aqua," has for Chapman a promise that Shakespeare betrays. In "Hymnus in Cynthiam," in the preparations for the narrative of *Euthymia,* Chapman first puts himself in the ecstatic mood and then, after praising Cynthia, invokes the Ovidian moment of Shakespeare's epigraph.

> Presume not then ye flesh confounded soules,
> That cannot beare the full Castalian bowles,
> Which sever mounting spirits from the sences,
> To looke in this deepe fount for thy pretenses:
> The juice more clear then day, yet shadows night,
> Where humor challengeth no drop of right:
> But judgement shall displaie, to purest eyes
> With ease, the bowells of these misteries. ("Hymnus in Cynthiam," 162–69)

The long tradition of reading these lines as alluding to Shakespeare misses the point when it sees Chapman as simply objecting to the sensuality of Shakespeare's poem.[5] The issue over which Chapman separates himself from Shakespeare is not the morality of sex but the purpose of poetry itself. The opposite of a "flesh confounded soul" is not a puritan ascetic but a furious initiate who uses sense to inspire spirit and, by a paradoxical energy that we by now are used to, "shadows night" with verse "more clear th[a]n day." The moral paradoxes of *euthymia* later in the poem are here anticipated in language recalling Chapman's first hymn: true poetry involves an enigmatic sensual spirituality. It is the emptiness of that sensuality in the Shakespeare poem, presented simply to flatter and entertain aristocratic idlers, that dismays Chapman. Like the ape in *Mother Hubberd's Tale,* who feeds "noble wits" with "fruitles follies and unsound delights" (823), Shakespeare in Chapman's eyes invokes sensuality for itself, as a style of aristocratic play. Such play has its Ovidian component, to be sure, but it lacks that quality of social struggle that Marlowe brings to the Ovidian tradition and that Chapman weaves throughout his early poems. The "flesh confounded soules" whom Chapman shoves away from the Castalian fount are not debauchees but—in Harold Bloom's sense of the term—weak poets.

Finally, we should remember that throughout the decade of the 1590s Marlowe himself is strongly linked with Ovid.[6] Marlowe's translation of Ovid's *Elegies* first appeared sometime around 1592, and yet its affront was such that the bishops still considered it subversive enough to warrant burning in 1599.[7] It is worth asking again why Marlowe's poem was considered dangerous while such equally lascivious poems as *Venus and Adonis* or *Parthenophile and Parthenophe* were tolerated. Clearly it is not a matter of simple regulation of sexual innuendo in literature; all these poems express an openness to pleasure that puritans must have found irritating and dangerous.[8] Shakespeare, however, respects authority; he dedicates this playful and amoral exercise to a nobleman; Barnes names a half-dozen nobles in his dedications; both these poems are licensed. Marlowe's translation of Ovid, by contrast, is mysterious and surreptitious; published abroad and without license, it gives an air of outlaw daring to what, if differently presented, might seem a rather innocuous, even pedantic text. The difference in address marks a difference in social meaning to which the bishops seem to have been alert. By his irregular publication Marlowe draws attention to the dangerous aspect of Ovid. It will not be forgotten by poor Ovidians that Ovid himself was a commoner who, as it was generally understood in the Renaissance, was exiled for his illicit relationship with Augustus Caesar's daughter, Julia, whom he calls Corinna in the *Amores*.[9] Like Semele in *Faustus,* or the shepherd lass in *Hero and Leander,* or Hymen in "The Tale of Teras," Ovid, driven by eros, disrupts social hierarchies, and if he is at one level a pathetic victim of a revenging and unjust authority, he is also a model of the poet who knows his worth despite society's censure. If Shakespeare's eroticism, appearing with license and dedicated to a nobleman, asks to be read as an expression of aristocratic freedom, Marlowe's rather similar eroticism speaks to a more precarious enterprise by which poetry becomes in itself a declaration of cultural presence and the poet constructs his own social importance, apart from the established hierarchies.

Ovid's worldliness, suggesting that intelligence and desire are always capable of teasing the social order and its decorum, inspires a pleasure in the infinite suggestibility of language. A paradigmatic moment for this awareness comes at the end of the notorious elegy 1.5 in which Ovid, after describing a dreamlike midday amour with Corinna, breaks off:

> Singula quid referam? nil non laudabile vidi
> et nudam pressi corpus ad usque meum.
> Cetera quis nescit? lassi requievimus ambo.
> proveniant medii sic mihi saepe dies! (1.5.23–26)

[Why recount each charm? Naught did I see not worthy of praise, and I clasped her undraped form to mine. The rest, who does not know? Outwearied, we both lay quiet in repose. May my lot bring many a midday like to this!][10]

The "cetera quis nescit" trope defines Ovidian "knowing": there is always something implied beyond what is being said. The worldly reader who knows all already enjoys proving his or her sophistication by catching the innuendo. Reading such a voice sometimes means knowing what does not need saying. It can also involve a kind of skepticism, an awareness that it may be the antithesis of what is being said that lurks in the saying. Thus, in the first of a pair of elegies, when accused of making love to Corinna's maid, Ovid declares his innocence, and then in the second he warns the maid they must be more careful (2.7, 8). Language suggests, and it also lies and conceals. But even in the lie, the relentless desire speaks; the lie is still at some level "true." The "quis nescit" trope is not just a moment of sexual innuendo; it points to an openness that means that for those "who know," verse is always saying more than it says it says. As Ithamore says in *The Jew of Malta*, "The meaning has a meaning" (2000).[11] Ovid represents a very potent model of a poet whose poetry is important not because it serves power but because it audaciously speaks its own eccentric and independent value and place in the world.

In the light of the discussion in the previous chapter, the traditional reading of the character of Ovid in "Ovids Banquet of Sence" as a furious initiate makes considerable sense. It is worth reminding ourselves at this point, in the face of the strong current treating Chapman's Ovid ironically, how reasonable it is to read the poem as describing with some eloquence poetic furor:

> Now Muses come, repayre your broken wings,
> (Pluckt, and prophan'd by rusticke Ignorance,)
> With feathers of these notes my Mistres sings:
> And let quick verse hir drooping head advance
>   From dungeons of contempt to smite the starrs;
>   In *Iulias* tunes, led forth by *furious trance*
>   A thousand Muses come to bid you warrs,
> Dive to your Spring, and hide you from the stroke,
> All *Poets furies* will her tunes invoke. (16, emphasis added)

The beginning of this stanza will be echoed in the "Coronet" when Chapman rebukes the muses whom "fames loose feathers beautify" (9.14, 10.1). We are here at the origin of poetry itself. A few stanzas later Ovid exclaims of Corynna's sounds:

> And now my soule in *Cupids* Furnace blazeth,
>   Wrought into furie with theyr daliance:
> And as the fire the parched stuble burns,
> So fades my flesh, and into spyrit turns. (22.6–9)

There may be room for irony here—Spenser might well suspect that this is lust—but from what we have seen of Chapman's ideal of fury and its similarity to *in-*

sania, it is not enough to invoke Spenser to read him. The rapturous quality which makes Spenser uneasy is exactly what identifies furor for Chapman, and throughout the poem this quality is recalled. Thus, when in the fourth course of the banquet (taste) Corynna kisses him, Ovid, "imaginde *Hebes* hands had brusde / A banquet of the Gods into his sence, / Which fild him with this furious influence" (97.7–9). Like Chapman inspired by Homer, Ovid is in touch with a heavenly insight that no ordinary poet can capture or imitate.

Traditionally, "Ovids Banquet of Sence" was read as just such a strange, difficult poem about using the senses to achieve a Platonic rapture.[12] However, given the other traditional idea of Chapman as a severe stoic moralist, such a rapturous reading of the "Banquet" posed a puzzle. The inquiry into this difficulty was derailed in 1957 when Frank Kermode simply erased one side of the contradiction by making the case that far from preaching Platonic inspiration the poem was ironic and taught the danger of sensual indulgence. By making *touch* the last sense that Ovid indulges, Kermode reasons, Chapman inverts the Ficinian order of the senses. Therefore, "Ovids Banquet of Sense" depicts "a fall into bestiality" rather than an ascent to divine furor. Kermode's reading, which I am calling the "moral" reading, has become the norm for most later interpretations.[13] Once the ironic moral reading is in place, the hermeneutic circle quickly closes; the ironic reading is said to be correct because the readings it generates are "typical of Chapman."[14]

A central procedure for the recovery of "Ovids Banquet of Sence" into moral orthodoxy is to treat Ovid himself as unreliable and to establish other voices in the poem as offering a standard by which to judge Ovid.[15] The moralist usually interprets the narrator's voice without irony and as a rebuke to Ovid, though the narrator's verse is stylistically indistinguishable from Ovid's. And there is a third voice, that of the annotator who speaks from the glosses on the margins of the poem, a voice which, unless we are to see the poem as a kind of Swiftian game, must be of undoubted authority. Most of the time this last voice is neutral about moral issues, testifying only to the classical authority of the imagery. Typical is the gloss to stanza 41, which flags the "Allusion to the transformation of *Acteon* with the sight of *Diana*," but leaves the interpretation ambiguous.[16]

Once, however, according to Kermode's argument, the voice of the gloss gives evidence of the moralist interpretation. About halfway through the poem Ovid dares to look on Corynna, and he sees her in heavenly terms:

> Shee lay at length, like an immortall soule
> At endlesse rest in blest Elisium:
> And then did true felicitie enroule
> So fayre a Lady, figure of her kingdome. (57.1–4)

The gloss explains the image: "The amplification of this simile, is taken from the blisfull state of soules in *Elisium,* as *Virgill* faines: and expresseth a regenerate beauty in all life & perfection, not intimating any rest of death. But in peace of that eternal spring, he poynteth to that life of life thys beauty-clad naked Lady." While drawing our attention to the Vergilian allusion, the obvious purpose of this gloss is to prevent us from reading the passage morbidly. Ovid says exactly what the gloss says when he compares Corynna's body to "Sweet fields of life which Deaths foote dare not presse" (58.3),[17] and when, later in the stanza, he declares that "Her body doth present those fields of peace / Where soules are feasted with the soule of ease" (58.8–9). Everything in the poem at this point speaks to the extraordinary power of naked beauty. Kermode, however, bent on proving Ovid unreliable, ingeniously and arbitrarily constructs an alternative point of view here. Though the word is repeated by Ovid (58.8), Kermode changes *peace* in the last sentence of the gloss to *place* and then reads the annotation as contrasting the Vergilian Elisium, which is a "regenerate beauty in all life," with this "naked Lady."[18]

The moralists must finally confront the fact that in the Elisium stanza the narrator himself makes Ovid his model for inspiration:

> Now *Ovids* Muse as in her tropicke shinde,
> And hee (strooke dead) was meere heaven-borne become,
> So his quick verse in equall height was shrinde:
> Or els blame mee as his submitted debter,
> That never Mistresse had to make me better. (57.5–9)

One way to read this is as a description of Ovid's poetic furor inspired by the vision of Corynna and the narrator's explanation that if the full effect of Ovid's "quick verse" is not conveyed the reason is the narrator unfortunately has not received similar inspiration from a "Mistress."[19] The "Coronet for His Mistresse, Philosophie," which immediately follows the "Banquet" might seem to be the narrator's rather more abstract inspiration.[20] As I have argued in earlier chapters, that second poem is hardly a rejection of the first. At this very moment of identification between the narrator and Ovid it is the erotic Ovid who attracts the narrator. This moment anticipates the notorious moment in Marston's *The Metamorphosis of Pygmalion's Image* when the narrator hopes that for him too a cold maiden will turn soft in his embrace. It is, thus, not enough to see Chapman's poem as simply Platonic; it is finally Ovidian with the social implications developed earlier in this chapter.

The gloss is not the only point at which the defenders of the moral interpretation must strain to disqualify Ovid's energy and prove him an object of narrative disapproval. A number of critics have made the claim that the narrator's digression in the middle of the poem is a moment of moral stability when the anti-Ovidian position is established.[21] Just before the digression we are told, "Heere *Ovid* sold his freedome for a looke." This is not the sure sign of moral failure sometimes supposed.[22] As we have seen, Ficino himself sanctions "alienation of soul" in the hope that, if the love is reciprocated, the insights of *furor amoris* will be available. The danger in loving, Ficino warns, is not sin but lack of reciprocity: if the love is not returned the conclusion is death.[23] This is exactly the point that the poet himself makes in the next stanza, the first of his digression:

> This beauties fayre is an enchantment made
> By natures witchcraft, tempting men to buy
> With endles showes what endlessly will fade,
> Yet promise chapmen all eternitie:
> But like to goods ill got a fate it hath,
> Brings men enricht therewith to beggerie
> *Unlesse* th'enricher be as rich in fayth,
> Enamourd (like good selfe-love) with her owne,
> Seene in another, then tis heaven alone. (51, emphasis added)

Far from simply condemning Ovid, this stanza charts the two roads that are open to him when he loves: in giving up his freedom Ovid may have committed himself to waste and frustration, or, if the love is mutual, he may have entered on the road to "heaven alone." The praise of "sacred beauty" that follows in stanza 52, though it may well make us reinspect what is going on, is too general to be applied as a gauge by which to measure Corynna's virtue.

Then, in the next stanzas (53–54), the poet argues that, though a state of contentment is the goal of the lover, the process of attaining it entails constant unrest.[24] This is a basic tenet of Ficino's theory of love: love is important as a prod, a lure, a motive to try to know God, and that goal is rarely and only momentarily achieved by any human in life.[25] Thus, the "keener edge" (stanza 110) that the satisfaction of each sense gives to Ovid's longings toward the end of the poem, while to a stoic or even a decorous courtier such as Spenser might appear as evidence of the frustrations of lust, would clearly betoken for an enthusiastic Platonist the more important unrest of divine furor.

Finally, the poet concludes his digression on love with lines which reject a moralism that is blind to the philosophic possibilities of love:

> And to conduce that compasse is reposde;
> More force and art in beautie joyned with love,

> Then thrones with wisdome, joyes of them composde
>   Are armes more proofe gainst any griefe we prove,
> Then all their vertue-scorning miserie
> Or judgments graven in Stoick gravitie. (54.4–9)

I touched on this passage in the introduction, but now we are in a position to appreciate its real audacity. "Beautie joyned with love" is stronger than the power of a wise king. The combination produces a joy more secure than those of either "vertue-scorning miserie" or "Stoick gravitie." Given Chapman's Nennian sense of "virtue," sensuality is not the issue here; the pronoun "their," like other instances of deniable assertion in other poems we have looked at, floats ambiguously: one reading would say that kings, even wise ones, are miserable and unvirtuous next to the "force and art in beautie joyned with love." The last line reproves readers who, like Lysias in *Phaedrus* and like many modern interpreters of Chapman, assuming a posture of "Stoick gravitie," deny the "force and art" of love. The digression, far from settling the question of point of view, describes the "twofold" nature of rapture and the possibilities of love.

A moralist will always find evidence of dissipation in a description of such furor precisely because such a moralist finds furor itself dissipation. But furor as the expression of the highest poetic seriousness can be described only in language that will alarm the conventional moralist. Near the end of the poem, after having kissed Corynna, Ovid desires to touch her:

> And thus with feasting, love is famisht more,
> Without my touch are all things turnd to gold,
> And till I touch, I cannot joy my store:
> To purchase others, I my selfe have sold,
>   Love is a wanton famine, rich in foode,
> But with a richer appetite controld,
>   An argument in figure and in Moode,
> Yet hates all arguments: disputing still
> For Sence, gainst Reason, with a senceless will. (101)

It is easy enough to see how this stanza can be interpreted as an expression of the self-destructive frustration of mere sensual passion.[26] One can also, however, see it as an ingenious, paradoxical expression of the restless urging to higher things that divine furor generates. The passage offers a double perspective of the sort we observed in "Hymnus in Noctem." Ovid is a Midas, but a Midas in reverse, one who creates life out of gold, not gold out of life. If his desire is for flesh, it is for a flesh higher than that sought by the usual human appetites. In one sense he has been reduced to a famished, lustful beast; in another he has gone beyond the "food" and the "reason" that are the ordinary goods of humanity, and in the midst of sensual food he experiences a spiritual longing, and his "unreasonable" sensuality is directed by a will which is free from the tyranny of the senses. Such a language of paradox, which inverts the conventional terms of discourse in order to transcend them, is a fitting one for describing the divine furor that leads to understandings beyond the reach of normal language and reason.

Perhaps the most outrageous instance of the poem as perspective picture is Corynna's song in stanza 12. Here cynical anti-intellectual praise of "beauty's sorcerie" and transcendent intellection are rendered in identical words:

> T''is better to contemne then love,
> And to be fayre then wise;
> For soules are rulde by eyes:
> And *Joves* Bird, ceaz'd by *Cypris* Dove,
> It is our grace and sport to see,
> Our beauties sorcerie
> That makes (like destinie)
> Men followe us the more wee flee;
> That sets wise Glosses on the foole,
> And turns her cheekes to bookes,
> Where wisdome sees in lookes
> Derision, laughing at his schoole,
> > Who (loving) proves, prophanenes, holy;
> > Nature, our fate, our wisdome, folly.

By seeing only the disruption of Stoic reason the song describes, the moral interpretation misses entirely the song's powerful Platonic suggestions. It is not a question of choosing one way or the other to divine insight; without the lure of beauty the human mind is confined to the diminished possibilities of mere human thought. "Beauties sorcerie," like the "enchantment" in stanza 51 at the beginning of the poet's digression, exerts a necessary and dangerous attraction—Ficino can compare it to a trap or to bait for a trap[27]—that inverts the conventional modes of wisdom so that beauty becomes the source for true understanding, and the wisdom of the "schoole" becomes an object of derision. While to a Stoic the final couplet of the song may reveal the complete impropriety of Corynna's powers and intentions, to a Platonist it announces the radical, paradoxical promise of *furor amoris*. As Chapman says in the "Coronet," "loves prophaned dart / Feedes the chaste flames of *Hymens* firmament" (4.8–9): a truly inspired love transforms profane sensual energies. Similarly, to assert that Nature is our fate, rather than denying the spirituality of love, is to affirm the essential intelligence that determines even Nature.[28] At this point, in fact, the Platonic version overlaps a possible Stoic reading, for it is a Stoic commonplace that virtue lies in living according to Nature.[29] Finally, the idea that there is a folly that transcends the "wisdome" of the world recurs frequently in the Renaissance and has the sanction of St. Paul.[30] A Stoic, therefore, may discover in Corynna's song only improper, worldly, cynical ideas, but if one is prepared to see it one can perceive also a daringly optimistic assertion of the power of divine furor.

The last stanza of "Ovids Banquet of Sence," rather than resolving the poem's ambiguity, intensifies it. Ovid, having progressed in his acquaintance with Corynna through four senses to the fifth, touch, has been "interrupted with the view / Of other Dames" and has retired complaining, like Alexander, "that there were no more worlds to subdue":

> But as when expert Painters have displaid,
> To quickest life a Monarchs royall hand
> Holding a Scepter, there is yet bewraide
> But halfe his fingers; when we understand
>   The rest not to be seene; and never blame
> The Painters Art, in nicest censures skand:
>   So in the compasse of this curious frame,
> *Ovid* well knew there was much more intended,
> With whose omition none must be offended.
>   *Intentio, animi actio*
>   Explicit convivium.[31]

Ovid's sense that "there was much more intended" recalls the "quis nescit" trope, but the obscure meanings we are to pick out range far beyond just sexual detail.[32] We may remember Chapman's use of painting to describe the nature of his own art in the epistle to Roydon that precedes the "Banquet": "it serves not a skilfull Painters turne, to draw the figure of a face onely to make knowne who it represents; but hee must lymn, give luster, shaddow, and heightening; which though ignorants will esteeme spic'd, and too curious, yet such as have the judiciall perspective, will see it hath, motion, spirit and life" (*Poems,* 49). The "expert Painters" referred to in the last stanza of the poem are engaged in just this sort of serious artistic translation of a three-dimensional reality into two, which those with "the judicial perspective" will understand. Thus, even at its close the poem yokes the lascivious and the deeply philosophical, and we are invited to follow in our own imaginations the discrepant courses that lie open to Ovid about which, for reasons of moral decorum or in acknowledgment of the limits of his art or per-haps for reasons of social diplomacy, the artist cannot speak.

As we observed in the previous chapter,[33] in the third stanza of the poem Chapman offers us a model for such complexity: an emblematic statue of Niobe "So cunningly to optick reason wrought" that it can be viewed in two ways. Elizabeth Story Donno suggests that "Ovid's nearer view becomes a symbol of what 'searching wits' apprehend rather than what the 'profane multitude' sees from afar."[34] The poem itself is a perspective picture. One can never entirely dismiss the possibility of Kermode's irony, but the poem's real puzzle is posed not as the moral dichotomy Barnes represents with his erotic and spiritual books—that is, as acceptance or rejection of eros—but as the difference between a merely sensual poetry and an erotic poetry that speaks beyond the obvious.

It remains for us to understand why a serious poet should write such an ambiguous poem. If the ambiguity serves for deniability, it is hard to think that Chapman would need this kind of escape if the only offense were a strong Platonism. Kermode was certainly correct in his intuition that the strangeness of "Ovids Banquet of Sence" meant that something was going on beyond the description of amorous furor. His moral reading underestimates how serious Chapman's main purpose is. Once we free ourselves from a narrow moral perspective, we can see that something more than Platonism is concealed here. Furor opens the poem to a number of levels of meaning, one of the most important of which is the one that has motivated this study. As we saw in the previous chapter, poetic rapture implies a restructuring of social rank, elevating the inspired poet above traditional inherited ranks. Plato offers the example of Ion, the reciter of Homer, as the model for inspiration. Chapman catches the social difficulty of furor, its insolence, by making his rapturous poet Ovid, *praeceptor amoris*.

By ending with a version of "quis nescit" "Ovids Banquet of Sence" reminds us that it depicts with extraordinary bravura the very scene of *Amores* 1.5, Ovid's encounter with Corinna. And we may also remember that according to common tradition *Amores* 1.5 depicts the sexual trespass that caused Ovid's banishment. The banishment lies behind Chapman's poem at a number of points. We hear the crux near the center of "Ovids Banquet of Sence" when the poet remarks, as Ovid decides to look at Corynna, "Here Ovid sold his freedom for a look." We have already discovered the Ficinian implications of this line; now I would want to add the layer of Ovid's social situation. The line alludes to the mysterious moment in *Tristia* II in which Ovid regrets the act that seems to have caused

Augustus Caesar to banish him: "cur aliquid vidi? cur noxia lumina feci?" (line 103) [Why did I see anything? Why did I make my eyes guilty?][35] While it is possible to treat Ovid's look as a terrible error, it is also possible to see it as embodying the central issue of the importance of poetry and the injustice of the world of rank and power represented by Augustus. The poet, to be worthy the title, must "sell his freedom," though that does not mean that he cannot also complain. And at the end of the "Banquet" (113.5) the inspired Ovid promises to write the "Art of Love," the poem to which according to another aspect of the tradition Caesar objected and which most contributed to the poet's banishment. Chapman's poem is, therefore, not an imitation of Ovid so much as a study of the philosophical and social implications of Ovidianism, both as an erotic practice and, more particularly, as a style of social discourse, a rapturous, always enigmatic, often witty, gracefulness in the presence of power. And, finally, like Ovid himself, the poem poses a profound question: what is the value of poetry in relation to the other "goods" of society? The erotic ambiguity of the poem is never entirely separate from its social consciousness.

For the virtuous poet of "Ovids Banquet of Sence," the opposite of erotic rapture is not lust but avarice:

> Gentle and noble are theyr tempers framde,
> That can be quickned with perfumes and sounds,
> And they are cripple-minded, Gowt-wit lamde,
> That lye like fire-fit blocks, dead without wounds,
>   Stird up with naught, but hell-descending gaine,
> The soule of fooles that all theyr soules confounds,
>   The art of Pessants and our Nobles staine,
> The bane of vertue and the blisse of sinne.
> Which none but fooles and Pessants glorie in. (35)

Nobility here has almost the modern sense of taste: it is a sign of the noble soul that it can "be quickned with perfumes and sounds," and it is the definition of the peasant that he can rouse himself only for gain. The essential aristocratic paradigm that lies behind the Ovidian lines Shakespeare quotes before *Venus and Adonis* ("Vilia miretur vulgus") is recalled here, but remarkably free of the blood, ancestry, and power that are conventionally also invoked. For if sensitivity defines the noble, what are we to make of "The art of Pessants and our Nobles staine"? There are clearly nobles who are insensitive, who pursue "hell-descending gaine" and who are indistinguishable in their tastes from "fooles" and "Pessants." Typically of Ovidian logic, the invocation of nobility and gentility takes us in an unforeseen direction.

The attack on material wealth, in a Bourdieu-like insight into the way culture creates a mysterious nothing that is most useful because it cannot be grasped by those who are outside of culture, pervades the poem. In the narrative interlude at the center of the poem we find:

> Then in the truest wisdome can be thought,
> Spight of the publique *Axiom* worldings hold,
> That nothing wisdome is, that getteth nought,
> This all-things-nothing, since it is no gold.
>   Beautie enchasing love, love gracing beautie,
> To such as constant simpathies enfold,
>   To perfect riches dooth a sounder deutie
> Then all endevors, for by all consent
> All wealth and wisdome rests in true Content. (53)

Just as toward the end of "Hymnus in Noctem" the poem spirals in toward a "nothing" that is everything and a dream, so here "This all-things-nothing" becomes a "perfect riches." And, again like the hymn, no sooner has "true Content" been announced as the sum of "wealth and wisdom" than it is shown as impossible.

At one of the poem's major climaxes, when Corynna makes a point of the difference of their "birth and state" (89.7), Ovid accuses her of trivializing the affair and concludes:

> True dignities and rites of reverence,
> Are sowne in mindes, and reapt in lively deedes,
> And onely pollicie makes difference
>   Twixt States, since vertue wants due imperance,
> Vertue makes honor, as the soule doth sence,
>   And merit farre exceeds inheritance. (91.2–7)

The social point of this argument is liable to be overlooked because of the ambiguity of the term *vertue,* but Phyllis Bartlett was certainly right to hear *Nennio* in this passage: social distinctions are artificial ("onely pollicie makes difference / Twixt States"), and "Vertue," not in a narrow moral sense but in the broad Stoic sense of Fabricio's "Virtues of the mind," makes "honor." "Merit fare exceeds inheritance" means that nobility of virtue surpasses nobility of blood. We recall that Corynna is Julia, the emperor's daughter, and whatever other meanings we may want to grant her, she is the highest reach of the social scale. For Ovid to approach her is for him to risk a major violation of the social order. While it is not her social status that attracts him, nevertheless eros cannot be thought of without considering the social disruption it entails. Ovid's attraction to Corynna is, finally, an exercise in Nennian virtue, and such social transgression is intrinsically a source of poetry.

Corynna has anticipated Ovid's Nennian argument and coyly emblematizes the social consequences of this understanding with a jewel depicting the long shadows at sunset with the profoundly ambiguous motto, "Decrescente nobilitate, crescunt obscuri" (70.9). A gloss explains the optics of the situation, but leaves the interpretation of the enigma open. If to the privileged nobility it might seem to say that darkness follows nobility's decline, the opposite social perspective gives a very different reading, declaring that in a world of debased nobility the obscure become important. Just as the state of the nobility is ambiguous, so the pun on *obscure* that pervades "Hymnus in Noctem" recurs. Obscure verse identifies the true nobility of the learned but obscure poet.

In "Ovids Banquet of Sence" Chapman gives us two other emblems of this very difficulty. The second of Corynna's jewels depicts an eye covered by a laurel spray with the motto "*Medio caret.*" The poem explains the image, "To showe not eyes, but meanes must truth display" (71.4), and in the margin Chapman offers a prose explanation: "Sight is one of the three sences that hath his medium extrinsecally, which now (supposed wanting) lets the sight by the close apposition of the Lawrell: the application whereof hath many constructions." Though, as the gloss coyly observes, there are many ways to read it, one construction is to read this emblem as an assertion that obscure poetry (the laurel), though it seems to block vision, is the key to insight. The analogue to this emblem is the purple glass in "Coronet" 8:

> And as a purple tincture gyven to Glasse
> By cleere transmission of the Sunne doth taint
> Opposed subiects: so my Mistresse face
> Doth reverence in her viewers browes depaint,
> And like the Pansye, with a little vaile
> Shee gives her inward worke the greater grace. (5–10)

The third and last jewel almost seems an emblem from Donne's "The Sunrising," for it shows "*Apollo* with his Teme / About a Diall and a worlde in way, / The Motto was, *Teipsum et orbem*" (71.5–7), and again the prose gloss, while explaining at one level, opens it up: "The Sun hath as much time to compasse a Diall as the world, & therefore ye world is placed in the Dyall, expressing the conceite of the Emprese morally which hath a far higher intention." Enigmas like this are clearly not to be solved conclusively, but in the present context it makes sense to see one possibility of a "higher intention" as another statement of the equal "virtue" of the dial and the world, and thus of the equivalence between small and local meanings (*teipsum*) and large ones (*orbem,* the world).

As the poem closes Ovid is frustrated at a number of levels. Most obviously, he is interrupted, but more important to the philosophical theme of the poem is the failure of language:

> And feeling still, he sigh'd out this effect;
> Alas why lent not heaven the soule a tongue?
> Nor language, nor peculier dialect,
> To make her high conceits as highly sung,
>   But that a fleshlie engine must unfold
> A spirituall notion; birth from Princes sprung
>   Pessants must nurse, free vertue waite on gold
> And a profest though flattering enemie,
> Must pleade my honor, and my libertie. (111)

The difficulty of the "fleshlie engine" unfolding a "spiritual notion" seems clear, but the metaphors that follow importantly resituate the inexpressibility topos so that it becomes in part an image of the distribution of social value. Chapman is being very dense and obscure through here, and it is worth making possibilities explicit. The lines "birth from Princes sprung / Pessants must nurse" are enigmatic: is the wet nurse an image of decline (as the possibly contemptuous term "pessants" might imply) or is it an image of the way the obscure support the nobility? In the next line, "free vertue waite on gold," the verb *wait* shifts between meaning something like "depend on" to meaning "serve." This is familiar territory: the virtuous peasant is more noble than merely noble and wealthy "blood," and virtue must serve gold. In the poem to Harriot three years later Chapman repeats this exact ambiguity in lines that I have had occasion to quote before:

> Thus as the soule upon the flesh depends,
> *Vertue must wait on wealth;* we must make friends,
> Of the unrighteous Mammon, and our sleights,
> Must beare the formes of fooles or Parasites.
>   ("To M. Harriot," 27–30, emphasis added)

Ovid registers a similar awareness of the service "virtue" must perform and of the contortions such service entails. As in the case of Hero's torch, Chapman here renders an intricate and delicate sense of how power is served and preserved. The "fleshlie engine" of the tongue is, after all, the agent of language, just as the wet nurse is the nurturer of the prince, and as such it has a certain dignity even as its inadequacy is acknowledged. My "honor" and my "libertie" are defended by this "flattering enemie."

In *Ovids Banquet of Sence* the failure of the "fleshlie engine" becomes the motive for a general complaint about the state of patronage:

> In these dog-dayes how this contagion smoothers
> The purest bloods with vertues diet fined
> Nothing theyr owne, unlesse they be some others
> Spite of themselves, are in themselves confined
>   And live so poore they are of all despised,
> Theyr gifts, held down with scorne should be divined,
>   And they like Mummers mask, unknowne, unprised:
> A thousand mervailes mourne in some such brest
> Would make a kinde and worthy Patrone blest. (114)

At the climax of the poem it is issues of social evaluation and support that are being discussed. The true nobility whose blood is pure not by birth but by "vertues diet" are impoverished and therefore scorned. This is not a turn away from the poem's central theme, but the final realization of a line of thought implicit from the beginning. The poetic furor, the line of inspiration beginning with Corynna but importantly progressing through Ovid's poetic accomplishment, is finally an idea of social reformation.

In the next stanza, the last before Ovid is interrupted, the narrator's voice becomes indistinguishable from Ovid's, and Corynna becomes indistinguishable from Elizabeth:

> To mee (deere Soveraigne) thou art Patronesse,
> And I, with that thy graces have infused,
> Will make all fat and foggy braines confesse,
> Riches may from a poore verse be deduced:
>   And that Golds love shall leave them groveling heere,
> When thy perfections shall to heaven be Mused,
>   Deckt in bright verse, where Angels shall appeare
> The praise of vertue, love, and beauty singing,
> Honor to Noblesse, shame to Avarice bringing. (115)

Under the patronage of Corynna (Elizabeth) we are back to the familiar opposition between poetry and the values of the social world. The "Riches" found in a verse are a kind of cultural capital, quite different from the love of "Gold" that motivates avarice. The "noblesse" honored at the end is the familiar Nennian quality, the virtues of the mind, now given a Platonic turn by the supplement of "love and beauty."

Paradoxical as it may sound to a generation of scholars brought up with Kermode on the allegorization of Ovid—and this same paradox must have been strongly felt by the readers of the 1590s who had been educated in the same tradition—Ovid is for Chapman most important as an inspired poet-lover and an image of the social (not the moral) dangers such a poet risks. In this passage we are involved in the question of what makes "bright verse." That is perhaps an outrageous claim; but this is an outrageous poem, as is Marlowe's *Elegies,* as is Ovid's *Amores.* In both rejecting the pedantries of moralist instruction and at the same time appealing to classical tradition, Chapman's shocking poem lays claim to a social meaning. We are here close to the core of the unspeakable but clear-to-all-eyes enigma of social power, a core that has been alluded to in the work of Marlowe, Spenser, Roydon, Lodge, and Jonson, but has nowhere received this kind of statement. The commendatory poems affixed to the first edition of *Ovids Banquet of Sence*[36] all express a deep and complex admiration for the poem's accomplishment but at the same time obfuscate the exact cause of the enthusiasm. It is intrinsic to the central contradiction of such cultural capital that, while the need for labor and the paradoxes of light in darkness pervade the imagery of these commendatory poems, the interest in the thematics of social reward, which as we have seen pervades Chapman's poem, is left implicit.

Rather like Ezra Pound more than three centuries later, Marlowe and Chapman and the poets around them want to revive the classics as a way of dignifying style itself and thereby opening up the market for a new form of capital. Where these poets differ from their later manifestation is that they work in a field without the possibilities of cultural capital that distinguish modern art. In the culturally more restricted field of the 1590s with its powerful controlling forces of licensing and patronage, the social implications of economic distribution are harder to deny. And yet ironically, as the modern history of the interpretation of "Ovids Banquet of Sence" bears witness, the social anger that motivates this important poem and that runs through much of the poetry of the decade has been invisible to scholarship.

Chapman had to struggle for his whole career. If he may at one moment in "Ovids Banquet of Sence" assert that "All wealth and wisdome rests in true Content" (53.9), he can go on to recognize that "Contentment is our heaven, and all our deeds / Bend in that circle, seld or never closde" (54.1–2). The heaven of "Contentment" is seldom or never achieved. Poverty, after all, is one of the parents of love. Yet, if discontent is, finally, true to the movements of Platonic ascent, it also is a disconcerting fact of material life. Philosophy and poetry have social implications. In the later poem, *Euthymiae Raptus* (1609), Chapman's interlocutor describes a vision he has had of Justice carrying an open book with a single hidden verse in which "all Arts, were contracted, and explainde" (625). He is reminded of a verse he himself once wrote: "God hath made none (that all might be) contented" (635). This is hardly the contraction and explanation of "all Arts" that we might reasonably have expected, yet Peace responds that "for the capacitie it bears" this might be Justice's verse, "Since all lines to man's peace are drawn in it" (636, 639). She goes on to explicate the social meaning of the verse, showing that the rich are not content and averring that the poor can have their "cares richly eased" (648) by this very knowledge. Resentment has its rewards; in the midst of its discontent poverty can take some consolation in the discontentment of wealth. Thus, finally, behind the moral and philosophical issues of Chapman's poetry lurk the inescapable truths of economic life, and they motivate the meaning. Chapman's Ovid represents the possibility of an autonomous art of the sort Bourdieu describes in "The Market of Symbolic Goods." Independent of nonartistic institutions such as church or state—flaunting that independence even by his lascivious thematics—this Ovid, unlike the allegorized Ovids of the Middle Ages or of Golding, posits a "field of restricted production," identified by the very thematics we have examined: a resentment of boorish privileges, a recognition of a "true nobility" built on "virtue," an appreciation of obscurity as a means of speaking truth and as a mark of distinction, and a faith in inspiration as a charismatic identification of the authentic poet.

Postscript:
The Presumption of Aemilia Lanyer

At the time of the publication of Jones's translation of *Nennio* and Chapman's "Ovids Banquet of Sence" in 1595, some poets could envision a moment of utopian promise when Fabricio's "virtues of the mind" might seem a viable form of cultural capital, when an intellectual might reject both the rules of courtly discourse, which however much they reward style never forget pedigree, and the abrasive opposition of puritan anger, inspired by a claim to reject the social world in the name of a higher truth outside of time, in order to define a space in which learning, wisdom, and even the very refusal to compete in the social arena—to choose to recline like Bussy at the beginning of the play—can be advanced as sources of cultural power. Even Spenser can at moments modestly and cautiously urge a place for an obscure poetic that is outside the court and, even if the court does not recognize it, has dignity. Under James I, however, the possibilities available at the end of Elizabeth's reign seem to close down; the court tends to monopolize social reward, and compared with the earlier decade there are few options for the ambitious intellectual outside that source of cultural capital. Except for some members of the earlier generation who continue to invoke the values and vocabulary of the virtues of the mind, the tone of the age becomes less culturally ambitious and less daring. The routes of success are known and other routes closed.

There is however one new and slightly younger poet who in a subtle and yet clear way pays her homage to those earlier possibilities. Aemilia Lanyer, born Bassano, the daughter of a court musician, "of respectable birth but limited means,"[1] appears to have been a bold, adventurous, and creative woman, consorting with powerful men in her youth and with powerful women in her middle age. In 1611, when she was over forty, she produced a single book of poems, *Salve Deus Rex Judaeorum.* This is a socially confusing book; while the central title poem narrates Christ's passion, fully one-half of the volume is composed of commendatory poems to royal and titled women. On the surface Lanyer would seem to have abandoned the space of ambition we have been studying and opted for both the other positions sketched at the beginning of this book: religious piety and solicitation of the court and its patronage.[2] But, as we saw in the case of Phillip Stubbes nearly thirty years earlier, religious piety finds itself finally in a deep conflict with courtly values, a conflict to which patrons, thanks to the mechanisms of self-congratulation, may be deaf, but which the poet and other people viewing the situation from her vantage will hear with quite a different implication. Lanyer presents herself, finally, not only as a celebrator of courtly piety but as a humble yet important instance of a "woman's wit." That is, like Chapman she comes before us, without title or fortune, asking to be recognized as a poet.

In the middle of the poem commending Anne, countess of Dorset, Lanyer visits a line of argument with which we are now familiar. After what seem like orthodox assertions that "No worldly treasure can assure . . . place" and "All worldly honours there [i.e., in heaven, or perhaps, more ambiguously, in God's eyes] are counted base" (18, 20), Lanyer moves to a more politically challenging idea: "Titles of honour which the world bestowes, / To none but to the virtuous doth belong" (25–26). Since this ideal of Nennian justice does not in fact prevail, "Poore virtues friends indure the greatest wrong" (30). Lanyer then raises the issue of whence did nobility spring?

> What difference was there when the world began,
> Was it not Virtue that distinguisht all?
> All sprang but from one woman and one man,
> Then how doth Gentry come to rise and fall?
> Or who is he that very rightly can
> Distinguish of his birth, or tell at all,
>> In what meane state his Ancestors have bin,
>> Before some one of worth did honour win?
>
> Whose successors, although they beare his name,
> Possessing not the riches of his minde,
> How doe we know they spring out of the same
> True stocke of honour, beeing not of that kind?
> It is faire virtue gets immortall fame,
> Tis that doth all love and duty bind:
>> If he that much enjoyes, doth little good,
>> We may suppose he comes not of that blood.[3]

The "indignity" of the world's rewards becomes the unambiguous argument, and the Nennian view of the artificiality of rank becomes explicit.[4] Lanyer avoids the insult of a pure Nennian line, however, by fading back into ambiguity in the next stanza and allowing the interpretation—a common one, to be sure, one we see in Jones's own dedication of *Nennio* to Essex—that the subject of the poem, Anne, countess of Dorset, in this instance will show the nobility of her blood by her doing good. The barb of the last two lines can easily be taken as a compliment by the patron who understands Lanyer to be including her in the "True stocke of honour." But we may suspect we are back recalling Chapman's scorn for the "blood without soul of false nobility."

It is the invocation of God's "kingdom" that licenses Lanyer's otherwise insulting assertions of the dignity of virtue. The Christian perspective allows her to dismiss rank, even avowing her disinterest in her own social position, but some strange effects are generated by such a piety. In the opening poem to Queen Anne one finds such strong ironies that if they fail to offend, it is simply because they are so intrinsic to the Christian perspective that royalty has become inured to them. Nevertheless, in the pointed logic of the poem they stand out as challenging declarations. Lanyer begins by observing the rarity of "a Womans writing of divinest things" (4) and worrying that if it is "defective" (5) the queen may take what is intended as praise as something else. After praising the queen for three stanzas, she then reverses the polarity and asks the queen to be the support of the poet's dignity: "To virtue [i.e., Lanyer's intention and poem] yet / Vouchsafe that splendor which my meannesse bars" (27–28). The term "meannesse" would seem to be a recognition of the social gap that defines the patronage situation, but it also opens up a rather different and surprising strategy of social questioning, because Lanyer is not the only "mean" person in the poem. The term recurs over the next six stanzas denoting qualities that identify Christ's virtue: he "tooke our flesh in base and meanest berth" (46); he is "The hopefull haven of the meaner sort" (50); he represents "that faire Virtue, though in meane attire, / All Princes of the world doe most desire" (65–66). The humility implicit in Lanyer's worry about her own meanness turns into the essence of Christian virtue. Again we may think of Chapman's "Mistress Philosophy" who "thus deprest doth knock at heaven's gate."

The embedded theme of rank pervades the poem "Salve Deus Rex Judaeorum" itself, and conventional Christian pieties are presented with a particularly political vigor: "Unto the Meane he makes the Mightie bow, / And raiseth up the Poore out of the dust" (123–24). Christ is repeatedly praised for his "great humility" (473), and being "counted of so meane a birth" (476) allows him "To purge our pride by [his] Humilitie" (480). Mary's "meane estate" (1034) is emphasized. If on the one hand flesh is "Too base a roabe for Immortalitie" (1112), Christ, "for our gaine . . . is content with losses / Our ragged clothing scornes he not to weare" (1124–25). Christ is a leveler; "He judgeth all alike, both rich and poore" (1646). When a number of times through the poem Lanyer turns to the countess of Cumberland, she praises her for her disregard of worldly wealth and position.

At one point Lanyer seems to invoke a more snobbish sense of the term "mean" when she emphasizes that Christ as the son of God was not mean. But the argument that seems simple in its premises is intricate and it is his very refusal of the privileges that might been seen as belonging to his rank that makes him Christ. At the beginning of the following quotation I italicize the word "mean" to emphasize the pointedness of Lanyer's wordplay:

> Yet, had he beene but of a *meane* degree,
> His suffrings had beene small to what they were;
> *Meane* minds will shew of what *meane* mouldes they bee;
> Small griefes seeme great, yet Use doth make them beare:
> But ah! tis hard to stirre a sturdy tree;
> Great dangers hardly puts [*sic*] great minds in feare:
> > They will conceale their griefes which mightie grow
> > In their stout hearts untill they overflow.
>
> If then an earthly Prince may ill endure
> The least of those afflictions which he bare,
> How could this all-commaunding King procure
> Such grievous torments with his mind to square,
> Legions of Angells being at his Lure?
> He might have liv'd in pleasure without care:
> > None can conceive the bitter paines he felt,
> > When God and man must suffer without guilt. (1233–48)

It is exactly the difference between Christ and "an earthly Prince," whose whole definition involves exercising the power that holds off affliction and grievous torments, that comes home here: Christ's nobility entails refusing those very elements that commonly identify the nobility. It is a connection that no one would point to, but the logic of these lines finally argue that earthly princes have "meane minds" for they make "small griefes seeme great." The opening line of the passage reveals a rather extraordinary meaning: had Christ been of "a meane degre" he would have acted the way any earthly prince acts and called on his army. *Mean* here, while to a casual reading it speaks to Christ's rank as the Son of God, in fact denies rank and distinguishes not between the great and the mean but between "great minds" and "mean minds." For Lanyer Christ is very much in the tradition we have been examining: a man who, while he might have appealed to "birth," earns his title by his virtue, which consists of not making that appeal to the privileges his birth entitles him. And just as Christ is here entirely indifferent to rank, the countess of Cumberland is herself praised for her Christian indifference to earthly rewards.

At moments in *Salve Deus Rex Judaeorum* Lanyer seems to be comforting the countess for her difficulties in preserving her late husband's inheritance for her daughter, Anne, countess of Dorset. It is a nice mode of flattery to praise someone for their indifference to the world and at the same time console them for their suffering in that world. We do not need to think of Lanyer as devious in using such a rhetorical strategy. As poets like Chapman, Jonson, and herself begin to invent the modern idea of cultural capital they express their ambitions in a moral ("virtue" is Chapman's favorite) or pious ("mean" is Lanyer's) vocabulary that refers to such culturally undoubted goods that the social contradictions analysis uncovers do not present themselves as problems. If this means that they do not see their ambitions as "subversive," it also means they may not entirely understand themselves what they are seeking. Like Faustus, they want their "cunning" to be respected, but what exactly that means is not clear. They shun the vulgar. Chapman addresses a fellow poet—in Bourdieu's terms, he appeals to the judgment of producers, not the titled and idle audience. Lanyer seems more conventional in that she commends royal and titled patrons, but by ignoring men, by recounting in "To Cooke-ham" a moment of feminine intellectual community, and in isolating the women's parts in the Passion, she clearly, just as much as Chapman, puts herself in a a position of creating the social space which has not previously existed in which her accomplishment will be valued.

If in *Salve Deus Rex Judaeorum* Lanyer can dignify great women for their virtue apart from their rank, in "The Description of Cooke-ham," the concluding poem in the 1611 volume, she shows that the consciousness of rank is never entirely absent. The countess of Dorset, who is granted a genuinely Nennian integrity in the poem dedicated to her before *Salve Deus Rex Judaeorum,* is now identified more conventionally as "sprung from *Cliffords* race / Of noble *Bedfords* blood" (93–94) "to honorable *Dorset* now espous'd" (95) and a woman of "true virtue" (96).[5] Ordinarily, it comes as no surprise that a woman of such pedigree is praised for her virtue, but it does come as a surprise that Lanyer does so when one considers how much she earlier praised Dorset and Cumberland for their indifference to rank and privilege. One may perhaps sense a note of irony in Lanyer's praise of Anne's "virtue" in "Cooke-ham," and that note is made more plausible by the remarkable and bitter passage that follows, lamenting how their difference in rank now keeps them apart. It is an audacious and moving passage in which Lanyer speaks about the realities of social difference in a way that one seldom hears.[6] She blames her separation from the countess first on "Unconstant Fortune," "Who casts us downe into so lowe a frame: / Where our great friends we cannot dayly see, / So great a diffrence is there in degree" (104–6). But more angry and personal charges develop when she implies a hypocrisy in the great who are "Neerer in show, yet farther off in love, / In which, the lowest always are above" (109–10).[7] This is dangerous territory, and Lanyer quickly retracts the claim: "But whither am I carried in conceit? / My Wit too weake to conster of the great" (111–12). And she then resigns herself to the memory of "pleasures past." We see here Lanyer's understanding—an understanding that belongs especially to those without power—of the frustrating and inescapable meaning of obscurity. In such unequal relationships as this between a countess and a commoner, the obscure love more not because they are in some mysterious way more loving but because they have more to gain socially by the relationship's continuation.[8] Yet, if for a moment ambition drives Lanyer to articulate a complaint about the injustice and inequality of the system, her obscurity also allows a retreat, in Lanyer's case a double obscurity of rank and gender. The reference to her "Wit too weake" takes us back to the opening poem to the queen and her dwelling on the tropes of incapacity: her apology for "My weake distempred braine and feeble spirits" (139) and her calling "presumption" the thought that she might "compare with any man" (145, 148).[9] Our age has become familiar with the ironies of such gendered presumption, but the other social element involved—that Aemilia Lanyer, the brilliant poet of common background, could claim any kind of equality with titled women—is a gesture involving considerable risk. What particularly distinguishes Lanyer's complaint is that, despite her economic difficulties, she does not want money from Anne; she wants love. This is a claim of obligation way beyond patronage, but it matches the claims of equality of earlier poets, whose ambition is hard to define but in some sense would be satisfied, not by economic success, but by being accepted by the elite. At this level Jonson's ploy of speaking familiarly with nobility, when it does not stimulate rejection, turns itself into a sign of his success. Contrarily, Barnes's or Gossen's claims of equality with Sidney get taken in a different manner, and quickly become the marks that identify their social inferiority. Lanyer disappears from our view after this poem; we cannot know how her appeal was received, though we do know that Anne, while she raised monuments to Spenser and Daniel, the poets whom her deceased mother, the countess of Cumberland, had patronized, is not on record as recognizing Lanyer.[10]

More than two decades after Lanyer's poem Chapman will publish his translation of Juvenal's Fifth Satire as a bitter comment on a patronage situation that has, if anything, declined over the years since he first enunciated the hope for a serious poetry. The humiliations of clienthood always entail a difficult rhetorical posture; even Dr. Johnson's great letter to the earl of Chesterfield accounts the earl's belated attention an "honour" and closes with expressions of conventional servility.[11] It isn't until the nineteenth century with the further decline of aristocratic privilege and the development of an independent market for symbolic goods that artists can afford to express openly their sense of their own dignity to the class that has hitherto sustained art. In Lanyer's daring gesture of companionship with the countess of Dorset we can recognize the whole world of utopian cultural possibilities that Chapman and his fellows hoped to open up but that will remain for yet another century and a half a source only of teasing hope for obscure and ambitious poets.

Notes

Preface

1. Daniel Javitch, *Poetry and Courtliness in Renaissance England* (Princeton: Princeton University Press, 1978), and Frank Whigham, *Ambition and Privilege: The Social Tropes of Elizabethan Courtesy Theory* (Berkeley: University of California Press, 1984).

2. Richard Helgerson, *Self-Crowned Laureates: Spenser, Jonson, Milton and the Literary System* (Berkeley: University of California Press, 1983).

3. See especially Louis Adrian Montrose, "'The Perfecte Paterne of a Poete': The Poetics of Courtship in *The Shepheardes Calender,*" *Texas Studies in Literature and Language* 21 (1979): 34–67.

4. Stephen Greenblatt, *Renaissance Self-Fashioning: From More to Shakespeare* (Chicago: University of Chicago Press, 1980).

5. Annabel Patterson, *Censorship and Interpretation: The Conditions of Writing and Reading in Early Modern England* (Madison: University of Wisconsin Press, 1984).

6. I will have occasion to refer to a number of Bourdieu's works, but the central texts for me have been: Pierre Bourdieu, *Outline of a Theory of Practice,* trans. Richard Nice (Cambridge: Cambridge University Press, 1977); Pierre Bourdieu, *Distinction: A Social Critique of the Judgement of Taste,* trans. Richard Nice (Cambridge: Harvard University Press, 1984); and Pierre Bourdieu, *The Field of Cultural Production,* ed. Randal Johnson (New York: Columbia University Press, 1993).

7. Millar MacLure, *George Chapman: A Critical Study* (Toronto: University of Toronto Press, 1966); Raymond B. Waddington, *The Mind's Empire: Myth and Form in George Chapman's Narrative Poems* (Baltimore: Johns Hopkins University Press, 1974); Richard S. Ide, *Possessed with Greatness: The Heroic Tragedies of Shakespeare and Chapman* (Chapel Hill: University of North Carolina Press, 1980); Gerald Snare, *The Mystification of George Chapman* (Durham, N.C.: Duke University Press, 1989).

8. Vincent W. Beach Jr., *George Chapman: An Annotated Bibliography of Commentary and Criticism* (New York: G. K. Hall, 1995).

Introduction

1. Bourdieu, *Distinction,* 250.

2. Classic studies of the professional writer are Phoebe Sheavyn, *The Literary Profession in the Elizabethan Age* (1909; reprint, New York: Haskell House, 1964); Edwin Haviland Miller, *The Professional Writer in Elizabethan England: A Study of Nondramatic Literature* (Cambridge: Harvard University Press, 1959); and J. W. Saunders, *The Profession of English Letters* (London: Routledge and Kegan Paul, 1964). The issue of how social rank reveals itself in English Renaissance literature has been studied recently by Lauro Martines, *Society and History in English Renaissance Verse* (Oxford: Basil Blackwell, 1985); Ralph Berry, *Shakespeare and Social Class* (Atlantic Highlands, N.J.: Humanities Press International, 1988); and Peter Holbrook, *Literature and Degree in Renaissance England: Nashe, Bourgeois Tragedy, Shakespeare* (Newark, N.J.: University of Delaware Press, 1994).

3. Frank Whigham, *Ambition and Privilege,* has articulated the ways the dominant faction used rhetoric to maintain its privilege.

4. The University Wits have long been recognized as such a social formation. Richard Helgerson begins the exploration of this group in *Elizabethan Prodigals* (Berkeley: University of California Press, 1976), though he tends to link them by age and career pattern rather than by economic class. The sign of his disregard for economic issues is his inclusion of Sidney in the group.

5. See G. K. Hunter, *John Lyly: The Humanist as Courtier* (London: Routledge and Kegan Paul, 1962).

6. The story is told in full in Mark Eccles, "Chapman's Early Years," *Studies in Philology* 43 (1946): 181–90. The text of Chapman's petition for relief can be found in *A Seventeenth Century Letter-Book: A Facsimile Edition of Folger MS. V.a.321,* ed. A. R. Braunmuller (Newark, N.J.: University of Delaware Press, 1983), item 138.

7. To speak anachronistically, the paradigm for such a strategy is Flaubert, whom Bourdieu sees as inventing a new tactic for art as a way of "refus[ing] to belong to one or the other group situated at one or the other of the poles" of social space (Bourdieu, "Field of Power, Literary Field and Habitus" [trans. Claud DuVerlie] in *Field of Cultural Production,* 173).

8. William Ringler, *Stephen Gosson: A Biographical and Critical Study* (Princeton: Princeton University Press, 1942). For Barnes, see chap. 1, below.

9. Sidney was not always seen as exemplary. In fact in the early nineteenth century he was treated as a fairly minor poetaster. But in this century his canonization, especially as the great Elizabethan theorist of poetry, has become increasingly common.

10. Francis Meres, *Palladis Tamia* (London: P. Short for C. Burbie, 1598), 286v.

11. See S. K. Heninger Jr., who observes that whatever artistic sympathies Sidney and Spenser may have shared, they could not have been friends in the modern sense: "The social disparity between them is difficult for the modern mind to comprehend" (*Sidney and Spenser: The Poet as Maker* [University Park: Pennsylvania State University Press, 1989], 11).

12. *The Poems of George Chapman,* ed. Phyllis Brooks Bartlett (1941; reprint, New York: Russell and Russell, 1962), 19. This edition is hereafter cited as Chapman, *Poems.* In quotations throughout I have regularized u/v and i/j and expanded contractions to conform to modern usage.

13. Sigmund Freud, *Civilization and Its Discontents,* trans. James Strachey (New York: W. W. Norton, 1961), 68.

14. Chapman, *Poems,* 49.

15. The social complexity of Roydon's elegy for Sidney is studied in detail in chap. 5.

16. Raymond Williams, *The Sociology of Culture* (New York; Schocken Books, 1982), 70.

17. Saunders, *Profession of English Letters,* 60.

18. Marlowe, *Hero and Leander: A Facsimile of the First Edition, London 1598,* ed. Louis L. Martz (New York: Johnston Reprint Corp., 1972).

19. See Lawrence Stone, *The Crisis of the Aristocracy, 1558–1641,* abridged ed. (London: Oxford University Press, 1967); G. R. Elton, *England under the Tudors,* 3d ed. (New York: Routledge, 1991); J. A. Sharpe, *Early Modern England: A Social History, 1550–1760* (London: Edward Arnold, 1987); and Joyce Youings, *Sixteenth-Century England* (London: A. Lane, 1984).

20. "The more fluid society became, the more passionately [Elizabethan social critics] urged the necessity and naturalness of fixed, hierarchically ordered estates" (Anthony Esler, *The Aspiring Mind of the Elizabethan Younger Generation* [Durham, N.C.: Duke University Press, 1966], 34).

21. The evidence is everywhere, but see in particular Alvin Kernan, *Shakespeare, the King's Playwright: Theater in the Stuart Court, 1603–1613* (New Haven: Yale University Press, 1995).

22. This is a pervasive thesis for Greenblatt, but see in particular Stephen Greenblatt, "Invisible Bullets," in *Shakespearean Negotiations: The Circulation of Social Energy in Renaissance England* (Berkeley: University of California Press, 1988), 21–65.

23. I distinguish my sociological approach from the more explicitly activist political approach of such major recent collections as *Political Shakespeare: New Essays in Cultural Materialism,* ed. Jonathan Dollimore and Alan Sinfield (Ithaca, N.Y.: Cornell University Press, 1985).

24. In addition to Bourdieu's emphasis on "practice," we should acknowledge Michel de Certeau, *The Practice of Everyday Life,* trans. Steven F. Rendall (Berkeley: University of California Press, 1984).

25. Pierre Bourdieu, "The Market of Symbolic Goods," *Poetics* 14 (1985): 42.

26. The difference can be overemphasized: Bourdieu is fond of showing how the supposedly egalitarian structures of modern education and culture cloak mechanisms of reproduction that are almost identical to those of inherited nobility. The homology between the traditional aristocracy of birth and the modern, democratically generated "nobility of culture" is central to "The Aristocracy of Culture" (*Distinction,* 11–96).

27. Bourdieu, "Market of Symbolic Goods," 15.

28. Russell Fraser, *The War against Poetry* (Princeton: Princeton University Press, 1970).

29. Thus, in accord with the neo-Marxist argument for the importance of the super-structure for social reproduction as developed by Louis Althusser (in "Ideology and Ideo-logical State Apparatuses," in *Lenin and Philosophy and Other Essays,* trans. Ben Brewster [New York; Monthly Review Press, 1971], 136) and Raymond Williams ("Base and Su-perstructure in Marxist Cultural Theory," *Problems in Materialism and Culture: Selected Essays* [London: Verso, 1980], 31–49), we can argue that even in the early modern transi-tion to capitalism, despite the almost unchallenged dominance of a small aristocracy, the ideology that supports the circle of privilege must be promulgated energetically, in church-es, in schools, in civic pageants, as well as in the codes and laws.

30. This is a strategy familiar in the twentieth century, and it is no accident that in the 1920s and 1930s Chapman was appreciated by T. S. Eliot or that he was invoked as a proto-modernist by Margaret Bottrall in *The Criterion* ("George Chapman's Defence of Difficulty in Poetry," *Criterion* 16 [1939]: 638–54).

31. John Guillory, *Cultural Capital: The Problem of Literary Canon Formation* (Chica-go: University of Chicago Press, 1993), 85–133.

32. Bourdieu has some acute observations about why such social dynamics are difficult for later readers to reconstruct. See Pierre Bourdieu, "The Field of Cultural Production," trans. Richard Nice, in *Field of Cultural Production,* 29–73.

33. The classic instance of offensive dedication may be Gosson's dedication of *The School of Abuse* to Sidney, though the issue here is not a criticism of the patron's class but a mis-guided sense of his political sympathies. For a description of the difficulties we have de-termining the meaning of an act of dedication, see Michael Brennan, *Literary Patronage in the English Renaissance: The Pembroke Family* (London: Routledge, 1988), 13.

34. In Bourdieu's conception, *habitus* is that cluster of values and expectations learned early in life that shapes one's behavior even as one moves into different class situations. The concept points to a hysteresis by which as a person's economic conditions change, behavior, which a simple materialist analysis would expect also to change to match the new class position, continues to enact attitudes and practices that are incongruent with those of the new class. *Habitus* is intrinsic to Bourdieu's thought, and he meditates on it throughout his work. For an early definition, see *Outline of a Theory of Practice,* 78–86.

35. Gary Waller, *English Poetry of the Sixteenth Century* (London: Longman, 1986), 39.

36. Jonathan Goldberg, *James I and the Politics of Literature* (Baltimore: Johns Hop-kins University Press, 1983), 155–56.

37. Chapman, *Poems,* 50.

38. *The Plays and Poems of George Chapman,* vol. 2: *The Comedies,* ed. Thomas Marc Parrott (London: Routledge and Sons, 1913), 270–71 (3.2.471–88).

39. There is room for much stage business on Bassiolo's part suggesting that he hears this as saying he is in Margaret's good graces.

40. Quoted in Cyndia Susan Clegg, *Press Censorship in Elizabethan England* (Cam-bridge: Cambridge University Press, 1997), 202. Emphasis added.

Chapter 1: Morality, Rank, and the Cultural Field

1. Fraser, *War against Poetry,* 155.

2. See also Patterson, *Censorship and Interpretation;* Janet Clare, *"Art Made Tongue-tied by Authority": Elizabethan and Jacobean Dramatic Censorship* (Manchester: Manchester University Press, 1990); and Richard Dutton, *Mastering the Revels: The Regulation and Censorship of English Drama* (Iowa City: University of Iowa Press, 1991).

3. For purposes of the following analysis I have used the first edition of Stubbes's polemic—Phillip Stubbes, *The Anatomie of Abuses: Contayning a Discoverie, or Briefe Summarie of such Notable Vices and Imperfections, as now raigne in many Christian Countreyes of the Worlde* . . . (London: R. Jones, 1583). This first edition includes a preface to the reader that softens the attack on the theater and was dropped from later editions. Traditionally the preface has been treated as part of a first draft which, after he had competed the main text, Stubbes realized he did not mean (see Furnivall's edition). It seems equally plausible to suppose that it was inserted in the first edition as a cautious disclaimer, and when the printer was assured that the angry text did not bring the law down on him he eliminated the preface and let the puritan sense that the stage itself is an abuse stand as the book's position.

4. Jean Howard, *The Stage and Social Struggle in Early Modern England* (London: Routledge, 1994), 32–34, 99–100; Laura Levine, *Men in Women's Clothing: Anti-theatricality and Effeminization, 1579–1642* (Cambridge: Cambridge University Press, 1994), 22.

5. Bourdieu, *Distinction,* 374–84.

6. In the Stationers' Register on June 1, 1599, the following were identified for burning: Hall's *Satires,* Marston's *Pygmalion* and *The Scourge of Villainy,* Guilpin's *Skialetheia,* T.M.'s *Snarling Satires,* Cutwode's *Caltha Poetarum,* the book containing Davies' *Epigrams* and Marlowe's *Elegies, Of Marriage and Wyving, The 15 Joyes of Marriage,* and all the works of Nash and Harvey. On June 4 *Caltha Poetarum* and Hall's *Satires* were "staid" and "WILLOBIES *Adviso*" was added to the list (*A Transcript of the Registers of the Company of Stationers of London: 1554–1640,* ed. Edward Arber, 5 vols. [London: Privately printed, 1876], vol. 3, 677–78).

7. Richard McCabe, "Elizabethan Satire and the Bishop's Ban of 1599," *Yearbook of English Studies* 11 (1981): 189.

8. Arthur Acheson first proposed Matthew Roydon as the author (*Shakespeare's Sonnet Story* [1922; reprint, London: Haskell House, 1971]). G. B. Harrison adds further evidence supporting the claim in *Willobie, His Avisa* (1924; reprint, New York: Barnes and Noble, 1966), 225–28. As will become apparent, I do not think Roydon would have written such a poem.

9. For a sense of how sensitive the authorities were to social disrespect, see Susan Dwyer Amussen, *An Ordered Society: Gender and Class in Early Modern England* (Oxford: Blackwell, 1988). "The most threatening refusal of deference was the claim to judge the social order, which included an implicit claim of equality" (147).

10. "Penelope clara est, veneranda fidelis: Avisa / obscura, obscuro fœmina nata loco. / Penelope satrapæ est conjux illustris: Avisa / conjux cauponis, filia pandochei" (Peter Colse, *Penelope's Complaint: or A Mirrour for wanton Minions* [London: H. Jackson, 1596], sig. A4).

11. The passages I have referred to are all quoted by Harrison in appendix 1 of his edition. Perhaps because he wants to see *Avisa* as the manifesto of an aristocratic faction, Harrison makes little of the sense of class anger in Colse.

12. Quotations from *Willobie, His Avisa* are from B. N. de Luna's edition in *The Queen Declined: An Interpretation of Willobie His Avisa, with the Text of the Original Edition* (Oxford: Clarendon Press, 1970). The lines of the poem are not numbered, so I have had to cite by page number. Harrison posits two editions (the second and third) of which we have no copies or explicit record. The poem is signed by Henry Willobie's supposed brother, Thomas. The mechanisms of anonymity are pretty hackneyed. Hadrian Dorrell claims that *Avisa* is a thirty-five-year-old poem that he found, and now, when we might ask what the author intended, he reveals that the author is dead.

13. Guillory, *Cultural Capital,* 3–38.

14. The poem's relation to Shakespeare is more intricate than I can develop here. In a recent essay John Roe has made the argument that "When as thine eye hath chose the dame," poem 18 in *The Passionate Pilgrim,* is a parody response to canto 47 of *Avisa* (John Roe, "*Willobie His Avisa* and *The Passionate Pilgrim:* Precedence, Parody, and Development," *Yearbook of English Studies* 23 [1993]: 111–25). I would argue that in treating the verses in which Willobie refers to Shakespeare as "a fulsome compliment" (111) Roe has initially misinterpreted *Avisa's* relation to *Lucrece.* Furthermore, because he misses the social issue in these poems, Roe sees them only in terms of how one woos a reluctant woman.

15. For the tradition of this line of thought, see Stephanie H. Jed, *Chaste Thinking: The Rape of Lucretia and the Birth of Humanism* (Bloomington: Indiana University Press, 1989), 39–50; Carolyn D. Williams. "'Silence, like a Lucrece Knife': Shakespeare and the Meanings of Rape," *Yearbook of English Studies* 23 (1993): 94. As the experience of the rape victims in the Bosnian war reminds us, this archaic sense of the rape victim's pollution lives on. In Shakespeare's poem, we should note, Lucrece sees herself as irreparably sullied.

16. Coppélia Kahn, "The Rape in Shakespeare's 'Lucrece,'" *Shakespeare Studies* 9 (1976): 45–72; Philippa Berry, "Woman, Language, and History in *The Rape of Lucrece,*" *Shakespeare Survey* 44 (1992): 34.

17. Joyce Green MacDonald notes that "social rank was a significant indicator of an individual woman's relative ability to subvene the gendered rule of silence" ("Speech, Silence, and History in *The Rape of Lucrece,*" *Shakespeare Studies* 22 (1994): 84.

18. The other time the threat is voiced the phrase is "some worthless slave of thine" (515).

19. William Shakespeare, *The Poems,* ed. F. T. Prince (London: Routledge, 1988), note to line 1334.

20. One other character of humble origin figures in the poem. Lucrece's maid is immediately in sympathy with the raped Lucrece even though she has no idea what precisely has happened. The women's weeping leads to a meditation on female mentality (1233–60).

When the maid cautiously seeks to know the reason for her mistress's "heaviness" ("But lady, if your maid may be so bold" [1282]), she is abruptly dismissed by Lucrece.

21. Kahn, "Rape in Shakespeare's 'Lucrece,'" 55; Katherine Eisaman Maus, "Taking Tropes Seriously: Language and Violence in Shakespeare's *Rape of Lucrece*," *Shakespeare Quarterly* 37 (1986): 73; Jane O. Newman, "'And Let Mild Women to Him Lose Their Mildness': Philomela, Female Violence, and Shakespeare's *The Rape of Lucrece*," *Shakespeare Quarterly* 45 (1994), 324. Newman makes a complicated case that hidden in the reference to Philomel as speechless victim is a darker "tradition of violent women" (326).

22. It is precisely this double quality of suicide that Othello emphasizes when he makes himself both the heroic soldier and "a malignant and a turbaned Turk." Coppélia Kahn quotes Antony, "A Roman by a Roman valiantly vanquished" ("*Lucrece:* The Sexual Politics of Subjectivity," in *Rape and Representation,* ed. Lynn A. Higgins and Brenda R. Silver [New York: Columbia University Press, 1991], 156).

23. Just as Brutus's suicide in *Julius Caesar* testifies to his integrity, or as Cleopatra's and Antony's suicides dignify them despite their self-indulgence.

24. Recent criticism of *Lucrece* makes much of Augustine's argument that by her suicide Lucrece herself committed a crime. I find little evidence for this line of argument in *Avisa,* and it is striking that suicide never enters Avisa's moral consideration.

25. Heather Dubrow, "A Mirror for Complaints: Shakespeare's *Lucrece* and Generic Tradition," in *Renaissance Genres: Essays on Theory, History, and Interpretation,* ed. Barbara Lewalski (Cambridge: Harvard University Press, 1986), 406; C. Williams, "'Silence, like a Lucrece Knife,'" 95.

26. De Luna reads this as Thomas Seymour, who sought to marry Elizabeth before she became queen (*Queen Declined,* 47–54). De Luna does not mention or account for the audacious (and one would think rather dangerous if it is the queen who is thus being spoken of) claims and insults of the nobleman.

27. This is a complex social and psychological strategy of dominated social space. It offers another instance of what Pierre Bourdieu describes as the "choice of the necessary" and "not for us" (*Distinction,* 272–96).

28. Such a gesture is fitting for the aristocratic sense of middle-class comedy. For instance, the practical economics of specific numbers occurs in *The Merry Wives of Windsor,* 1.1.43–60. One would not find such calculations in *Lucrece.* It is, I am arguing, a sign of *Avisa*'s commoner's sensibility that specific numbers can be discussed in what is clearly not a comic poem.

29. This is not the first time Avisa has sounded like Ralegh's Nymph's reply. See *Avisa,* 138.

30. Harrison's identifying the author of *Avisa* as Matthew Roydon seems to me to become completely implausible at this point, for by all evidence we have Roydon represents an idea of high culture, not this Christian suspicion.

31. Sir Philip Sidney, *An Apology for Poetry,* ed. Forrest G. Robinson (Indianapolis: Library of the Liberal Arts, 1970), 21. Dubrow notes that *Lucrece* is exceptional among the complaints of the period for the complexity of its depiction of virtue: *Lucrece,* she argues,

"teaches us above all . . . the danger of the simplified values promoted in other works in its genre" ("Mirror for Complaints," 407). This complexity, which makes Shakespeare's poem attractive to some modern readers, would be precisely the quality that would offend Willobie.

32. *Campion's Works,* ed. Percival Vivian (Oxford: Clarendon Press, 1909), 239 (no. 17, "In Barnum"), 46 (epigram no. R8). More than a decade after these gibes, however, Barnes can proudly place epigrams from Campion in the frontmatter of his *Four Bookes of Offices* (1606). These later poems praise him for being "Vertuous, and honest": "Here is the Scoole of *Temperance,* and *Wit,* / Of *Justice,* and all formes that tend to it; / Here *Fortitude* doth teach to live and die, / Then, Reader, love this Booke, or rather buy" (*Campion's Works,* 352). Campion seems ready to praise the cleric Barnes who has given up amorous sonneteering, though there is room for irony even here.

33. *The Letters and Epigrams of Sir John Harington, Together with The Prayse of Private Life,* ed. Norman Egbert McClure (Philadelphia: University of Pennsylvania Press, 1930), 173.

34. Thomas Nash, *Have With You to Saffron-walden,* (London: J. Danter, 1596), 89.

35. There is remarkably little modern criticism of Barnes. The major recent work, aside from Doyno's edition, is Thomas Roche's chapter in *Petrarch and the English Sonnet Sequences* (New York: AMS Press, 1989), 244–71. In an attempt to make moral sense of Barnes's leering, Roche reads the poems ironically, as cautionary anti-poems. I do not find this a plausible approach. The arguments I bring against the moralist reading of Chapman's "Ovids Banquet of Sense" later would apply to such a reading of Barnes.

36. Gabriel Harvey, *Foure Letters, and certaine sonnets especially touching R. Greene* (London: John Wolfe, 1592), 192.

37. Gabriel Harvey, *Pierces Supererogation, or a new prayse of the old asse* (London: John Wolfe, 1593), 187. While he may at one time have admired Marlowe's "Highest minde," by late 1593, after Marlowe's death, Harvey tended to treat Marlowe as an atheist who got his due. See Virginia F. Stern, *Gabriel Harvey: A Study of His Life, Marginalia, and Library* (Oxford: Clarendon Press, 1979), 117–18.

38. Harvey, *Pierces Supererogation,* 164, 204–5, 212.

39. Nash seized on this passage to attack both Barnes and Harvey (see *Have With You to Saffron-walden,* [Q2v–Q3]), but we need to be skeptical of Nash's version of Barnes: I cannot imagine Harvey praising Barnes's French service if it were in the least bit as embarrassing as Nash describes it. And certainly, admiring as this is, it does not place Barnes above Spenser.

40. By exchanging compliments with Barnes in the same book, Harvey is clearly here trying to repeat the success of the earlier exchanges between himself and Spenser. To create the illusion that the reader is overhearing great men's flattering small talk, Harvey and his allies pat each others' backs. It is an awkward fiction that Nash turned to his own advantage.

41. Clark Hulse, *Metamorphic Verse: The Elizabethan Minor Epic* (Princeton: Princeton University Press, 1981), 269–70. Hulse's main emphasis is on the *Metamorphoses* rather

than the *Amores*. In his modern edition of *Parthenophil and Parthenophe,* Victor Doyno carefully annotates Barnes's debt to Ovid and to the *Anacreontea* (Barnabe Barnes, *Parthenophil and Parthenophe,* ed. Victor A. Doyno [Carbondale: Southern Illinois University Press, 1971], xxx–xlii). All quotations from *Parthenophil and Parthenophe* are from this edition.

42. Jonathan Bate, *Shakespeare and Ovid* (Oxford: Clarendon Press, 1993), 46.

43. *Amores* 1.4 serves as the basis for the Malbecco, Paridell, Helinore episode.

44. G. K. Hunter, *John Lyly,* 31.

45. Doyno discusses this in his introduction, li–lii. See Barnes's sonnet 48.

46. Nash, too, finds it safe to assume a strong moral position as a hedge against the risk of his more daring literary plunge. *Christ's Tears Over Jerusalem* represents his version of Barnes's spiritual sonnets. Charles Nicholl sees *Christ's Tears* as a sign of a nervous breakdown (*A Cup of News: The Life of Thomas Nashe* [London: Routledge and Kegan Paul, 1984], 169).

Chapter 2: "Midas Brood Shall Sit in Honor's Chaire"

1. Elsewhere Bourdieu notes that the social dynamic as rendered in subtle plays of connotation is often lost to scholars. "Ignorance of everything which goes to make up the 'mood of the age' produces a derealization of works: stripped of everything which attached them to the most concrete debates of their time (I am thinking in particular of the connotations of words), they are impoverished and transformed in the direction of intellectualism or an empty humanism" ("Field of Cultural Production," 32).

2. The satire has been recently edited in Richard Corballis, *George Chapman's Minor Translations: A Critical Edition of His Renderings of Musaeus, Hesiod and Juvenal* (Salzburg: Institut für Anglistik und Amerikanistic, 1984). Corballis notes local departures from Juvenal's text, some of them mistranslations (e.g., 15–16, 90), others elaborations of the sort Chapman defends in his prefatory epistle "To the Reader." "Smell-feast" is not Chapman's coinage; Hall uses the term in *Virgidemiarum* 6.1.47, as does Davies in epigram 40.

3. In "To Penshurst" Jonson makes it a virtue of the Sidneys that the distinctions Juvenal complains of do not occur at the lord's table at Penshurst, "Where comes no guest but is allowed to eat, / Without his fear, and of thy lord's own meat; / Where the same beer and bread, and selfsame wine, / That is his lordship's shall be also mine, / And I not fain to sit (as some this day / At great men's tables), and yet dine away. / Here no man tells my cups; nor, standing by, / A waiter doth my gluttony envy" (61–68); *The Complete Poetry of Ben Jonson,* ed. William B. Hunter (New York: Norton, 1968), 80. All quotations of Jonson's poetry are from this edition. We do not know when Chapman performed his translation, but at the end of his life he was angry at Jonson and in his papers was found an "Invective" against Jonson. It is possible that he chose to translate Juvenal's Fifth Satire as a response to "Penshurst."

4. Eccles, "Chapman's Early Years," 176.

5. Roydon, too, had problems of debt, and was at times entangled with people in league

with the Wolfalls. See G. C. Moore Smith, "Matthew Roydon," *Modern Language Review* 10 (1909): 97–98; and Eccles, "Chapman's Early Years," 187.

6. Chapman, *Poems,* 19.

7. Ibid., 49.

8. Thomas Lodge, *A Fig for Momus* (London: Clement Knight, 1595), [C4]–D2. For these identifications, see Eliane Cuvelier, *Thomas Lodge: Témoin de son temps (c. 1558–1625)* (Paris: Didier Erudition, 1984), 111. For drawing my attention to Lodge's reference to Roydon, I am indebted to a note in Braunmuller's *Seventeenth Century Letter-Book,* 423–24.

9. This passage echoes Chapman's language (especially in the phrases "with-drawne to studie" and "earthlie thoughts," and in the anger at how "ignorance" interprets). To a remarkable extent, however, this passage seems to anticipate a majestic passage in Chapman's 1598 poem to M. Harriot before *Achilles Shield* (*Poems,* 381, lines 15–30), discussed below.

10. Spenser had anticipated some of this in the tenth eclogue of *The Shepheardes Calender,* but though he laments the absence of a Maecenas, he does not enter into the kind of economic analysis of patronage that distinguishes Lodge's poem. Toward the end of Spenser's eclogue, the issue shifts from patronage to love (which is praised by Piers and criticized by Cuddy), and at the poem's close, inspiration seems to replace patronage as the source of verse. Spenser's poem is discussed further in chap. 5, below.

11. The final phrase, "my muse shall flie the light," may, however, suggest something other than retirement. It could say that he will change his style and instead of writing a clear verse designed to please the patrons who have so disappointed him, he will write a "dark" verse which abjures the game of patronage altogether.

12. *The Complete Works of Thomas Watson (1556–1592),* ed. Dana F. Sutton, 2 vols. (Lewiston: Edwin Mellen Press, 1996), vol. 1, 152.

13. See Nash's preface to Robert Greene's *Menaphon* in *The Life and Complete Works in Prose and Verse of Robert Greene,* ed. Alexander B. Grosart, 15 vols. (London, 1881–86), vol. 2, 26. In 1598 Meres can include Roydon in a list of minor English poets who parallel the great Italian poets. "As Italy had *Dante, Boccace, Petrarch, Tasso, Celiano* and *Ariosto:* so England had *Matthew Roydon, Thomas Atchelow, Thomas Watson, Thomas Kid, Robert Greene* & *George Peele*" (*Palladis Tamia,* 282v).

14. Thomas Kyd in his forced confession to the Lord Keeper just before Marlowe's death links Roydon with Marlowe, Harriot, and Warner, and at the end reports that Marlowe intended to go to the king of Scots, "whether I heare Royden is gon." Quoted in *Marlowe: The Critical Heritage, 1588–1896,* ed. Millar MacLure (London: Routledge and Kegan Paul, 1979), 32–36.

15. Chapman may have this line in mind when he mocks those who "quemishlie commend [poetry] for a pretie toy" (*Poems,* 19).

16. Quotations from Marlowe's works, except *Doctor Faustus,* are from *The Works of Christopher Marlowe,* ed. C. F. Tucker Brooke (Oxford: Clarendon Press, 1910).

17. The social resentment I am emphasizing can be seen as a dimension of what Leah Marcus calls "the Marlowe effect," a mark of sensationalism that both markets and gives coherence to the plays ("Textual Indeterminacy and Ideological Difference: The Case of

Doctor Faustus," first published in *Renaissance Drama* 20 [1989], 1–29, and reprinted in *Critical Essays on Chistopher Marlowe,* ed. Emily C. Bartels [New York: G. K. Hall, 1997], 15–38). Marlowe's impoverished origins have never been hidden, but the modern interest in Marlowe as represented in Bartel's useful anthology tends to look elsewhere and emphasize his religious, political, racial, and sexual outrageousness.

18. In his introduction to a facsimile edition of Marlowe's part of *Hero and Leander,* Louis Martz, arguing for the completeness of the fragment, emphasizes the importance of the Mercury myth to the poem. It establishes "a universe where everyone from Jove and the Fates to the country maid and the poor scholar have their lives ruled by the effects of love," thereby providing "the pivot upon which the lovers turn from the social world of ceremonies and conventions to create their private world of 'unknowne joy.'" Martz, however, discounts these final lines as "a querulous digression that provides a bathetic conclusion to the Mercury episode" (*Hero and Leander: Facsimile*). A more recent critic, W. L. Gotshalk, has found the digression on Mercury and the Fates inept and the ground for a reading of the poem's narrator as untrustworthy ("*Hero and Leander:* The Sense of an Ending," in *A Poet and a Filthy Play-maker: New Essays on Christopher Marlowe,* ed. Kenneth Friedenreich, Roma Gill, and Constance B. Kuriyama [New York: AMS Press, 1988], 308).

19. Quotations from *Faustus* are from *Marlowe's Doctor Faustus, 1604–1616,* ed. W. W. Greg (Oxford: Clarendon Press, 1950).

20. Annabel Patterson argues that just this kind of deniability occurs in Jonson's *Sejanus* a decade or so later (*Censorship and Interpretation,* 65).

21. Patrick Cheney quotes these lines as if they were the voice of Marlowe himself (*Marlowe's Counterfeit Profession: Ovid, Spenser, Counter-Nationhood* [Toronto: University of Toronto Press, 1997], 21).

22. Cf. the discussion in *Tamburlaine,* part 1, on whether or not to become kings, beginning with the famous lines, "Is it not passing brave to be a King / And ride in triumph through *Persepolis?*" (758–59). Theridimas, when asked if he wants to be a king, can say "though I praise it, I can live without it" (771).

23. Joseph Hall, *Virgidemiarum,* 1.3.11–12. Arnold Davenport, Hall's modern editor, notes that "Hall is here contrasting the orthodox neo-classical theory of the tragic hero . . . and Marlowe's tendency to choose commoners and upstarts as his heroes" (*Poems of Joseph Hall,* ed. A. Davenport [Liverpool: Liverpool University Press, 1949], 165). Hall might also have been offended by *Edward II* and shared the anger of that play's nobility at Gaveston's presumptuous rise. For the argument that it is Gaveston's preferment more than his sexuality that offends, see Stephen Orgel, "Nobody's Perfect: Or Why Did the English Stage Take Boys for Women?" *South Atlantic Quarterly* 88 (1989): 25.

24. Faustus's confusion is a recurrent concern for critics. The Christian readings attribute the confusion to Faustus's lack of faith. "The questions [Faustus] asks can be poignant or ludicrous; in either case they reveal an aspiration stunted by the narrow scope of a mind that will not climb after knowledge infinite" (Lawrence Danson, "Christopher Marlowe: The Questioner," *English Literary Renaissance* 12 [1982], 27). I find more congruent with my social reading the psychological reading of Edgar A. Snow, "Marlowe's *Doctor Faus-*

tus and the Ends of Desire," in *Two Renaissance Mythmakers: Christopher Marlowe and Ben Jonson,* ed. Alvin Kernan (Baltimore: Johns Hopkins University Press, 1977), 70–110. "Every time the drama raises the issue of what Faustus wants, it does so in a way that subtly deflects attention away from the ostensible objects of his desire toward the ontological ambiguities at its origin" (70).

25. This is a commonplace in Bourdieu: "The field of power is organized according to a *chiasmatic structure.* The distribution according to the dominant principle of hierarchization—economic capital—is, as it were, 'intersected' by the distribution based on a second principle of hierarchization—cultural capital—in which the different fields line up according to an inverse hierarchy, that is, from the artistic field to the economic field" (Pierre Bourdieu, *The State Nobility: Elite Schools in the Field of Power,* trans. Lauretta C. Clough [Stanford: Stanford University Press, 1996], 270).

26. Chapman, "Hymnus in Noctem," 119–20 (*Poems,* 22).

27. *The Three Parnassus Plays (1598–1601),* ed. J. B. Leishman (London: Ivor Nicholson and Watson, 1949).

28. Just as Marlowe's complain about gold and boors can offend Martz, the Parnassus trilogy's sympathy with impoverished art can be dismissed by recent critics as "self defeating" (Paula Glatzer, *The Complaint of the Poet: The Parnassas Plays* [Salzburg: Institut für Englische Sprache and Literatur, 1977], 16).

29. In sonnet 74 of *Astrophel and Stella* Sidney pointedly confesses he "never drank of Aganippe Well." See the discussion of furor in chap. 5, below.

30. Fritz Caspari, *Humanism and the Social Order in Tudor England* (Chicago: University of Chicago Press, 1954), 141.

31. Arber quotes Hazlitt in 1820, "It contains . . . the earliest denunciation (I know of) of the miseries and unprofitableness of a scholar's life" (*The Returne from Pernassus: Or The Scourge of Simony. The English Scholar's Library of Old and Modern Works,* no. 6, ed. Edward Arber [London: Unwin Bros., 1879], xvi).

32. For our present purposes the issue of whether Marlowe considered *Hero and Leander* complete is irrelevant: the text as Marlowe left it gave Chapman his opening. For the argument for Marlowe's part as complete, see Martz's edition cited above (intro., n. 18) and Marion Campbell, "'Desunt Nonnulla': The Construction of Marlowe's *Hero and Leander* as an Unfinished Poem," *ELH* 51 (1984): 241–68.

33. The text has "Nobles," but I agree with Stephen Orgel's reading of this as "Noblesse" (*Christopher Marlowe: The Complete Poems and Translations,* ed. Stephen Orgel [Harmondsworth: Penguin Books, 1971], 42).

34. D. J. Gordon, "The Renaissance Poet as Classicist: Chapman's *Hero and Leander,*" in Gordon, *The Renaissance Imagination: Essays and Lectures,* ed. Stephen Orgel (Berkeley: University of California Press, 1975), 102–33.

35. In "The Serious Trifle: Aphorisms in Chapman's *Hero and Leander,*" *Studies in the Literary Imagination* 9 (1978): 111, I read this simile as a meditation on the need to "feede on men" and to burn torches in order to realize their virtues. This is also an important theme, but in the present argument it is not relevant.

36. I omit here seven and a half lines comparing the gallant to a ship tacking down the Thames.

37. In the introductory letter to Roydon before *The Shadow of Night* (Chapman, *Poems*, 19, lines 11–12).

38. Ibid., 381–84.

39. The reference here is to the Platonic doctrine of remembrance, which occurs frequently in Chapman's early work.

40. We have seen it before in the phrase "absolute Poems" in Chapman's epistle to Roydon before "Ovids Banquet of Sence" (*Poems*, 49).

41. "He [i.e., Marlowe] affirmeth that Moyses was but a Jugler, & that one Heriots being Sir W Raleighs man Can do more than he" (*Marlowe: Critical Heritage*, 36–37).

Chapter 3: Virtue and the Critique of Nobility

1. Chapman, *Poems*, 85.

2. To be accurate, I should observe that, as Bartlett's note reminds us, Arthur Acheson found in these lines evidence of Chapman's envy of Shakespeare's coat of arms (*Shakespeare's Sonnet Story*, 227).

3. Albert Rabil, ed., *Knowledge, Goodness, and Power: The Debate over Nobility among Quattrocento Italian Humanists* (Binghamton: Medieval and Renaissance Texts and Studies, 1991), 41.

4. Charles Trinkaus, *Adversity's Noblemen: The Italian Humanists on Happiness* (1940; reprint, New York: Octagon Books, 1965), x. We know of at least twelve treatises on nobility written in Italy in the fifteenth century, though only three (by Buonaccorso da Montemagno, Poggio Bracciolini, and Bartolomeo Sacchi) were printed, and of these, only Buonaccorso's *Disputatio de nobilitate* was translated into English (to be printed by Caxton in 1481) (Rabil, *Knowledge, Goodness, and Power*, 2, 30–31). Trinkaus's argument that these humanists were motivated by a social insecurity seems plausible despite Lauro Martines's demonstration (*The Social World of the Florentine Humanists, 1390–1460* [Princeton: Princeton University Press, 1963]) that they were all economically secure. See also Paul F. Grendler, *Schooling in Renaissance Italy: Literacy and Learning, 1300–1600* (Baltimore: Johns Hopkins University Press, 1989), and Anthony Grafton and Lisa Jardine, *From Humanism to the Humanities: Education and the Liberal Arts in Fifteenth- and Sixteenth-Century Europe* (London: Duckworth, 1986). The economic and social situation of Chapman more than a century later is significantly different from that of the Italian humanists, and that difference changes the implications of the arguments about nobility.

5. Lawrence Humphrey, *The Nobles, or of Nobilitye* (London: Thomas Marshe, 1563).

6. Annibale Romei, *The Courtier's Academy*, trans. John Kepers (London: V. Sims, 1598), 187.

7. John Ferne, *The Blazon of Gentrie* (London: John Windet, 1586), 9.

8. See Frank Whigham, "Tropes of Personal Rivalry," *Ambition and Privilege*, 137–84.

9. "Solum sapientem esse divitem" is the sixth of the *Paradoxa stoicorum*, in *Cicero*, vol.

4, trans. H. Rackham (Cambridge: Harvard University Press, 1942), 294–303. The claim "that only the wise man is rich" is central to stoicism, but it also has a Platonic tradition. See Socrates' prayer at the end of the *Phaedrus* 279C.

10. "[W]here virtue is in a gentleman it is commonly mixed with more sufferance, more affability, and mildness, than for the more part it is in a person rural or of a very base lineage" (Sir Thomas Elyot, *The Book named The Governor,* ed. S. E. Lehmberg [New York: Dutton, 1962], 14).

11. Quentin Skinner, *The Foundations of Modern Political Thought,* vol. 1: *The Renaissance* (Cambridge: Cambridge University Press, 1978), 238–39. Whigham analyzes the rhetorical techniques by which this identity of virtue and rank is promoted in the sixteenth century in his chapter "Tropes of Social Hierarchy" in *Ambition and Privilege* (63–87).

12. The great exception to this generalization is Thomas More's *Utopia,* but for a number of reasons we can see that the exception makes sense. First of all, though he is not an aristocrat, More is not in the usual sense dependent on patronage. Of course, insofar as all citizens and civil servants depend on the king, he must be careful not to offend. But since the king may take some pleasure in seeing the nobility criticized, More is in a good position to perform a modest analysis and critique of the system. Second, *Utopia's* critique appears in an explicitly paradoxical and ambiguous fiction, so that More can always claim that the joke is aimed against the very position set forth. Third, as Skinner argues, More's criticism of degree is motivated by the logic of a justice that is critical of humanists with their "comfortable social philosophy" of degree (Skinner, *Renaissance,* 259).

13. Jones's translation appeared in print three years after Marlowe's death. The translation may have circulated earlier, or in England *Nennio* may well have been read in Italian or perhaps even French. Chapman's commendatory sonnet seems aware of a French edition (*Poems,* 353).

14. *Nennio* has been reprinted in a facsimile edition, edited with an introduction by Alice Shalvi (*Nennio, or, A treatise of nobility* [Jerusalem: Israel Universities Press, 1967]). The four commendatory sonnets were clearly a late addition in the printing of the volume. The two pages fall between sigs. A4 and B1. In the 1595 *Nennio,* the commendatory poems are in a larger font than the rest of the text, and the printing is inferior. Alice Shalvi notes in her introduction to the facsimile edition that the dedicatory poems are not included in the 1600 reprint of Jones's translation (xiv).

Because the pages of the Jones translation of *Nennio* are numbered consecutively on the recto sheet only and because there are numerous errors in pagination, I have found it simplest to identify pages by signatures.

Of Chapman scholars, only Bartlett, in her notes to Chapman's complimentary sonnet (*Poems,* 467), and A. R. Braunmuller (*Natural Fictions: George Chapman's Major Tragedies* [Newark: University of Delaware Press, 1992], 42], have paid this book any attention. Bartlett does not observe that Spenser, Daniel, and Day also wrote poems for the edition. Braunmuller focuses on a moment when the virtues of the active and of the contemplative life are debated.

15. Shalvi reads *Nennio* as an unremarkable instance of a generic convention: "Nenna's work is noteworthy not for its originality but rather for the way it summarises the arguments of both sides in the debate on honor" (*Nennio*, x). Skinner, on the contrary, reads the book as an exceptional and radical critique of inherited nobility (*Renaissance*, 237). I clearly disagree with Shalvi about what makes *Nennio* noteworthy, but I would consider her sense of the book's conventionality an important testament to its success in obscuring its critique. Michael McCanles suggests a reading of *Nennio* congruent with mine: the proposition that "those who possess true nobility are aristocrats" "makes explicit the position that writers like Jonson were always skirting but could never allow themselves to venture into overtly" (*Jonsonian Discriminations: The Humanist Poet and the Praise of True Nobility* [Toronto: University of Toronto Press, 1992], 54). This seems to me true of Jonson; Chapman takes greater risks.

16. Nenna of Bari, *Il Nennio, Nel Quale Si Ragiona di Nobilita* (n.p., 1542). Shalvi, in her apparatus for the facsimile edition of Jones's translation, has some observations on the relation of the original to the translation. She includes her own translation of Nenna's original dedicatory preface (*Nennio*, xvii–xix).

17. It is very unclear from these descriptions what is the actual social rank and background of either disputant. How noble is Possidonio? How common Fabricio? Such ambiguity seems crucial to a text that wants to raise serious questions about rank.

18. This kind of ambiguity is difficult to identify or prove, and it has not been much studied. For an important beginning, see Annabel Patterson's *Censorship and Interpretation*.

19. Virginia Cox, in *The Renaissance Dialogue: Literary Dialogue in its Social and Political Contexts, Castiglione to Galileo* (Cambridge: Cambridge University Press, 1992), does not analyze *Nennio*, and it is unclear to me where it would fit in her generic scheme. It gestures toward both the "dialogic" models of the beginning of the sixteenth century and the more authoritarian ones of the end of the century. The expressive use of unauthorized voices, unacknowledged contradiction, and unresolved lines of thought makes *Nennio* resemble Cox's reading of *The Courtier*. See her chap. 5: "Castiglione's *Cortegiano:* The Dialogue as a Drama of Doubt."

20. See Richard Strier's analysis of the dilemma of obedience in "Faithful Servants: Shakespeare's Praise of Disobedience," in *The Historical Renaissance: New Essays on Tudor and Stuart Literature and Culture,* ed. Heather Dubrow and Richard Strier (Chicago: University of Chicago Press, 1988), 104–33.

21. Nobles, members of the titled peerage, constitute a distinct group in the sixteenth century, but the term *nobility* has some ambiguity. See Sharpe, *Early Modern England,* 152–53. The distinction between the nobility and the gentry was in danger of being blurred by the increased number of knights, though *Nennio* is published before the inflation caused by Essex's Irish expedition and James I's creation of Scottish knights. See G. E. Mingay, *The Gentry: The Rise and Fall of a Ruling Class* (New York: Longman, 1976), 4–5; Youings, *Sixteenth-Century England,* 113–15; Lawrence Stone, "The Anatomy of the Elizabethan Aristocracy," *Economic Review* 28 (1948): 1–41.

22. Jones's translation is quite literal, and generally he uses the obvious English equivalents of the Italian. See Shalvi's introduction (*Nennio*, xii). In these particular instances where the Italian uses *nobile* the English uses *noble*.

23. A version of this argument that since we are all descended from Adam, nobility is not inherent in God's scheme or in the blood appears in earlier treatises. For example, in Poggio Bracciolini, "If nobility is conferred by a long line of ancestors, all are equally nobles, inasmuch as the origin of every person goes back equally far" (Rabil, *Knowledge, Goodness, and Power,* 73). Bracciolini uses this argument to deny blood as the sole determinant of nobility, but he leaves it ambiguous how much genealogy may enrich nobility. Rabil sees here an allusion to Dante, *Convivio* 4. Behind this argument lies the folk wisdom embodied in the distich: "When Adam delved and Eve span, Who was then the gentleman?" The Gravedigger in *Hamlet* plays on this difficulty when, to the question of whether Adam was a gentleman, he responds, "A was the first that ever bore arms" (5.1.27).

24. A more blatant insult to the nobility is made by a secondary character who jokes that the ugliness and deformity of the nobility prove that they are related to the earliest creation; more beautiful, ignoble people were produced later by a more practiced nature (*Nennio*, F4v–G1).

25. The potential for such an anthropology also appears in Bracciolini (Rabil, *Knowledge, Goodness, and Power,* 68–69).

26. Fabricio has casually but explicitly rejected this whole line of argument. He concedes that "whosoever is descended of Noble bloud, wee call him a Noble man; but generallie I denie this to containe a trueth. . . . The bad custome of men, therein is much to be blamed" (*Nennio*, K1–K1v).

27. It is strange for Nennio to invoke Gismond at the end, for just a few pages earlier John Francisco had recalled that Gismond, when asked to confer nobility on a non-noble, declared "I may make thee free and rich, but noble I cannot make thee; as being a gift not under his commaund, but in the power of nature" (*Nennio*, Bb3v). Nennio clarifies this claim by saying Gismond meant he could not make a man virtuous, for of course, so Nennio argues, any ruler can confer other kinds of nobility.

28. The practice I am here describing resembles rather closely one aspect of "signifyin(g)" in African American culture which uses "antiphonal structures to reverse their apparent meaning, as a mode of encoding for self-preservation" (Henry Louis Gates, *The Signifying Monkey: A Theory of African-American Literary Criticism* [Oxford: Oxford University Press, 1988], 67).

I would distinguish this practice from the method of reading frequently invoked by analysts of contemporary popular culture, whereby the audience, by a process Michel de Certeau calls "poaching," reads its own meaning into a hegemonic text. See Michel de Certeau, *The Practice of Everyday Life,* trans. Stephen F. Rendall (Berkeley: University of California Press, 1984), and John Fiske, *Understanding Popular Culture* (Boston: Unwin Hyman, 1989). Gates and I are describing a very different kind of coding operation whereby meanings are consciously expressed (in whatever disguised form) by the sender, not manufactured by the receiver.

Greenblatt's reading of Holbein's *The Ambassadors* is not unlike the procedure of selecting a special angle of vision I am arguing *Nennio* demands: "we must throw the entire painting out of perspective [i.e., both view it from the side and magnify details] in order to bring into perspective what our usual mode of perception [i.e., a conventional reading] cannot comprehend" (*Renaissance Self-Fashioning*, 19).

29. One of the alternate voices that must be mentioned is an explicitly feminist one that speaks strongly at the beginning of *Nennio*. A woman with the suggestive name of Cassandra, arguing against Possidonio's claim that nobility descends from the father rather than the mother, concludes with the passionate assertion: "But you men make laws as you list, & draw your reaso[n]s as liketh you best, setting us silly women aside, as if we were none of the number of the world: but if it were lawfull for us to be present at your counsels, peradventure matters would go otherwise, and so many things would not passe for currant . . . as they do" (C3v). As in the case of Fabricio's arguments, this one is never adequately put to rest.

30. For Daniel's enthusiasm for Essex, see Richard McCoy, *The Rites of Knighthood: The Literature and Politics of Elizabethan Chivalry* (Berkeley: University of California Press, 1989), 103ff.

31. Inserted after A4, lines 10–14. The poems by Spenser and Chapman are also quoted from these two sheets inserted after A4.

32. See Frances A. Yates, *John Florio: The Life of an Italian in Shakespeare's England* (Cambridge: Cambridge University Press, 1934), 50.

33. "Sir Phillip Sidney, his honorable life, his valiant death, and true vertues," in *Elegies for Sir Philip Sidney (1587)*, introduction by A. J. Colaianne and W. L. Godshalk (Delman, N.Y.: Scholars Facsimiles and Reprints, 1980), sig. B2.

34. For Roydon, see chaps. 4 and 5, below.

35. *Chapman's Homer*, 2 vol., ed. Allardyce Nicoll (New York: Bollingen Foundation, 1956) vol. 1, 503, 547. Despite the insistence on the term in the prefatory matter, Chapman's early Homeric translations are noticeably silent about "virtue," neither using the word nor praising a warrior; there is therefore a certain enigma in the phrase "Achilleian vertue."

36. Simone Weil, *The Iliad; or, The Poem of Force*, trans. Mary McCarthy (Wallingford, Pa.: Pendle Hill, 1956).

37. See especially Richard Ide's discussion in *Possessed with Greatness*, 21–33, 75–79.

38. *Seaven Bookes of the Iliades*, in *Chapman's Homer*, vol. 1, 511 (line 71). In his revision of the translation of book 1, published in 1611, Chapman turns the phrase "prophetic force" to "prophetic rage." See *Iliad 1*, line 66, in *Chapman's Homer*, vol. 1, 25. See the discussion of furor below for the significance of such rage.

39. My reading of Achilles here is much indebted to Richard Ide's interpretation of this moment "as a conflict between a just, independent spirit and a lustful, covetous tyrant" (*Possessed with Greatness*, 26). I differ with Ide in that I see the dedication to Essex as important as an instance of a broad social dynamic implicit in Nennian values and not as a sign of Chapman's soon-to-be-disappointed enthusiasm for Essex himself. See ibid., 75–76, for this argument.

40. Spondanus notes in his commentary that in Homer the argument takes two forms, whose difference Chapman heightens so as to emphasize the earned basis of social benefits. See Spondanus's translation of *Iliad 12* in *Homeri Quae Exstant Omnia Ilias, Odyssea . . . cum Latina versione.* Io Spondani Mauleonensis Commentariis (Basel: Per Sebastianum Henricpetri, n.d.), 235. For Chapman's debt to Spondanus, see Frank L. Schoell, *Études sur l'humanisme continental en Angleterre à la fin de la Renaissance* (Paris: Librairie Ancienne Honoré Champion, 1926), 132–77.

41. Homer, *The Iliad,* trans. A. T. Murray, 2 vols. (Cambridge: Harvard University Press, 1924–25), vol. 1, 567.

42. *The Complete Poetry of Ben Jonson,* ed. William B. Hunter Jr. (New York: W. W. Norton, 1968), 197.

43. The position here echoes attitudes in the *Parnassus* plays in which Sir Raderick and his Ovid-reading son, Amoretto, whose only real occupations are selling benefices, avoiding patronage seekers, and displaying their knowledge of hunting technicalities, are precisely the frivolous aristocracy that Jonson abhors. The irony is most pointed when Amoretto ridiculously claims to be a scholar: "Faith Sir, you must pardon mee, it is my ordinarie custome to be too studious, my Mistresse hath tolde me of it very often, and I finde it to hurt my ordinary discourse. But say sweete Sir, do yee affect the most gentleman-like game of hunting?" ("The Second Part of the Return from Parnassas," lines 789–93, in *Three Parnassus Plays,* 274–75).

44. *Ben Jonson,* ed. C. H. Herford and Percy Simpson, 11 vols. (Oxford: Clarendon Press, 1952), vol. 4. Frank Kermode, in an important argument which we will deal with in chap. 6, suggests that Jonson disapproves of Ovid. His main evidence, however, comes from the much later *New Inn* (see his essay, "The Banquet of Sense," in Kermode, *Shakespeare, Spenser, Donne: Renaissance Essays* [New York: Viking Press, 1971], 90–92). Kermode's argument about Jonson has been usefully qualified in James D. Mulvihill, "Jonson's *Poetaster* and the Ovidian Debate," *Studies in English Literature* 22 (1982): 239–55.

45. If Augustus Caesar is ever criticized by Horace, it is for being too morally earnest, for banishing Ovid for a scene of "innocent mirth / And harmless pleasures, bred, of noble wit" (*Poetaster* 4.6.41–42). Again there is room for complication: this is said to Lupus who has falsely suggested earlier that Ovid and the masquers were planning treason, and it is not clear whether or not he is criticizing Caesar's severity.

46. John Dryden, dedication of *The Spanish Friar,* 1681. Quoted in *The Plays and Poems of George Chapman,* vol. 1: *The Tragedies,* ed. Thomas Marc Parrott (London: Routledge and Sons, 1910), 541.

47. *The Plays of George Chapman: The Tragedies,* gen. ed. Allan Holaday (Cambridge: D. S. Brewer, 1987), 1.1.20–33. With Nicholas Brooke I have preferred the first quarto of 1607 to the second of 1641, though Parrott and Lordi have given the latter authority. See George Chapman, *Bussy D'Ambois* (Revels edition), ed. N. Brooke (Cambridge: Harvard University Press, 1964); *Plays and Poems of George Chapman,* vol. 1: *Tragedies,* ed. Parrott; George Chapman, *Bussy D'Ambois,* ed. Robert J. Lordi (Lincoln: University of Nebraska Press, 1964). This is not the place to develop the textual argument, but it says something

about how the world had changed between 1607 and 1641 (Chapman, of course, was dead by then) that many of the Nennian sentiments have been excised from the later quarto. Cf. Ide, *Possessed with Greatness,* 79.

48. Moments like this may seem to support a Jacobean ideology of divine right and customary nobility (see Goldberg, *James I and the Politics of Literature*). Achillean virtue is, however, hostile to inherited power, just as it scorns the democratic idea of power "from the people." "Virtue" in this situation is a statement of self-achieved independence.

49. The historical Bussy was not noble by his bloodline. As Brooke's note observes, the cardinal was Bussy's great-uncle, not his father, so the issue of his birth is doubly confused by the charge.

Later Clermont D'Ambois in *The Revenge of Bussy D'Ambois* makes a claim for noble birth, but even then the terms are ambiguous: "I note how dangerous it is / For any man to press beyond the place / To which his birth, or means, or knowledge ties him; / For my part, though of noble birth, my birthright / Had little left it" (3.4.48–52). Later, when he is abducted, he asserts to his captors, "you know me nobly born, / Use ye t'assault such men as I with lackeys?" (4.1.80–81)

50. In *The Painful Passage to Virtue: A Study of George Chapman's The Tragedy of Bussy D'Ambois and The Revenge of Bussy D'Ambois* (Lund Studies in English 61 [Lund: GWK Gleerup, 1982]), Gunilla Florby develops this issue of empty greatness in considerable detail as an instance of the deceptive confusion of appearance and reality. Hers is the most recent and complete instance of the possibility of reading these works as a moral and psychological comment without reference to the dynamics of the implicit social critique or to the consequences of such a comment for the disadvantaged poet himself.

51. Jean Jacquot explicates Monsieur's argument by referring to Aristotle's *Ethics,* 8.7–12, and the issue of Monsieur's different ranks as subject and as brother to Henry. Despite this attempt to read Monsieur's argument as valid, Jacquot concedes that in the verses that follow the terms *virtue* and *greatness* acquire "un sens nouveau, et désignent les qualités morales que devrait posséder un vrai roi" (Jean Jacquot, ed. and trans., *Bussy D'Amboise* [Paris: Aubier, 1960], 182 [note to 2.1.141–48]).

52. Guise's argument may be in response to and agreement with Ulysses in *Troilus and Cressida.*

53. In "Hymnus in Noctem" Chapman had, very covertly, made the same claim. See below, chap. 4. Gunilla Florby gives these speeches little emphasis in her detailed examination of the Bussy plays. For her, they express a "myth of the golden age" that, along with the Prometheus and Hercules myths, serves to elevate Bussy. See *Painful Passage to Virtue,* 94–96.

54. Goldberg, *James I and the Politics of Literature,* 156.

Chapter 4: Virtues Obscured

1. Sidney, *Apology for Poetry,* 57.

2. "Culture is the site, par excellence, of misrecognition, because, in generating strate-

gies objectively adapted to the objective chances of profit of which it is the product, the sense of investment secures profits which do not need to be pursued as profits; and so it brings to those who have legitimate culture as a second nature the supplementary profit of being seen (and seeing themselves) as perfectly disinterested, unblemished by any cynical or mercenary use of culture" (Bourdieu, *Distinction*, 86).

3. Sidney's aristocratic position might hardly seem to need remarking, but it is seldom acknowledged how he uses that position in his rhetoric. For the tone that I am terming aristocratic, see Catherine Barnes, "The Hidden Persuader: The Complex Speaking Voice of Sidney's *Defense of Poetry*," *PMLA* 86 (1971): 422–27; and Ronald Levao, "Sidney's Feigned *Apology*," *PMLA* 94 (1979): 223–33. Richard Dutton captures the social issue: "Here, as elsewhere, Sidney projected himself not as a professional writer, but as an aristocrat 'provoked to say something unto you in defence of that my unelected vocation'— the 'you' clearly addressing a circle of friends and social peers among whom the *Defense* was meant to circulate in manuscript, rather than indiscriminately among the reading public at large" (*Ben Jonson, Authority, Criticism* [New York: St. Martin's Press, 1996], 17).

Though a Protestant agenda may underlie the *Apology*, I take it as a sign of Sidney's skill in the game of culture that the issue is always implicit. He never gets down on Gosson's level to debate moral behavior. See Andrew Weiner, *Sidney's Protestant Poetics* (Madison: University of Wisconsin Press, 1978); and Alan Sinfield, "The Cultural Politics of *The Defense of Poetry*," in *Sir Philip Sidney and the Interpretation of Renaissance Culture*, ed. Gary F. Waller and Michael D. Moore (London: Croom Helm, 1984), 124–43.

4. Bourdieu quotes Molière's *Les femmes savantes* (1672) on the conflict of "Court Wit and Fusty Learning" (*Distinction*, 69). In the early seventeenth century in France the debate between the *doctes* and the *mondains*, or between the anti-Ciceronian Parliamentarians and the aulic courtiers (Marc Fumaroli, *L'age de l'eloquence: Rhétorique et "res literarie" de la Renaissance au seuil de l'epoque classique* [Geneva: Librairie Droz, 1980]), is much like the less-institutionalized struggle I am describing in England in the 1590s. The fact that the *doctes* and the *mondains* ally themselves against the vulgar makes it easy to overlook their difference (Bourdieu, *Distinction*, 74).

In Sidney's passage we see a pure instance of the conflict between the court and humanists that Javitch's *Poetry and Courtliness* and G. K. Hunter's *John Lyly* have studied. Javitch quotes Sidney's passage to defend the courtier's sense of the sophistication the court encourages (*Poetry and Courtliness*, 52n); see also Muriel Bradbrook, "No Room at the Top: Spenser's Pursuit of Fame," *Stratford-Upon-Avon Studies 2: Elizabethan Poetry* (London: Edward Arnold, 1960), 93.

5. Clark Hulse has suggested to me that Sidney may well have been thinking of Gabriel Harvey in his reference to "some professors of learning." That seems plausible. Chapman's rebuttal, however, is not to a personal attack but to the courtier idea of poetry.

6. "Persuasion lies at the heart of Sidney's entire theory of poetry" (Neil Rudenstein, *Sidney's Poetic Development* [Cambridge: Harvard University Press, 1967], 152).

7. Rosamund Tuve conflates the "professor of learning" and the "smally learned courtier" and finds in Chapman's passage a familiar Renaissance poetic idea: the *enargia* here

advocated, she says, is essential to the rhetorician's task of making the audience "realize clearly" what the poet is saying, of conveying "a poet's exact and whole meaning, with force, to a reader." Such "clearness," Tuve argues, does not preclude that kind of obscurity "in which the poet's invention is high and complex but delivered in images whose connection with his interpretation is not left vague or tenuous to a careful reader" (*Elizabethan and Metaphysical Imagery* [Chicago: University of Chicago Press, 1947], 31–32). Such an attempt to squeeze Chapman into the mainstream of the rhetorical tradition, as I will argue in what follows, will not stand up to close inspection.

Both Tuve and MacLure (*George Chapman*, 46n) have tried to derive Chapman's concept of *enargia* from Puttenham, but there is no basis for this genealogy. Puttenham describes *enargia* as imparting "glorious luster and light" to verse, and he poses no association between *enargia* and "significance" or "high invention." He carefully limits the "luminosity" generated by *enargia* to the sound of the verse. It is the very cognitive *insig*nificance of *enargia*—to "satisfy and delight th'eare onely"—that defines it. He reserves the cognitive dimension of poetry for *energia* (George Puttenham, *The Art of Poetry*, in *Elizabethan Critical Essays*, ed. Gregory Smith [Oxford: Clarendon, 1904], vol. 2, 148).

8. Quintilian, *Institutes*, trans. H. E. Butler (Cambridge: Harvard University Press, 1932), III.245.

9. Quintilian's concern that "our language" be "clear to the uneducated" is echoed by Sidney, who praises the English language for its ease and clarity. He thinks "it was a piece of the Tower of Babylon's curse, that a man should be put to school to learn his mother tongue" (*Apology for Poetry*, 85).

10. John Harington, "Preface, or rather a Brief Apologie of Poetrie," in *Elizabethan Critical Essays*, vol. 2, 203. E.K. makes a similar argument in defense of Spenser's style in his "Epistle" to *The Shepheardes Calender:* "It is round without roughnesse, and learned wythout hardnes, such indeede as may be perceived of the leaste, understoode of the moste, but judged onely of the learned" (*The Yale Edition of the Shorter Poems of Edmund Spenser*, ed. William Oram, Einar Bjorvand, Ronald Bond, Thomas Cain, Alexander Dunlop, Richard Schell [New Haven: Yale University Press, 1989], 17). Not surprisingly, Chapman will at times invoke a version of this medieval idea of levels of interpretation. Thus, an explanatory gloss to an emblem in "Ovids Banquet of Sence" explains that it expresses the conceit "morally which hath a far higher intention" (Chapman, *Poems*, 71).

11. *Spenser's Faerie Queene*, ed. J. C. Smith, 2 vols. (Oxford: Clarendon Press, 1909), vol. 2, 487. Wayne Erickson finds Spenser playing an elaborate and self-consciously ironic game in such a claim ("Spenser's Letter to Ralegh and the Literary Politics of *The Faerie Queene*'s 1590 Publication" [*Spenser Studies* 10 (1992): 139–74]).

12. Patterson, *Censorship and Interpretation*, 53–68.

13. See Chapman's *A Free and Offenceles Justification of Andromeda Liberata*, in *Poems*, 325–35.

14. Ernest B. Gilman analyzes the tautological balance of this line in *Twelfth Night* as an expressly artistic device defining a particular kind of comedy (*The Curious Perspective: Literary and Pictorial Wit in the Seventeenth Century* [New Haven: Yale University Press,

1978], 129–51). As we shall see, Chapman uses the perspective picture to represent a more problematic relation of different visions.

15. For the importance to Chapman of the perspective picture, a painting that renders different images when viewed from different perspectives, see *Poems,* 431 (note to *Ovids Banquet of Sence* 3.6), 456 (note to *Eugenia* 173), and Waddington, *Mind's Empire,* 119–30.

16. *Plays and Poems of George Chapman,* vol. 1: *Tragedies,* ed. Parrott, 276–77 (1.1.68–72).

17. Chapman, *Poems,* 231–32.

18. "The Masque of the Middle Temple," in *Plays and Poems of George Chapman,* vol. 2: *Comedies,* ed. Parrott, 570.

19. See the dedication of the *Odyssey* (Chapman, *Poems,* 408), Chapman's note to line 116 of *Odyssey 12* (*Chapman's Homer,* vol. 2, 211), and the dedicatory epistle to *The Hymns of Homer* (*Poems,* 416). See Schoell, *Études sur l'humanisme continental en Angleterre à la fin de la Renaissance,* 4–5.

20. Chapman, *Poems,* 276.

21. We see a briefer version of this same enigma in *Hero and Leander* when Ceremony appears to Leander: "Her face was changeable to everie eye; / One way lookt ill, another graciouslie" (Chapman, *Poems,* 137, lines 125–26).

22. Richard Burt, *Licensed by Authority: Ben Jonson and the Discourses of Censorship* (Ithaca: Cornell University Press, 1993), xi.

23. Edgar Wind, *Pagan Mysteries in the Renaissance,* rev. ed. (New York: Barnes and Noble, 1968); Don Cameron Allen, *Mysteriously Meant: The Rediscovery of Pagan Symbolism and Allegorical Interpretation in the Renaissance* (Baltimore: Johns Hopkins University Press, 1970).

24. Bourdieu argues that the illusion of "distance from necessity" is crucial to dominant class aesthetics. In modern taste culture the members of the dominated fraction of the dominant class, even if they cannot in fact claim such distance, must do their best to blend with the dominant fraction to prevent their being dismissed as vulgar (*Distinction,* 34).

25. Both poems are accompanied by an apparatus of marginalia and endnotes drawing the reader's attention to the authentic sources for Chapman's imagery and testifying to the seriousness of the project. The models of Spenser's *Shepheardes Calender* and Watson's *Hekatompathia* may have been in Chapman's mind, but the comparisons do not take us very far. E.K.'s commentary is much fuller and designed to highlight Spenser's accomplishment. The Watson volume comes somewhat closer, in that the notes point to sources without going on to explain meaning. For the argument that Chapman's glosses are designed to draw attention to the aesthetic accomplishment of the poem, rather than its meaning, see Snare, *Mystification of George Chapman,* 139–67.

All scholars of Chapman are indebted to Roy Battenhouse's pioneering Neoplatonic reading of the poem, "Chapman's *The Shadow of Night,*" *Philological Quarterly* 39 (1941): 584–608. See also MacLure's reasoned summary (*George Chapman,* 32–48) and Waddington's extended reading (*Mind's Empire,* 24–112).

26. Bourdieu, *Distinction*, 173–75.

27. Waddington, ignoring the perspective implied in "Some farre off observing," reads this passage as a Breugel-like picture of bacchanalian excess (*Mind's Empire*, 106).

28. Thus Bussy challenges Guise: "Here would I make thee cast that popular purple, / In which thy proud soul sits and braves thy Sovereign" (*Bussy D'Ambois*, 3.2.69–70).

29. Ibid., 2.2.88–97.

30. These lines have led some scholars to see this book as the manifesto for the "School of Night" that Shakespeare is supposed to have mocked in *Love's Labour's Lost*, 4.3.246–51. See Acheson, *Shakespeare's Sonnet Story;* Muriel Bradbrook, *The School of Night: A Study in the Literary Relationships of Sir Walter Ralegh* (Cambridge: Cambridge University Press, 1936); and Frances Yates, *A Study of Love's Labour's Lost* (Cambridge: Cambridge University Press, 1936).

31. Chapman, *Poems,* 83–86.

32. The process is often described chronologically, as beginning in the senses and then rising to the mind. The sensual attraction of the individual leads to the intellectual love of and understanding of the universal, the Idea. One finds this idea throughout Ficino's *Commentary;* see Marsilio Ficino, *Commentary on Plato's Symposium,* trans. Sears Jayne, *University of Missouri Studies* 19 (1944): 164–65. Paul Oskar Kristeller describes it as the central epistemological concept of Ficino's thought (*The Philosophy of Marsilio Ficino,* trans. Virginia Conant [1943; reprint, Gloucester, Mass.: Peter Smith, 1964], 111).

33. Jean Jacquot remarks how the lines of sonnet 7, by their sanction of "sentiment" and "exaltation," reveal an attitude quite unlike that of classical Stoicism (*George Chapman (1559–1634): sa vie, sa poésie, son théâtre, sa pensée* [Paris: Société d'Édition les Belles Lettres, 1951], 263).

34. We should observe that one of the paradoxes of this sonnet is that while the basic idea is Platonic, in line 4 Philosophy is also described in terms perfectly congruent with the Stoicism of Plutarch, Seneca, and even Epictetus.

Chapter 5: "Nobler Than Nobility"

1. *Colin Clouts Come Home Again,* in *Yale Edition of the Shorter Poems of Edmund Spenser,* 549, lines 620–23. All citations from Spenser's shorter poems are from this edition.

2. For Spenser, the word *fury,* when it means rage rather than divine rapture, often attracts the word *insolent,* and in such cases the word clearly has negative implications. For instance, the phrase "fury insolent" occurs in *Faerie Queene,* 3.3.38 and 3.3.52, both times describing outrageous behavior. All citations are to *The Faerie Queene,* ed. J. C. Smith, 2 vols. (Oxford: Clarendon Press, 1909).

3. See Louis Adrian Montrose's "The Elizabethan Subject and the Spenserian Text," in *Literary Theory/Renaissance Texts,* ed. Patricia Parker and David Quint (Baltimore: Johns Hopkins University Press, 1986), 323.

4. A quarter of a century ago Edgar Wind warned of the "stoic frost [that] has so often invaded the garden of Plato" (*Pagan Mysteries in the Renaissance,* 142). Since then the topic

has not received much attention as it relates to English poetry, though Michael J. B. Allen's works on Ficino have supplied evidence that should support a significant revision of the older moral readings. See in particular Allen's *Marsilio Ficino and the Phaedran Charioteer* (Berkeley: University of California Press, 1981).

5. Baldassare Castiglione, *The Book of the Courtier,* trans. Sir Thomas Hoby, Everyman's Library (London: Dent, 1928), 307, 315.

6. Paul Friedlander quotes Porphyry describing his master Plotinus as "like one ashamed to be in the flesh" and points out that Plotinus, in treating the ascent toward intellectual love, sees it as beginning only when one turns away from physical beauty (*Plato: An Introduction,* trans. Hans Meyerhoff [New York: Harper Torchbooks, 1958], 56).

7. Marsilio Ficino, *Opera Omnia,* 2 vols. (Basel, 1576; facsim., Turin, 1959), vol. 2, 1281. My translation.

8. *Euthyphro, Apology, Crito, Phaedo, Phaedrus,* trans. H. N. Fowler (Cambridge: Harvard University Press, 1953). This *fool* (Ficino uses the term *demens*) is carefully distinguished from the person experiencing *furor.*

9. M. Allen, *Marsilio Ficino and the Phaedran Charioteer,* 142.

10. This tension between reason and a more ecstatic furor is analogous to that which William Kerrigan studies in Milton, but as Kerrigan observes, Milton, working in an explicitly prophetic tradition, is talking of a bolder flight (*The Prophetic Milton* [Charlottesville: University of Virginia, 1974], 10).

11. Sidney, *Apology for Poetry,* 88. Plato, Sidney says elsewhere in the *Apology,* "attributeth unto poesy more than myself do, namely, to be a very inspiring of a divine force" (67). John Guillory observes the way the essentially medieval conception of poetic inspiration degenerates in the Renaissance into "a weak metaphor," and he argues that Sidney in the *Apology* tries to "redeem poetry from its fallen state, its secularity, without returning, as Tasso did, to the mystified notion of the inspired poet" (*Poetic Authority: Spenser, Milton, and Literary History* [New York: Columbia University Press, 1983], 3, 11). For Sidney's importance to the courtly ideal of poetry, see Javitch, *Poetry and Courtliness,* 93–104.

12. See Levao, "Sidney's Feigned *Apology.*"

13. O. B. Hardison, "The Two Voices of Sidney's *Apology for Poetry,*" *English Literary Renaissance* 2 (1972): 83–99.

14. Sidney, *Astrophel and Stella,* sonnet 74, in *The Poems of Sir Philip Sidney,* ed. William Ringler (Oxford: Clarendon Press, 1962), 203–4.

15. See Javitch, *Poetry and Courtliness,* 97. In addition to the claim to inspiration, Astrophel goes on to denounce learned allusion ("I am no pick-purse of another's wit"). Sidney may here by attacking another mode by which nonaristocratic poets generate cultural capital. E.K., of course, takes pride in annotating Spenser's allusions in *The Shepheardes Calender.* See Evelyn Tribble, "Glozing the Gap: Authority, Glossing Traditions and *The Shepheardes Calender,*" *Criticism* 34 (1992): 155–72. Some years after Sidney wrote *Astrophel and Stella* Thomas Watson would carefully annotate the agreement in imagery between his poems in *Hekatompathia* and those of the Italian masters, and Chapman would proudly display the "authenticity" of his imagery in his notes to *The Shadow of Night.*

16. Shakespeare, sonnet 86, lines 9–10. In *A Midsummer Night's Dream* Theseus's famous speech at the beginning of the last act refers to something like furor, but it is hard to see the "fine frenzy" of the poet's eye as much more than an energetic version of the "tricks of strong imagination" (5.1.19). It is noteworthy that one serious use of "fury" in Shakespeare is Othello's description of the making of the handkerchief: a sibyl "in her prophetic fury sew'd the work" (3.4.72). Given Shakespeare's apparent skepticism about furor, we may see signs of superstition in Othello's use of the term.

17. It is this belief in rapturous inspiration that has made Chapman a popular candidate for the position of rival poet. Years ago F. L. Schoell annotated Chapman's debt to Ficino for the idea of furor (*Études sur l'humanisme continental en Angleterre à la fin de la Renaissance,* 1–20). Recent critics of Chapman have treated his claim to inspiration, when they have bothered to observe it, as a minor element in his poetic. See MacLure, *George Chapman* 37, 40; Waddington, *Mind's Empire,* 186, 213; Ide, *Possessed with Greatness,* 6; Braunmuller, *Natural Fictions,* 146–48. Clark Hulse recognizes the centrality of inspired furor to Chapman's (and Marlowe's) poetic project, though he does not treat it as a social gesture (*Metamorphic Verse* 93–99, 124–26).

18. Chapman, *Poems,* 408, lines 68–85. For Chapman's Platonism, see Jacquot, *George Chapman.* Frank Kermode, who begins his analysis of the Platonic basis of "Ovids Banquet of Sence" with Ficino, slides easily to Castiglione and Spenser as the basis for his moral reading of the poem. See *Shakespeare, Spenser, Donne,* 95.

19. "Ut non sine Maximo favore Dei comparari queat. Pla. in Ione" (Chapman, *Poems,* 416). Chapman does not distinguish between Plato's and Ficino's words.

20. *Plays and Poems of George Chapman,* vol. 2: *Comedies,* ed. Parrott, 570.

21. See the discussion in chap. 4.

22. *Ion,* in *Statesman, Philebus, Ion,* trans. H. N. Fowler, W. R. M. Lamb (Cambridge: Harvard University Press, 1952), 533d–536d. In his *epitome* of *Ion* Ficino does not explain why one man attains divine furor while another succumbs to *insania.* While Chapman would argue that through moral purification and study one prepares oneself for the highest insights, there is no trace of this in Plato's *Ion* and the doctrine there presented does not require it. As Kerrigan observes, Ficino was true to Plato in this respect and at times allowed that insane and uneducated poets might be truly inspired (*Prophetic Milton,* 51). See also Michael Murrin, *The Veil of Allegory* (Chicago: University of Chicago Press, 1969), 71–72.

23. Furor is not a systematic concept for Ficino. For his changes in the order and relation of the four furors (poetic, mystic, prophetic, and amorous), see Michael J. B. Allen, *The Platonism of Marsilio Ficino* (Berkeley: University of California Press, 1984), 47–50.

24. Ficino, *Opera Omnia,* vol. 2, 1282; my translation.

25. *The Letters of Marsilio Ficino,* trans. by members of the Language Department of the School of Economic Science, London (New York: Gingko Press, 1985), vol. 1, letter 7, 18. See also Kristeller, *Philosophy of Marsilio Ficino,* 308–9. André Chastel observes that Christoforo Landino, who also invokes the doctrine of furor, explicitly rejects "sweetness of words" as a quality of inspired poetry and demands both obscurity and surprise (*Mar-*

sile Ficin et l'art [Geneva: Droz, 1954], 132). The hints of a psychology of sound make this passage a part of the tradition studied by Frances Yates in *Giordano Bruno and the Hermetic Tradition* (Chicago: University of Chicago Press, 1964), and D. P. Walker in *Spiritual and Demonic Magic* (London: Warburg Institute, 1954). I do not pursue this line because it seems clear to me that none of these struggling English poets were much concerned with this dimension of the problem.

26. For rhetoric as magic, see William A. Covino, *Magic, Rhetoric, and Literacy: An Eccentric History of the Composing Imagination* (Albany: State University of New York Press, 1994), 17–20.

27. To be sure, Chapman's exclusionary gesture has a rhetorical force, but I am here interested in defining how Chapman's Platonism is serving a social purpose different from the psychological and stylistic considerations of Puttenham, Quintilian, Aristotle, or even, as in *Ion,* Plato, and from the formalism that Wesley Trimpi sees as "characteristic of the Neoplatonic influence on the arts as a whole" (*Muses of One Mind: The Literary Analysis of Experience and Its Continuity* [Princeton: Princeton University Press, 1983], 165).

28. Chapman, *Poems,* 19. In the passage from the end of the second letter to Roydon quoted early in the present chapter, Chapman again expresses the idea that "darkness" is the fault of the uninspired audience rather than of the inspired poet (*Poems,* 50).

29. See the prefatory matter for *Seaven Bookes of the Iliades* and *Achilles Shield* in *Chapman's Homer,* vol. 1, 543, 507, and 548. Jonson assumes a similar stance and will frequently invoke the "understander" as a privileged and valued reader.

30. For the more common picture of the cult of Sidney created by Sir Henry Lee, see Alan Hagar, "The Exemplary Mirage: Fabrication of Sir Philip Sidney's Biographical Image and the Sidney Reader," *ELH* 48 (1981): 1–16. The elegies that were published immediately after Sidney's death have been reprinted in *Elegies for Sir Philip Sidney.* Roydon's elegy for Sidney was published in two important collections, first in *The Phoenix Nest* (1593) and then again in the group of Sidney elegies in *Colin Clouts Come Home Again* (1595), but it was known earlier, for Nash praises "the immortall epitaph" in 1589 in his preface, "To the Gentlemen Students of both Universities," before Robert Greene's *Menaphon* (Robert Greene, *Life and Complete Works,* ed. Alexander B. Grosart [New York: Russell and Russell, 1964], vol. 2, 26). Quotations from Roydon's "An Elegie, or Friend's Passion, for His Astrophill" are from *Spenser's Minor Poems,* ed. Ernest de Selincourt (Oxford: Clarendon Press, 1910), 357–63.

31. William Ringler argues that Roydon "probably knew no more than the titles of Sidney's works, for he has him taking pleasure 'on the mountain Parthenie' in Arcadia, which is a detail found in Sannazaro's story but not in Sidney's" (*Poems of Sir Philip Sidney,* lxii).

32. In the tenth eclogue (October) of *The Shepheardes Calender* Spenser has Cuddie explicitly connect inspiration and inebriation, "For *Bacchus* fruit is frend to *Phoebus* wise" (106).

33. Oram notes (in reference to line 55 of Spenser's "Astrophel") that until 1598 Stella was generally assumed to be Sidney's wife (*Yale Edition of the Shorter Poems of Edmund Spenser,* 572).

34. See James Phares Myers Jr., "'This Curious Frame': Chapman's *Ovid's Banquet of Sense*," *Studies in Philology* 65 (1968): 202; Elizabeth Story Donno, *Elizabethan Minor Epics* (New York: Columbia University Press, 1963), 13; and John Huntington, "Philosophical Seduction in Chapman, Davies, and Donne," *ELH* 40 (1977): 45. Frank Kermode, who inverts the traditional reading of *Ovids Banquet of Sence* as a poem about furor and reads it as a cautionary fable, explicitly rejects such a reading of this stanza (*Shakespeare, Spenser, Donne*, 10–11).

35. "The Forrest: XII. Epistle" (*Complete Poetry of Ben Jonson*, 102–5).

36. Robert Ellrodt's analysis of the Platonism of the *Fowre Hymnes* corrects the ascetic interpretation that would see Spenser's Platonism as entirely intellectual (*Neoplatonism in the Poetry of Spenser* [Geneva: Librairie Droz, 1960]). Ellrodt's reading finds "wedded love" the culmination of Spenser's unorthodox Platonic progress. However, Ellrodt's argument for "Spenser's frank acceptance of physical love" (145), while welcome as a corrective, distracts attention from the more basic issue of the loss of control that furor entails. Ellrodt recognizes this limit: "The originality of Spenser's philosophy of love lies in the association of Platonic idealism with an acceptance of bodily union limited by ethical standards. The 'Englishness' of this attitude is obvious. It rejected the worldly game and mere pretense of courtly Platonism, but it also excluded the higher flights of mysticism" (146).

37. The problematic importance of the concept of "gentle blood" to Spenser is discussed at some length by Humphrey Tonkin in connection with book 6 of *The Faerie Queene*. See *Spenser's Courteous Pastoral: Book Six of The Faerie Queene* (Oxford: Clarendon Press, 1972), 63–64, 166–69, and 223–24.

38. G. C. Moore Smith, *Gabriel Harvey's Marginalia* (Stratford-upon-Avon: Shakespeare Head Press, 1913), 105, 119.

39. Disillusion with the court and a questioning of the position of the poet has been the theme of much criticism of *Colin Clouts Come Home Again*. See Thomas Edwards, *Imagination and Power: A Study of Poetry on Public Themes* (New York: Oxford University Press, 1971), 56; David Shore, "The Shepherd and the Court: Pastoral Poetics in Spenser's *Colin Clout* and Tasso's *Aminta*," *Canadian Review of Comparative Literature* 4 (1980): 394–410; and David Miller, "Spenser's Vocation, Spenser's Career," *ELH* 50 (1983): 197–231.

40. This enigmatic episode has generated a wide variety of readings. One group, which we might call the positive reading, is summarized by Humphrey Tonkin: "Calidore learns true courtesy through the device [of the Graces] and he sees in Pastorella the earthly representative of courtesy's true flower: the vision on Mount Acidale in effect confirms his correctness in falling in love with the shepherdess" (*The Faerie Queene* [London: Unwin Hyman, 1989], 187). Other critics have sought to understand how Calidore fails. Richard Neuse, it seems to me, catches the difficulty of the passage precisely: "The entire scene suggests Calidore's fundamental inability to appreciate the ideal on which Spenser's version of courtesy is founded" ("Book VI as Conclusion to *The Faerie Queene*," *ELH* 35 [1968]: 349). Critics writing since Neuse can argue that the issue is one of defining true ("Spenser's version") courtesy. See George E. Rowe, "Privacy, Vision, and Gender in Spens-

er's Legend of Courtesy," *Modern Language Quarterly* 50 (1989), 309–36. Daniel Javitch combines these two positions by arguing that the episode affirms "that the poet is uniquely endowed to understand as well as teach courtesy" (*Poetry and Courtliness*, 150). It may be, as I am arguing, that Spenser is secretly of the devil's party and would say that in the final analysis all courtesy falls short of furious vision.

41. Exactly such privileges of rank are the subject of Tristram's slaying of a knight in the second canto of book 6 (see especially stanza 7). Spenser's rendering of Calidore's generosity to a social inferior is both pointed and exceptional.

42. I am taking Calidore's "pleasaunce" as purely "aesthetic," but as Paul Alpers observes, the nakedness of the dancers is pointed (*The Poetry of the Faerie Queene* [Princeton: Princeton University Press, 1967], 12). There may be an erotic component to Calidore's rapture, in which case his concern for *insania* is all the more proper.

43. Chapman, *Euthymiae Raptus*, 75–80, in *Poems*, 174–75.

44. Barnabe Barnes, *A Divine Century of Spirituall Sonnets* (London: John Windet, 1595), A3v.

45. Joshuah Sylvester, *The Complete Works*, ed. Alexander B. Grosart (1880; reprint, Hildesheim: Georg Olms Verlagsbuchhandlung, 1969), vol. 2, 4.

46. Though in denigrating secular verse he may dismiss "idle *Fame*" (34.4), for most of "Urania" Du Bartas seems to account ambition (8.1) admirable: "*Excelling Works* preserve the Memory / Of those that make them" (63.1–2). For other instances in the poem of his hope for fame and eternal verse, see also 17.4, 31.2, 65–66, 73.4, and 81.

47. The word *prince* is itself ambiguous in England. See Susan Frye's *Elizabeth I: The Competition for Representation* for a discussion of the important ambiguity in the title of "The Princely Pleasures at the Courte at Kenelwoorth" ([New York: Oxford University Press, 1993], 63). Furthermore, on the Continent there are princes who are clearly not royal.

48. Bartlett, apparently following Liddell and Scott, calls ευθυμία "cheerefulness" (Chapman, *Poems*, 426, note to 218). Janet Spens says that Euthymia may be "equivalent either to 'Human love' . . . or to Peace" ("Chapman's Ethical Thought," *Essays and Studies by Members of the English Association* 11 [1925]: 166). MacLure calls it "contentment or peace of soul" (*George Chapman*, 43), and Jacquot calls it "contentment" (*George Chapman*, 62).

49. "On Tranquillity of Mind," *Plutarch's Moralia*, trans. W. C. Helmbold (Cambridge: Harvard University Press, 1957), VI, 166–241.

50. Seneca, "De tranquillitate Animi," *Moral Essays*, trans. J. W. Basore (Cambridge: Harvard University Press, 1935), I, 213.

51. Ennis Rees, *The Tragedies of George Chapman: Renaissance Ethics in Action* (Cambridge: Harvard University Press), 13. The linking of Platonism to Stoicism has a long tradition through Cicero and, following him, St. Augustine, who found that the distinctions that the Greek Stoics repeatedly made between their position and that of the Platonists concerning the Good were trivial plays on words. "I judge that the Stoics themselves hold exactly the same view of the Platonists and Peripatetics, in so far as the gist of

the matter is concerned and not the mere jingle of words" (*City of God,* trans. David S. Wiesen [Cambridge: Harvard University Press, 1968], 3.159). Cf. Cicero, *De finibus,* IV.

52. We can see these stages at work in Ficino's commentary on the *Symposium:* "Hence, two kinds of virtues are delineated: moral virtues, so to speak, and intellectual virtues, prior to them. The intellectual virtues are: Wisdom, Knowledge, and Prudence; the moral virtues: Justice, Courage, and Temperance. The moral virtues, because of their functions and public applications, are better known. The intellectual virtues, because of their recondite truth, are more esoteric. . . . Know also that you will rise immediately above moral virtue to the clear truth of wisdom, conceded to the soul brought up in the best rule of a moral life" (*Commentary on Plato's Symposium,* 213–15). From here Ficino goes on to treat the intellectual virtues which allow one first to perceive the multiform truths of the world, then to rise to an understanding of the single truth of the world, which Ficino calls the beauty of the Angelic Mind, and finally, at the highest possible realm of insight, to perceive the absolute unity, "which we call the One Itself." The moral virtues precede and sustain this intellectual ascent to perfect understanding, but they are not the goal of the process.

53. Consolation is more important for Ficino than I can develop here. See George W. McClure, "Grief and Melancholy in Medicean Florence: Marsilio Ficino and the Platonic Regimen," *Sorrow and Consolation in Italian Humanism* (Princeton: Princeton University Press, 1991), 132–54.

54. In his paraphrase of *Alcibiades II,* a dialogue to which Chapman explicitly refers in his *Justification of Andromeda Liberata,* Ficino gives us a Platonist's catechism: "What did Socrates seek? Good. What Good? Wisdom, that is knowledge of divine truth which only God is able to give, which only the pure, that is the temperate, clean, and chaste soul, is able to receive. What did he desire first? That He make him worthy of knowledge, for surely it is a rash man who seeks any reward for which he is unworthy. Who is worthy of divine wisdom? He who is prepared to bear its light. Who is prepared? He who through continence first, then through temperance, finally through sanctity—that is he who through law, purgation, and the virtue of the purged soul—thus clears his soul so that beautiful, that is totally pure and gleaming, he should ascend and choose now exemplary virtue, namely divine wisdom alone, seeing that it is the treasure house of all riches" (Ficino, *Opera Omnia,* vol. 2, 1281; my translation).

55. Battenhouse relates the panther to pride and the boar to lust and argues that they mask "the two sorts of sin (sin of the spirit and sin of the flesh) which arise when joy takes beastly form." "The story of Cynthia's activity as a huntress is an allegory of World-Soul acting in her role of providential governor of men and punisher of the wicked" ("Chapman's *The Shadow of Night,* 604).

56. Giordano Bruno, *The Heroic Frenzies,* trans. Paul Eugene Memmo Jr. (Chapel Hill: University of North Carolina Press, 1966), 225–26. In stanza 41 of "Ovids Banquet of Sence" something like the Bruno reading of the Acteon story is recalled. See Huntington, "Philosophical Seduction in Chapman, Davies, and Donne," 44–45; and chap. 6, below.

Chapter 6: Ovid and the Social Value of Literature

1. Yates, *Study of Love's Labour's Lost,* 23. Yates goes on to discover Shakespeare in *Love's Labour's Lost* satirizing Chapman and the supposed "School of Night" surrounding Ralegh.

2. As Eccles notes ("Chapman's Early Years," 167), Barnes's and Shakespeare's poems were licensed within a month of each other, and both are dedicated to the earl of Southampton. I would not want to push this similarity too far, however: Barnes also writes dedicatory sonnets to the earls of Northumberland and Essex, the countess of Pembrooke, Lady Strange, and Lady Brigett Manners. Like many other impoverished young poets, he sprays dedications to get attention.

3. Gary Schmidgal, *Shakespeare and the Courtly Aesthetic* (Berkeley: University of California Press, 1981), 115. Schmidgal treats Chapman as part of this courtly aesthetic (117).

4. I will take this dimension of Shakespeare's poem as a given and will not bother to defend it. Central studies of Ovid are William Keach, *Elizabethan Erotic Narratives: Irony and Pathos in the Ovidian Poetry of Shakespeare, Marlowe, and Their Contemporaries* (New Brunswick: Rutgers University Press, 1977); Hulse, *Metamorphic Verse;* and Bate, *Shakespeare and Ovid.* I will not pursue one other reading of Shakespeare's epigraph: that it is part of the flattery of Southhampton. Ovid in *Amores* 1.15, the source for Shakespeare's quotation, is clearly talking about poetry.

5. Bartlett in her notes observes that these lines may be a "rebuke to Shakespeare for his erotic *Venus and Adonis*" (Chapman, *Poems,* 426). See also Hudston and Rowland's edition, *George Chapman: Plays and Poems* (Harmondsworth: Penguin Books, 1998), 388.

6. This link is central for Cheney, *Marlowe's Counterfeit Profession.*

7. For the mysterious history of Marlowe's translation of the *Elegies,* see *The Complete Works of Christopher Marlowe,* vol. 1, ed. Roma Gill (Oxford: Clarendon Press, 1987).

8. "It becomes quite clear that this [i.e., "Venus and Adonis"] is a poem about transgressive sexuality" (Bate, *Shakespeare and Ovid,* 60).

9. Ovid's banishment remains something of a mystery. See John C. Thibault, *The Mystery of Ovid's Exile* (Berkeley: University of California Press, 1964); Alessandro Barchiesi, *The Poet and the Prince: Ovid and Augustan Discourse* (Berkeley: University of California Press, 1997); and M. L. Stapleton, *Harmful Eloquence: Ovid's* Amores *from Antiquity to Shakespeare* (Ann Arbor: University of Michigan Press, 1996).

10. Ovid, *Heroides and Amores,* trans. Grant Showerman (Cambridge: Harvard University Press, 1914). Marlowe's curious rendering of "cetera quis nescit" as "Judge you the rest" directs us more than Ovid's original does to the different possibilities for judgment involved in the scene: "To leave the rest, all liked me passing well; / I clinged her naked body, down she fell. / Judge you the rest: being tired she bade me kiss; / Jove send me more such afternoons as this." Patrick Cheney, who sees Marlowe in constant rivalry with Spenser, finds elsewhere Acrasian parallels with Corinna, but Marlowe's translation here seems to ignore the similarities between this scene of erotic relaxation and the scene of "lewd loves, and wastfull luxuree" of the Bower of Bliss (*Marlowe's Counterfeit Profession,* 74).

11. To some extent the *Ovide moralisé* tradition capitalizes on precisely this quality of Ovid, finding deep allegorical significances in what appear to be unpretentious narratives. But the motive of the moralized Ovid is, at least in part, to impose a fixed meaning on the Ovidian text and to stop its relentlessly suggestive motion.

12. See Douglas Bush, *Mythology and the Renaissance Tradition in English Poetry*, rev. ed. (New York: W. W. Norton, 1963), 211–13; and C. S. Lewis, *English Literature in the Sixteenth Century, Excluding Drama* (Oxford: Clarendon Press, 1954), 513. The traditional reading is recently asserted in John Roe, "Italian Neoplatonism and the Poetry of Sidney, Shakespeare, Chapman and Donne" in *Platonism and the English Imagination*, ed. Anna Baldwin and Sarah Hutton (Cambridge: Cambridge University Press, 1994), 100–116.

13. The closest followers of Kermode are Myers in "'This Curious Frame,'" 196; and Darryl J. Gless in "Chapman's Ironic Ovid," *English Literary Renaissance*, 9 (1979): 24–28. MacLure and Waddington, while they never reject the reading, remain at a discreet distance from it. Donno explicitly rejects it in her preface to *Elizabethan Minor Epics*. In "Philosophical Seduction in Chapman, Davies, and Donne," I have argued an alternative reading that allows both the traditional and the moral understandings. Gerald Snare, more recently in *Mystification of George Chapman*, has focused attention on Chapman's art and has tried to talk outside the issue of moral behavior that has so dominated much of this century's reading not just of Chapman but of most Renaissance verse.

14. When Kermode was offering his ironic reading of "Ovids Banquet of Sence," Ennis Rees was developing a similar line on *Bussy D'Ambois*, suggesting that Bussy was not an exemplary hero at all, but an example of a fallen sensualist. See *Tragedies of George Chapman*, 31–50.

15. Thus, Waddington finds the emblem of the stick that appears bent in water, which appears on the title page of *Ovids Banquet of Sence*, as evidence for the moral reading, though, were one to argue that the moral reading itself is the illusion, then the emblem would imply something quite different. Waddington sees the moral reading as more interesting because it is ironic and the alternative is dull, "*no more complex* than a fictional embodiment of Chapman's viewpoint or philosophy, and the narrator's comments *merely* supplementary, not corrective" (*Mind's Empire*, 141, emphasis added). The aesthetic behind such a reading resembles Henry James's more than any Renaissance position.

16. For an analysis of the ambiguity of this image, see my "Philosophical Seduction in Chapman, Davies, and Donne," 44–45.

17. The phrase "Sweet fields" is itself glossed, explaining the imagery of paradise that follows in this and the next stanza.

18. The change has no textual basis, though Kermode manages to imply that it is somehow arbitrary to read *peace* (*Shakespeare, Spenser, Donne*, 109). Gless accepts Kermode's change without comment ("Chapman's Ironic Ovid," 38). In her edition of "Ovids Banquet of Sence," Elizabeth Story Donno silently follows Kermode's alteration (*Elizabethan Minor Epics*, 225). Despite this change, however, Donno in her introduction rejects Kermode's moral interpretation of the poem, thus showing that even the changed gloss is

compatible with a rapturous reading of the poem. Hudston and Rowland's Penguin edition retains *peace*.

Kermode further distinguishes the voice of the gloss from that of Ovid by ignoring the gloss's phrase, "life of life," and thereby reducing Corynna simply to "the vital beauty of this lady." But "life of life" is a favorite locution of Chapman's to describe the ineffable quintessence. At the beginning of stanza 58 the narrator describes Ovid's banquet as "that feast of feasts" (2). One can find many other examples of this favorite locution in Chapman, but one of the clearest occurs at the end of "Hymnus in Noctem," "This traine, / with meteors, comets, lightenings, / The dreadfull presence of our Empresse sings: / Which grant for ever (ô eternal Night) / Till vertue flourish in the light of light" (400–403).

19. The problems that arise here about inspiration and the difficulty of conveying inspiration in verse become major themes of the last part of the poem. See Snare's fine discussion of the issue of invention in the poem (*Mystification of George Chapman*, 119).

20. None of the critics who would make "A Coronet for His Mistresse, Philosophy" a corrective to "Ovids Banquet of Sence" makes reference to this final couplet of stanza 57.

21. Kermode, *Shakespeare, Spenser, Donne*, 14; MacLure, *George Chapman*, 59; Myers, "'This Curious Frame,'" 196; Gless, "Chapman's Ironic Ovid," 24–28.

22. Myers, "'This Curious Frame,'" 197, 201.

23. Ficino, *Commentary*, 144.

24. Gless sees Ovid's failure to be content as a sign of his moral failure, but the digression, while it dreams of the heaven of contentment, treats it as a rarely attained ("seld or never") goal. To see unrest as moral failure is to invoke the "stoic gravitie" that the Platonism of the poem rejects.

25. Kristeller, *Philosophy of Marsilio Ficino*, 211, 374.

26. See Kermode, *Shakespeare, Spenser, Donne*, 113.

27. Ficino, *Commentary*, 164, 183.

28. Kristeller, *Philosophy of Marsilio Ficino*, 171–99; Jacquot, *George Chapman*, 254.

29. J. M. Rist, *Stoic Philosophy* (Cambridge: Cambridge University Press, 1969), 186, 214, and passim. As Kermode observes, Chapman himself, in his gloss to stanza 84, quotes Theophrastus, "Natura est uniuscuiusque Fatum" (*Shakespeare, Spenser, Donne*, 106).

30. The basic text is 1 Cor. 3:18–19. Erasmus's *Moriae Encomium* is of course the great Renaissance development of the paradox.

31. The bawdy implications of this close have been noted by Kermode (*Shakespeare, Spenser, Donne*, 114). MacLure (*George Chapman*, 59) and Myers ("'This Curious Frame,'" 196) seem to agree with Kermode's reading.

32. In stanza 55 the poet, speaking in his own person, makes a similar point about the limitations of artistic expression of divine furor.

33. In chap. 5, in the discussion of the similarly ambiguous figure in Roydon's elegy for Sidney.

34. Donno, *Elizabethan Minor Epics*, 13. In his introduction to *Shakespeare, Spenser, Donne*, Kermode responds to Donno and rejects again the idea that the statue is a "per-

spective sculpture" (13). As Bartlett notes (Chapman, *Poems,* 431), however, though the phrase "optick reason" comes from Natalis Comes, Chapman also uses it in the descriptions of "perspective pictures" in *Chabot,* 1.1.68 and *Eugenia,* line 174. Also, the statue's doubleness is attributed to "cunning."

35. Ovid, *Tristia; Ex Ponto,* trans. Arthur Leslie Wheeler (Cambridge: Harvard University Press, 1953). Ovid in the next lines compares himself to Acteon. Cf. "Banquet," stanza 41.

36. John Davies wrote two commendatory sonnets for the volume. Richard Stapleton, who would remain a friend of Chapman's well into the next century, wrote one. Thomas Williams wrote two. All in one way or another praise the poem for expressing some sort of latent meaning under a manifest surface. Unfortunately, these poems are omitted from Hudston and Rowland's recent edition.

Postscript

1. Susanne Woods, *Lanyer: A Renaissance Woman Poet* (New York: Oxford University Press, 1999), 41.

2. Much of the recent interest in Lanyer has focused on her feminist piety. See especially Elaine V. Beilin, *Redeeming Eve: Women Writers of the English Renaissance* (Princeton: Princeton University Press, 1987), 177–207; and Wendy Wall, "Our Bodies/Our Texts? Renaissance Women and the Trials of Authorship" in *Anxious Power: Reading, Writing, and Ambivalence in Narrative by Women,* ed. Carol J. Singley and Susan Elizabeth Sweeney (Albany: State University of New York Press, 1993), 51–71.

3. *The Poems of Aemilia Lanyer: Salve Deus Rex Judaeorum,* ed. Susanne Woods (New York: Oxford University Press, 1993), 42–43 (lines 17–48). All quotations from Lanyer are from this edition.

4. Barbara Lewalski reads this stanza as distinguishing "male succession through aristocratic titles" from "a female succession grounded upon virtue and holiness" ("Re-writing Patriarchy and Patronage: Margaret Clifford, Anne Clifford, and Aemilia Lanyer," *Yearbook of English Studies,* vol. 21, ed. Andrew Gurr [London: Modern Humanities Research Association, 1991], 101).

5. Anne seems to have been a remarkable woman, though perhaps not the utopian Lanyer invokes. Daughter of the duke of Cumberland, one of Elizabeth's most powerful courtiers, she married two equally powerful courtiers, the earl of Dorset and later the earl of Pembroke. She fought church, court, and king for her paternal inheritance, which she gained, finally, not so much by her tenacity as by the good fortune of having all her male cousins die. She wrote a memoir in the 1650s, and she died after the Restoration, a wealthy matriarch. See Lewalski, "Re-writing Patriarchy."

6. As Lewalski observes, Lanyer was twenty years older than Anne Clifford, who must have been a child in her teens during the period Lanyer commemorates in "Cooke-ham,"

so "hardly her playmate" (Lewalski, "Re-writing Patriarchy," 105). Woods thinks the so-journ at Cooke-ham took place between 1603 and 1605, when Anne Clifford was thir-teen to fifteen (Woods, *Lanyer,* 29).

7. Woods's reading of these elliptical lines seems accurate: "circumstances may place the high and low near to each other, but their devotion is not reciprocally strong; the lower born are more devoted to the high than the reverse" (*Salve Deus Rex Judaeorum,* 134, note to lines 109–10).

8. Shakespeare, though often complacent about his friend's rank and emphatic about the continuation of their love, in "Farewell, thou art too dear for my possessing" (Sonnet 88) seems to have a sense of the problem this unequal dynamic poses.

9. Numerous recent critics have noted and discussed Lanyer's strategy of humility. Woods argues that "By collapsing her unworthiness as a woman into the general unwor-thiness of the lower-born in relation to the higher, and by seeking elevation from anoth-er woman, Lanyer effectively transcends the gender issue altogether" (*Lanyer,* 104).

10. Lewalski, "Re-writing Patriarchy," 105.

11. "To the Earl of Chesterfield, February 7, 1755," *Samuel Johnson: Rasselas, Poems, and Selected Prose,* ed. Bertrand H. Bronson (New York: Rinehart, 1958), 2–3.

Index

John Huntington, professor of English at the University of Illinois at Chicago, has taught Shakespeare and Renaissance poetry for many years and has published numerous articles on Chapman, Spenser, and Donne. His book on H. G. Wells, *The Logic of Fantasy: H. G. Wells and Science Fiction* (1982), won the Eaton Award in 1984. His interest in the social strategies of authors on the fringe of the canon is evidenced also in *Rationalizing Genius: Ideological Strategies in the Classic American Science Fiction Short Story* (1989).

Typeset in 10.5/13 Adobe Garamond
with Adobe Garamond display
Designed by Dennis Roberts
Composed by Jim Proefrock
at the University of Illinois Press
Manufactured by Thomson-Shore, Inc.

University of Illinois Press
1325 South Oak Street
Champaign, IL 61820-6903
www.press.uillinois.edu